Henry Augustin Beers

An Outline Sketch of English Literature

Henry Augustin Beers

An Outline Sketch of English Literature

ISBN/EAN: 9783337010485

Printed in Europe, USA, Canada, Australia, Japan

Cover: Foto ©Thomas Meinert / pixelio.de

More available books at **www.hansebooks.com**

AN

OUTLINE SKETCH

OF

ENGLISH LITERATURE.

BY

HENRY A. BEERS.

NEW YORK:
CHAUTAUQUA PRESS,
C. L. S. C. Department,
805 BROADWAY.
1886.

The required books of the C. L. S. C. are recommended by a Council of six. It must, however, be understood that recommendation does not involve an approval by the Council, or by any member of it, of every principle or doctrine contained in the book recommended.

Franklin Press:

RAND, AVERY, AND COMPANY,

BOSTON.

PREFACE.

IN so brief a history of so rich a literature, the problem is how to get room enough to give, not an adequate impression—that is impossible—but any impression at all of the subject. To do this I have crowded out every thing but *belles-lettres*. Books in philosophy, history, science, etc., however important in the history of English thought, receive the merest incidental mention, or even no mention at all. Again, I have omitted the literature of the Anglo-Saxon period, which is written in a language nearly as hard for a modern Englishman to read as German is, or Dutch. Cædmon and Cynewulf are no more a part of English literature than Vergil and Horace are of Italian. I have also left out the vernacular literature of the Scotch before the time of Burns. Up to the date of the union Scotland was a separate kingdom, and its literature had a development independent of the English, though parallel with it.

In dividing the history into periods, I have followed, with some modifications, the divisions made by Mr. Stopford Brooke in his excellent little *Primer of English Literature.* A short reading course is appended to each chapter.

HENRY A. BEERS.

CONTENTS.

CONTENTS

OUTLINE SKETCH

OF

ENGLISH LITERATURE.

CHAPTER I.

FROM THE CONQUEST TO CHAUCER,

1066–1400.

THE Norman conquest of England, in the 11th century, made a break in the natural growth of the English language and literature. The old English or Anglo-Saxon had been a purely Germanic speech, with a complicated grammar and a full set of inflections. For three hundred years following the battle of Hastings this native tongue was driven from the king's court and the courts of law, from parliament, school, and university. During all this time there were two languages spoken in England. Norman French was the birth-tongue of the upper classes and English of the lower. When the latter finally got the better in the struggle, and became, about the middle of the 14th century, the national speech of all England, it was no longer the English of King Alfred. It was a new language, a grammarless tongue, almost wholly

stripped of its inflections. It had lost a half of
its old words, and had filled their places with
French equivalents. The Norman lawyers had
introduced legal terms; the ladies and courtiers,
words of dress and courtesy. The knight had
imported the vocabulary of war and of the chase.
The master-builders of the Norman castles and
cathedrals contributed technical expressions proper to the architect and the mason. The art of
cooking was French. The naming of the living
animals, *ox*, *swine*, *sheep*, *deer*, was left to the Saxon
churl who had the herding of them, while the
dressed meats, *beef*, *pork*, *mutton*, *venison*, received
their baptism from the table-talk of his Norman
master. The four orders of begging friars, and
especially the Franciscans or Gray Friars, introduced into England in 1224, became interme-
diaries between the high and the low. They went
about preaching to the poor, and in their sermons
they intermingled French with English. In their
hands, too, was almost all the science of the day;
their *medicine*, *botany*, and *astronomy* displaced the
old nomenclature of *leechdom*, *wort-cunning*, and
star-craft. And, finally, the translators of French
poems often found it easier to transfer a foreign
word bodily than to seek out a native synonym,
particularly when the former supplied them with
a rhyme. But the innovation reached even to the
commonest words in every-day use, so that *voice*
drove out *steven*, *poor* drove out *earm*, and *color*,
use, and *place* made good their footing beside *hue*,

wont, and *stead*. A great part of the English words
that were left were so changed in spelling and
pronunciation as to be practically new. Chaucer
stands, in date, midway between King Alfred and
Alfred Tennyson, but his English differs vastly
more from the former's than from the latter's To
Chaucer Anglo-Saxon was as much a dead language as it is to us.

The classical Anglo-Saxon, moreover, had been
the Wessex dialect, spoken and written at Alfred's
capital, Winchester. When the French had displaced this as the language of culture, there was
no longer a " king's English " or any literary standard. The sources of modern standard English
are to be found in the East Midland, spoken in
Lincoln, Norfolk, Suffolk, Cambridge, and neigh-
boring shires. Here the old Anglian had been
corrupted by the Danish settlers, and rapidly threw
off its inflections when it became a spoken and
no longer a written language, after the Conquest.
The West Saxon, clinging more tenaciously to
ancient forms, sunk into the position of a local
dialect; while the East Midland, spreading to London, Oxford, and Cambridge, became the literary
English in which Chaucer wrote.

The Normans brought in also new intellectual
influences and new forms of literature. They
were a cosmopolitan people, and they connected
England with the continent. Lanfranc and An-
selm, the first two Norman archbishops of Canterbury, were learned and splendid prelates of a

type quite unknown to the Anglo-Saxons. They introduced the scholastic philosophy taught at the University of Paris, and the reformed discipline of the Norman abbeys. They bound the English Church more closely to Rome, and officered it with Normans. English bishops were deprived of their sees for illiteracy, and French abbots were set over monasteries of Saxon monks. Down to the middle of the 14th century the learned literature of England was mostly in Latin, and the polite literature in French. English did not at any time altogether cease to be a written language, but the extant remains of the period from 1066 to 1200 are few and, with one exception, unimportant. After 1200 English came more and more into written use, but mainly in translations, paraphrases, and imitations of French words. The native genius was at school, and followed awkwardly the copy set by its master.

The Anglo-Saxon poetry, for example, had been rhythmical and alliterative. It was commonly written in lines containing four rhythmical accents and with three of the accented syllables alliterating.

Reste hine thâ *rúm*-heort ; *ré*ced hlifade
*Ge*áp and *gó*ld-fâh, *gä*st inne swäf.

Rested him then the great-hearted ; the hall towered
Roomy and gold-bright, the guest slept within.

This rude energetic verse the Saxon *scóp* had sung to his harp or *glee-beam*, dwelling on the em-

phatic syllables, passing swiftly over the others
which were of undetermined number and position
in the line. It was now displaced by the smooth
metrical verse with rhymed endings, which the
French introduced and which our modern poets
use, a verse fitted to be recited rather than sung.
The old English alliterative verse continued, indeed, in occasional use to the 16th century. But
it was linked to a forgotten literature and an obsolete dialect, and was doomed to give way.
Chaucer lent his great authority to the more
modern verse system, and his own literary models
and inspirers were all foreign, French or Italian.
Literature in England began to be once more
English and truly national in the hands of Chaucer
and his contemporaries, but it was the literature
of a nation cut off from its own past by three centuries of foreign rule.

The most noteworthy English document of the
11th and 12th centuries was the continuation of
the Anglo-Saxon chronicle. Copies of these annals, differing somewhat among themselves, had
been kept at the monasteries in Winchester,
Abingdon, Worcester, and elsewhere. The yearly
entries were mostly brief, dry records of passing
events, though occasionally they become full and
animated. The fen country of Cambridge and
Lincolnshire was a region of monasteries. Here
were the great abbeys of Peterborough and Croy-
land and Ely minster. One of the earliest English
songs tells how the savage heart of the Danish

king Cnut was softened by the singing of the monks
in Ely.

> Merie sungen muneches binnen Ely
> Tha Cnut chyning reu ther by ;
> Roweth, cnihtes, noer the land,
> And here we thes muneches sang.

It was among the dikes and marshes of this fen
country that the bold outlaw Hereward, "the last
of the English," held out for some years against
the conqueror.   And it was here, in the rich
abbey of Burch or Peterborough, the ancient
Medeshamstede (meadow - homestead) that the
chronicle was continued for nearly a century after
the Conquest, breaking off abruptly in 1154, the
date of King Stephen's death.   Peterborough had
received a new Norman abbot, Turold, "a very
stern man," and the entry in the chronicle for
1170 tells how, Hereward and his gang, with his
Danish backers, thereupon plundered the abbey
of its treasures, which were first removed to Ely,
and then carried off by the Danish fleet and sunk,
lost, or squandered.   The English in the later
portions of this Peterborough chronicle becomes
gradually more modern, and falls away more and
more from the strict grammatical standards of the
classical Anglo-Saxon.   It is a most valuable historical monument, and some passages of it are
written with great vividness, notably the sketch of
William the Conqueror put down in the year of
his death (1086) by one who had " looked upon
him and at another time dwelt in his court."

" He who was before a rich king, and lord of many a land, he had not then of all his land but a piece of seven feet. . . . Likewise he was a very stark man and a terrible, so that one durst do nothing against his will. . . . Among other things is not to be forgotton the good peace that he made in this land, so that a man might fare over his kingdom with his bosom full of gold unhurt. He set up a great deer preserve, and he laid laws therewith that whoso should slay hart or hind, he should be blinded. As greatly did he love the tall deer as if he were their father."

With the discontinuance of the Peterborough annals, English history written in English prose ceased for three hundred years. The thread of the nation's story was kept up in Latin chronicles, compiled by writers partly of English and partly of Norman descent. The earliest of these, such as Ordericus Vitalis, Simeon of Durham, Henry of Huntingdon, and William of Malmesbury, were contemporary with the later entries of the Saxon chronicle. The last of them, Matthew of Westminster, finished his work in 1273. About 1300 Robert, a monk of Gloucester, composed a chronicle in English verse, following in the main the authority of the Latin chronicles, and he was succeeded by other rhyming chroniclers in the 14th century. In the hands of these the true history of the Saxon times was overlaid with an ever-increasing mass of fable and legend. All real knowledge of the period dwindled away until in Capgrave's *Chronicle of England*, written in prose in 1463–64, hardly any thing of it is left. In history as in literature the English had forgotten their past, and had turned to foreign sources. It is noteworthy that Shakspere, who borrowed his subjects and his heroes sometimes from authentic English history, sometimes from the legendary history of ancient Britain, Denmark, and Scotland, as in Lear, Hamlet, and Macbeth, ignores the Saxon period altogether. And Spenser, who gives in his second book of the *Faerie Queene*, a *resumé* of the reigns of fabulous British kings—the supposed ancestors of Queen Elizabeth, his royal patron—has nothing to say of the real kings of early England. So completely had the true record faded away that it made no appeal to the imaginations of our most patriotic poets. The Saxon Alfred had been dethroned by the British Arthur, and the conquered Welsh had imposed their fictitious genealogies upon the dynasty of the conquerors. In the *Roman de Rou*, a verse chronicle of the dukes of Normandy, written by the Norman Wace, it is related that at the battle of Hastings the French *jongleur*, Taillefer, spurred out before the van of William's army, tossing his lance in the air and chanting of " Charlemagne and of Roland, of Oliver and the peers who died at Roncesvals." This incident is prophetic of the victory which Norman song, no less than Norman arms, was to win over England. The lines which Taillefer sang were from the *Chanson de Roland*, the oldest and best of the French hero sagas. The heathen Northmen, who had ravaged the coasts of France in the 10th century, had become in the course of one hundred and fifty years, completely identified with the French. They had accepted Christianity, intermarried with the native women, and forgotten their own Norse tongue. The race thus formed was the most brilliant in Europe. The warlike, adventurous spirit of the vikings mingled in its blood with the French nimbleness of wit and fondness for display. The Normans were a nation of knights-errant, with a passion for prowess and for courtesy. Their architecture was at once strong and graceful. Their women were skilled in embroidery, a splendid sample of which is preserved in the famous Bayeux tapestry, in which the conqueror's wife, Matilda, and the ladies of her court wrought the history of the Conquest.

This national taste for decoration expressed itself not only in the ceremonious pomp of feast and chase and tourney, but likewise in literature. The most characteristic contribution of the Normans to English poetry were the metrical romances or chivalry tales. These were sung or recited by the minstrels, who were among the retainers of every great feudal baron, or by the *jongleurs*, who wandered from court to castle. There is a whole literature of these *romans d' aventure* in the Anglo-Norman dialect of French. Many of them are very long — often thirty, forty, or fifty thousand lines—written sometimes in a strophic form, sometimes in long Alexandrines, but commonly in the short, eight-syllabled rhyming couplet. Numbers of them were turned into English verse in the 13th, 14th, and 15th centuries. The translations were usually inferior to the originals. The French *trouvere* (finder or poet) told his story in a straightforward, prosaic fashion, omitting no details in the action and unrolling endless descriptions of dresses, trappings, gardens, etc. He invented plots and situations full of fine possibilities by which later poets have profited, but his own handling of them was feeble and prolix. Yet there was a simplicity about the old French language and a certain elegance and delicacy in the diction of the *trouveres* which the rude, unformed English failed to catch.

The heroes of these romances were of various climes: Guy of Warwick, and Richard the Lion Heart of England, Havelok the Dane, Sir Troilus of Troy, Charlemagne, and Alexander. But, strangely enough, the favorite hero of English romance was that mythical Arthur of Britain, whom Welsh legend had celebrated as the most formidable enemy of the Sassenach invaders and their victor in twelve great battles. The language and literature of the ancient Cymry or Welsh had made no impression on their Anglo-Saxon conquerors. There are a few Welsh borrowings in the English speech, such as *bard* and *druid*; but in the old Anglo-Saxon literature there are no more traces of British song and story than if the two races had been sundered by the ocean instead of being borderers for over six hundred years. But the Welsh had their own national traditions, and after the Norman Conquest these were set free from the isolation of their Celtic tongue and, in an indirect form, entered into the general literature of Europe. The French came into contact with the old British literature in two places: in the Welsh marches in England and in the province of Brittany in France, where the population is of Cymric race and spoke, and still to some extent speaks, a Cymric dialect akin to the Welsh.

About 1140 Geoffrey of Monmouth, a Benedictine monk, seemingly of Welsh descent, who lived at the court of Henry the First and became afterward bishop of St. Asaph, produced in Latin a so-called *Historia Britonum* in which it was told how Brutus, the great grandson of Æneas, came to Britain, and founded there his kingdom called after him, and his city of New Troy (Troynovant) on the site of the later London. An air of historic gravity was given to this tissue of Welsh legends by an exact chronology and the genealogy of the British kings, and the author referred, as his authority, to an imaginary Welsh book given him, as he said, by a certain Walter, archdeacon of Oxford. Here appeared that line of fabulous British princes which has become so familiar to modern readers in the plays of Shakspere and the poems of Tennyson: Lear and his

2

three daughters; Cymbeline, Gorboduc, the subject
of the earliest regular English tragedy, composed
by Sackville and acted in 1562; Locrine and his
Queen Gwendolen, and his daughter Sabrina, who
gave her name to the river Severn, was made immortal by an exquisite song in Milton's *Comus*,
and became the heroine of the tragedy of *Locrine*,
once attributed to Shakspere; and above all, Arthur, the son of Uther Pendragon, and the founder
of the Table Round.   In 1155 Wace, the author
of the *Roman de Rou*, turned Geoffrey's work into a French poem entitled *Brut d' Angleterre*,
"brut" being a Welsh word meaning chronicle.
About the year 1200 Wace's poem was Englished
by Layamon, a priest of Arley Regis, on the
border stream of Severn.   Layamon's *Brut* is in
thirty thousand lines, partly alliterative and partly
rhymed, but written in pure Saxon English with
hardly any French words.   The style is rude but
vigorous, and, at times, highly imaginative.   Wace
had amplified Geoffrey's chronicle somewhat, but
Layamon made much larger additions, derived,
no doubt, from legends current on the Welsh
border.   In particular the story of Arthur grew
in his hands into something like fullness.   He
tells of the enchantments of Merlin, the wizard;
of the unfaithfulness of Arthur's queen, Guenever;
and the treachery of his nephew, Modred.   His
narration of the last great battle between Arthur
and Modred; of the wounding of the king—"fifteen
fiendly wounds he had, one might in the least

three gloves thrust—"; and of the little boat with
" two women therein, wonderly dight," which
came to bear him away to Avalun and the Queen
Argante, " sheenest of all elves," whence he shall
come again, according to Merlin's prophecy, to rule
the Britons; all this left little, in essentials, for
Tennyson to add in his *Death of Arthur*. This
new material for fiction was eagerly seized upon
by the Norman romancers. The story of Arthur
drew to itself other stories which were afloat.
Walter Map, a gentleman of the Court of Henry
II., in two French prose romances, connected with
it the church legend of the Sangreal, or holy cup,
from which Christ had drunk at his last supper,
and which Joseph of Arimathea had afterward
brought to England. Then it miraculously disappeared and became thenceforth the occasion
of knightly quest, the mystic symbol of the object of the soul's desire, an adventure only to be
achieved by the maiden knight, Galahad, the son
of the great Launcelot, who in the romances had
taken the place of Modred in Geoffrey's history, as
the paramour of Queen Guenever. In like manner the love-story of Tristan and Isolde was
joined by other romancers to the Arthur-Saga.
This came probably from Brittany or Cornwall.
Thus there grew up a great epic cycle of Arthurian romance, with a fixed shape and a unity
and vitality which have prolonged it to our own
day and rendered it capable of a deeper and
more spiritual treatment and a more artistic hand-

ling by such modern English poets as Tennyson in his *Idyls of the King*, by Matthew Arnold, Swinburne, and many others. There were innumerable Arthur romances in prose and verse, in Anglo-Norman and continental French dialects, in English, in German, and in other tongues. But the final form which the Saga took in mediæval England was the prose *Morte Dartur* of Sir Thomas Malory, composed at the close of the 15th century. This was a digest of the earlier romances and is Tennyson's main authority.

Besides the literature of the knight was the literature of the cloister. There is a considerable body of religious writing in early English, consisting of homilies in prose and verse, books of devotion, like the *Ancren Riwle* (Rule of Anchoresses), 1225; the *Ayenbite of Inwyt* (Remorse of Conscience), 1340, both in prose; the *Handlyng Sinne*, 1303; the *Cursor Mundi*, 1320; and the *Pricke of Conscience*, 1340, in verse; metrical renderings of the Psalter, the Pater Noster, the Creed, and the Ten Commandments, the Gospels for the Day, such as the *Ormulum*, or Book of Orm, 1205; legends and miracles of saints; poems in praise of virginity, on the contempt of the world, on the five joys of the Virgin, the five wounds of Christ, the eleven pains of hell, the seven deadly sins, the fifteen tokens of the coming judgment, and dialogues between the soul and the body. These were the works not only of the monks, but also of the begging friars, and in smaller part of the secular or parish clergy. They are full of the ascetic piety and superstition of the Middle Age, the childish belief in the marvelous, the allegorical interpretation of Scripture texts, the grotesque material horrors of hell with its grisly fiends, the vileness of the human body and the loathsome details of its corruption after death. Now and then a single poem rises above the tedious and hideous barbarism of the general level of this monkish literature, either from a more intensely personal feeling in the poet, or from an occasional grace or beauty in his verse. A poem so distinguished is, for example, *A Luve Ron* (A Love Counsel) by the Minorite friar, Thomas de Hales, one stanza of which recalls the French poet Villon's *Balade of Dead Ladies*, with its refrain.

> "Mais ou sont les neiges d'antan?"
> "Where are the snows of yester year?"
> Where is Paris and Heléyne
> That weren so bright and fair of blee*
> Amadas, Tristan, and Idéyne
> Yseudë and allë the,†
> Hector with his sharpë main,
> And Cæsar rich in worldës fee?
> They beth ygliden out of the reign‡
> As the shaft is of the clee." §

A few early English poems on secular subjects are also worthy of mention, among others, *The Owl and the Nightingale*, generally assigned to the reign of Henry III. (1216–1272), an *Estrif*,

* Hue.   † Those.   ‡ Realm,   § Bowstring.

or dispute, in which the owl represents the ascetic
and the nightingale the æsthetic view of life.
The debate is conducted with much animation and
a spirited use of proverbial wisdom. *The Land of
Cokaygne* is an amusing little poem of some two
hundred lines, belonging to the class of *fabliaux*,
short humorous tales or satirical pieces in verse.
It describes a lubber-land, or fool's paradise, where
the geese fly down all roasted on the spit, bringing garlic in the bills for their dressing, and where
there is a nunnery upon a river of sweet milk, and
an abbey of white monks and gray, whose walls,
like the hall of little King Pepin, are " of pie-
crust and pastry crust," with flouren cakes for
the shingles and fat puddings for the pins.

There are a few songs dating from about 1300,
and mostly found in a single collection (Harl.
MS., 2253), which are almost the only English
verse before Chaucer that has any sweetness to
a modern ear.   They are written in French
strophic forms in the southern dialect, and sometimes have an intermixture of French and Latin
lines.   They are musical, fresh, simple, and many
of them very pretty.   They celebrate the gladness
of spring with its cuckoos and throstle-cocks, its
daisies and woodruff.

> "When the nightingalë sings the woodës waxen green
> Leaf and grass and blossom spring in Averil, I ween,
> And love is to my hertë gone with a spear so keen,
> Night and day my blood it drinks my hertë doth me tene.*

---

* Pain.

Others are love plaints to "Alysoun" or some other lady whose "name is in a note of the nightingale; " whose eyes are as gray as glass, and her skin as " red as rose on ris." * Some employ a burden or refrain.

> " Blow, northern wind,
> Blow thou me, my sweeting.
> Blow, northern wind, blow, blow, blow ! "

Others are touched with a light melancholy at the coming of winter.

> " Winter wakeneth all my care
> Now these leavës waxeth bare.
> Oft I sigh and mournë sare
> When it cometh in my thought
> Of this worldes joy, how it goeth all to nought."

Some of these poems are love songs to Christ or the Virgin, .composed in the warm language of earthly passion. The sentiment of chivalry united with the ecstatic reveries of the cloister had produced Mariolatry and the imagery of the Song of Solomon, in which Christ wooes the soul, had made this feeling of divine love familiar. Toward the end of the 13th century a collection of lives of saints, a sort of English *Golden Legend*, was prepared at the great abbey of Gloucester for uşe on saints' days. The legends were chosen partly from the hagiology of the Church Catholic, as the lives of Margaret, Christopher, and Michael; partly from the calendar of the English Church, as the

* Branch.

lives of St. Thomas of Canterbury, of the Anglo-Saxons, Dunstan, Swithin—who is mentioned by Shakspere — and Kenelm, whose life is quoted by Chaucer in the *Nonne Preste's Tale*. The verse was clumsy and the style monotonous, but an imaginative touch here and there has furnished a hint to later poets. Thus the legend of St. Brandan's search for the earthly paradise has been treated by Matthew Arnold and William Morris.

About the middle of the 14th century there was a revival of the Old English alliterative verse in romances like *William and the Werewolf*, and *Sir Gawayne*, and in religious pieces such as *Clannesse* (purity), *Patience* and *The Perle*, the last named a mystical poem of much beauty, in which a bereaved father sees a vision of his daughter among the glorified. Some of these employed rhyme as well as alliteration. They are in the West Midland dialect, although Chaucer implies that alliteration was most common in the north. " I am a sotherne man," says the parson in the *Canterbury Tales*. " I cannot geste rom, ram, ruf, by my letter." But the most important of the alliterative poems was the *Vision of William concerning Piers the Plowman*. In the second half of the 14th century French had ceased to be the mother-tongue of any considerable part of the population of England. By a statute of Edward III., in 1362, it was displaced from the law courts. By 1386 English had taken its place in the schools. The

Anglo-Norman dialect had grown corrupt, and Chaucer contrasts the French of Paris with the provincial French spoken by his prioress, "after the scole of Stratford-atte-Bowe." The native English genius was also beginning to assert itself, roused in part, perhaps, by the English victories in the wars of Edward III. against the French. It was the bows of the English yeomanry that won the fight at Crecy, fully as much as the prowess of the Norman baronage. But at home the times were bad. Heavy taxes and the repeated visitations of the pestilence, or Black Death, pressed upon the poor and wasted the land. The Church was corrupt; the mendicant orders had grown enormously wealthy, and the country was eaten up by a swarm of begging friars, pardoners, and apparitors. The social discontent was fermenting among the lower classes, which finally issued in the communistic uprising of the peasantry, under Wat Tyler and Jack Straw. This state of things is reflected in the *Vision of Piers Plowman*, written as early as 1362, by William Langland, a tonsured clerk of the west country. It is in form an allegory, and bears some resemblance to the later and more famous allegory of the *Pilgrim's Progress*. The poet falls asleep on the Malvern Hills, in Worcestershire, and has a vision of a "fair field full of folk," representing the world with its various conditions of men. There were pilgrims and palmers; hermits with hooked staves, who went to Walsingham—and

their wenches after them—great lubbers and long
that were loth to work : friars glossing the Gospel
for their own profit; pardoners cheating the people with relics and indulgences; parish priests
who forsook their parishes—that had been poor
since the pestilence time—and went to London to
sing there for simony; bishops, archbishops, and
deacons, who got themselves fat clerkships in the
Exchequer, or King's Bench; in short, all manner
of lazy and corrupt ecclesiastics. A lady, who represents holy Church, then appears to the dreamer,
explains to him the meaning of his vision, and
reads him a sermon the text of which is, " When
all treasure is tried, truth is the best."   A number
of other allegorical figures are next introduced,
Conscience, Reason, Meed, Simony, Falsehood,
etc., and after a series of speeches and adventures,
a second vision begins in which the seven deadly
sins pass before the poet in a succession of graphic
impersonations, and finally all the characters set
out on a pilgrimage in search of St. Truth, finding
no guide to direct them save Piers the Plowman,
who stands for the simple, pious laboring man, the
sound heart of the English common folk. The
poem was originally in eight divisions or " passus,"
to which was added a continuation in three parts,
Vita Do Wel, Do Bet, and *Do Best.* About 1377
the whole was greatly enlarged by the author.

Piers Plowman was the first extended literary
work after the Conquest which was purely English
in character. It owed nothing to France but the

allegorical cast which the *Roman de la Rose* had
made fashionable in both countries. But even
here such personified abstractions as Langland's
Fair-speech and Work-when-time-is, remind us less
of the Fraunchise, Bel-amour, and Fals-semblaunt
of the French courtly allegories than of Bunyan's Mr. Worldly Wiseman, and even of such
Puritan names as Praise-God Barebones, and
Zeal-of-the-land Busy. The poem is full of English moral seriousness, of shrewd humor, the
hatred of a lie, the homely English love for reality.
It has little unity of plan, but is rather a series of
episodes, discourses, parables, and scenes. It is
all astir with the actual life of the time. We see
the gossips gathered in the ale-house of Betun the
brewster, and the pastry cooks in the London
streets crying "Hote pies, hote! Good gees and
grys. Go we dine, go we!" Had Langland not
linked his literary fortunes with an uncouth and
obsolescent verse, and had he possessed a finer
artistic sense and a higher poetic imagination, his
book might have been, like Chaucer's, among the
lasting glories of our tongue. As it is, it is forgotten by all but professional students of literature
and history. Its popularity in its own day is
shown by the number of MSS. which are extant,
and by imitations, such as *Piers the Plowman's
Crede* (1394), and the *Plowman's Tale*, for a long
time wrongly inserted in the *Canterbury Tales*.
Piers became a kind of typical figure, like the
French peasant, *Jacques Bonhomme*, and was ap-

pealed to as such by the Protestant reformers of the 16th century.

The attack upon the growing corruptions of the Church was made more systematically, and from the stand-point of a theologian rather than of a popular moralist and satirist, by John Wiclif, the rector of Lutterworth and professor of Divinity in Baliol College, Oxford. In a series of Latin and English tracts he made war against indulgences, pilgrimages, images, oblations, the friars, the pope, and the doctrine of transubstantiation. But his greatest service to England was his translation of the Bible, the first complete version in the mother-tongue. This he made about 1380, with the help of Nicholas Hereford, and a revision of it was made by another disciple, Purvey, some ten years later. There was no knowledge of Hebrew or Greek in England at that time, and the Wiclifite versions were made not from the original tongues, but from the Latin Vulgate. In his anxiety to make his rendering close, and mindful, perhaps, of the warning in the Apocalypse, " If any man shall take away from the words of the book of this prophecy, God shall take away his part out of the book of life," Wiclif followed the Latin order of construction so literally as to make rather awkward English, translating, for example, *Quid sibi vult hoc somnium?* by *What to itself wole this sweven?* Purvey's revision was somewhat freer and more idiomatic. In the reigns of Henry IV. and V. it was forbidden to read or to have any of Wiclif's writings. Such of them as could be seized were publicly burned. In spite of this, copies of his Bible circulated secretly in great numbers. Forshall and Madden, in their great edition (1850), enumerate one hundred and fifty MSS. which had been consulted by them. Later translators, like Tyndale and the makers of the Authorized Version, or " King James' Bible " (1611), followed Wiclif's language in many instances; so that he was, in truth, the first author of our biblical dialect and the founder of that great monument of noble English which has been the main conservative influence in the mother-tongue, holding it fast to many strong, pithy words and idioms that would else have been lost. In 1415, some thirty years after Wiclif's death, by decree of the Council of Constance, his bones were dug up from the soil of Lutterworth chancel and burned, and the ashes cast into the Swift. " The brook," says Thomas Fuller, in his *Church History*, " did convey his ashes into Avon; Avon into Severn; Severn into the narrow seas; they into the main ocean. And thus the ashes of Wiclif are the emblem of his doctrine, which now is dispersed all the world over."

Although the writings thus far mentioned are of very high interest to the student of the English language, and the historian of English manners and culture, they cannot be said to have much importance as mere literature. But in Geoffrey Chaucer (died 1400) we meet with a poet of the first rank, whose works are increasingly read and will always continue to be a source of delight and refreshment to the general reader as well as a " well of English undefiled " to the professional man of letters. With the exception of Dante, Chaucer was the greatest of the poets of mediæval Europe, and he remains one of the greatest of English poets, and certainly the foremost of English story-tellers in verse. He was the son of a London vintner, and was in his youth in the service of Lionel, Duke of Clarence, one of the sons of Edward III. He made a campaign in France in 1359–60, when he was taken prisoner. Afterward he was attached to the court and received numerous favors and appointments. He was sent on several diplomatic missions by the king, three of them to Italy, where, in all probability, he made the acquaintance of the new Italian literature, the writings of Dante, Petrarch, and Boccaccio. He was appointed at different times Comptroller of the Wool Customs, Comptroller of Petty Customs, and Clerk of the Works. He sat for Kent in Parliament, and he received pensions from three successive kings. He was a man of business as well as books, and he loved men and nature no less than study. He knew his world; he " saw life steadily and saw it whole." Living at the center of English social and political life, and resorting to the court of Edward III., then the most brilliant in Europe, Chaucer was an eye-witness of those feudal pomps which fill the high-colored pages of his contemporary, the French chronicler,

Froissart. His description of a tournament in the *Knight's Tale* is unexcelled for spirit and detail. He was familiar with dances, feasts, and state ceremonies, and all the life of the baronial castle, in bower and hall, the " trompes with the loude minstralcie," the heralds, the ladies, and the squires,

> " What hawkës sitten on the perch above,
> What houndës liggen on the floor adown."

But his sympathy reached no less the life of the lowly, the poor widow in her narrow cottage, and that " trewe swynkere and a good," the plowman whom Langland had made the hero of his vision. He is, more than all English poets, the poet of the lusty spring, of " Aprillë with her showrës sweet " and the "foulës song," of " May with all her flourës and her greenë," of the new leaves in the wood, and the meadows new powdered with the daisy, the mystic Marguerite of his *Legend of Good Women*. A fresh vernal air blows through all his pages.

In Chaucer's earlier works, such as the translation of the *Romaunt of the Rose* (if that be his), the *Boke of the Duchesse*, the *Parlament of Foules*, the *Hous of Fame*, as well as in the *Legend of Good Women*, which was later, the inspiration of the French court poetry of the 13th and 14th centuries is manifest. He retains in them the mediæval machinery of allegories and dreams, the elaborate descriptions of palaces, temples, portraitures, etc., which had been made fashionable in France by such poems as Guillaume de Lorris's *Roman de la Rose*, and Jean Machault's *La Fontainé Amoureuse.* In some of these the influence of Italian poetry is also perceptible. There are suggestions from Dante, for example, in the *Parlament of Foules* and the *Hous of Fame,* and *Troilus and Cresseide* is a free handling rather than a translation of Boccaccio's *Filostrato.* In all of these there are passages of great beauty and force. Had Chaucer written nothing else, he would still have been remembered as the most accomplished English poet of his time, but he would not have risen to the rank which he now occupies, as one of the greatest English poets of all time. This position he owes to his masterpiece, the *Canterbury Tales.* Here he abandoned the imitation of foreign models and the artificial literary fashions of his age, and wrote of real life from his own ripe knowledge of men and things.

The *Canterbury Tales* are a collection of stories written at different times, but put together, probably, toward the close of his life. The frame-work into which they are fitted is one of the happiest ever devised. A number of pilgrims who are going on horseback to the shrine of St. Thomas à Becket, at Canterbury, meet at the Tabard Inn, in Southwark, a suburb of London. The jolly host of the Tabard, Harry Bailey, proposes that on their way to Canterbury, each of the company shall tell two tales, and two more on their way back, and

that the one who tells the best shall have a supper
at the cost of the rest when they return to the
inn. He himself accompanies them as judge and
" reporter." In the setting of the stories there is
thus a constant feeling of movement and the air
of all outdoors. The little " head-links " and
" end-links " which bind them together, give incidents of the journey and glimpses of the talk of
the pilgrims, sometimes amounting, as in the prologue of the *Wife of Bath*, to full and almost
dramatic character-sketches. The stories, too, are
dramatically suited to the narrators. The general
prologue is a series of such character-sketches,
the most perfect in English poetry. The portraits of the pilgrims are illuminated with the soft
brilliancy and the minute loving fidelity of the
miniatures in the old missals, and with the same
quaint precision in traits of expression and in cos-
tume. The pilgrims are not all such as one would
meet nowadays at an English inn. The presence of a knight, a squire, a yeoman archer, and
especially of so many kinds of ecclesiastics, a nun,
a friar, a monk, a pardoner, and a sompnour or ap-
paritor, reminds us that the England of that day
must have been less like Protestant England, as
we know it, than like the Italy of some thirty
years ago. But however the outward face of
society may have changed, the Canterbury pilgrims remain, in Chaucer's description, living and
universal types of human nature. The *Canterbury
Tales* are twenty-four in number. There were thirty-

3

two pilgrims, so that if finished as designed the whole collection would have numbered one hundred and twenty-eight stories.

Chaucer is the bright consummate flower of the English Middle Age. Like many another great poet, he put the final touch to the various literary forms that he found in cultivation. Thus his *Knight's Tale*, based upon Boccaccio's *Teseide*, is the best of English mediæval romances. And yet the *Rime of Sir Thopas*, who goes seeking an elf queen for his mate, and is encountered by the giant Sir Olifaunt, burlesques these same romances with their impossible adventures and their tedious rambling descriptions. The tales of the prioress and the second nun are saints' legends. The *Monk's Tale* is a set of dry, moral apologues in the manner of his contemporary, the " moral Gower." The stories told by the reeve, miller, friar, sompnour, shipman, and merchant, belong to the class of *fabliaux*, a few of which existed in English, such as *Dame Siriz*, the *Lay of the Ash*, and the *Land of Cokaygne*, already mentioned. The *Noune Preste's Tale*, likewise, which Dryden modernized with admirable humor, was of the class of *fabliaux*, and was suggested by a little poem in forty lines, *Dou Coc et Werpil*, by Marie de France, a Norman poetess of the 13th century. It belonged, like the early English poem of *The Fox and the Wolf*, to the popular animal-saga of *Reynard the Fox*. The *Franklin's Tale*, whose scene is Brittany, and the *Wife of Baths'*

Tale, which is laid in the time of the British Arthur, belong to the class of French *lais*, serious metrical tales shorter than the romance and of Breton origin, the best representatives of which are the elegant and graceful *lais* of Marie de France.

Chaucer was our first great master of laughter and of tears. His serious poetry is full of the tenderest pathos. His loosest tales are delightfully humorous and life-like. He is the kindliest of satirists. The knavery, greed, and hypocrisy of the begging friars and the sellers of indulgences are exposed by him as pitilessly as by Langland and Wiclif, though his mood is not like theirs, one of stern, moral indignation, but rather the good-natured scorn of a man of the world. His charity is broad enough to cover even the corrupt sompnour of whom he says,

"And yet in sooth he was a good felawe."

Whether he shared Wiclif's opinions is unknown, but John of Gaunt, the Duke of Lancaster and father of Henry IV., who was Chaucer's life-long patron, was likewise Wiclif's great upholder against the persecution of the bishops. It is, perhaps, not without significance that the poor parson in the *Canterbury Tales*, the only one of his ecclesiastical pilgrims whom Chaucer treats with respect, is suspected by the host of the Tabard to be a "loller," that is, a Lollard, or disciple of Wiclif, and that because he objects to the jovial innkeeper's swearing "by Goddes bones."

Chaucer's English is nearly as easy for a modern reader as Shakspere's, and few of his words have become obsolete. His verse, when rightly read, is correct and melodious. The early English was, in some respects, more " sweet upon the tongue " than the modern language. The vowels had their broad Italian sounds, and the speech was full of soft gutturals and vocalic syllables, like the endings ën, ës, and ë, which made feminine rhymes and kept the consonants from coming harshly together.

Great poet as Chaucer was, he was not quite free from the literary weakness of his time. He relapses sometimes into the babbling style of the old chroniclers and legend writers; cites " auctours " and gives long catalogues of names and objects with a *naïve* display of learning; and introduces vulgar details in his most exquisite passages. There is something childish about almost all the thought and art of the Middle Ages—at least outside of Italy, where classical models and traditions never quite lost their hold. But Chaucer's artlessness is half the secret of his wonderful ease in story-telling, and is so engaging that, like a child's sweet unconsciousness, one would not wish it otherwise.

The *Canterbury Tales* had shown of what high uses the English language was capable, but the curiously trilingual condition of literature still continued. French was spoken in the proceedings of Parliament as late as the reign of Henry

VI. (1422–1471). Chaucer's contemporary, John Gower, wrote his *Vox Clamantis* in Latin, his *Speculum Meditantis* (a lost poem), and a number of *ballades* in Parisian French, and his *Confessio Amantis* (1393) in English. The last named is a dreary, pedantic work, in some 15,000 smooth, monotonous, eight - syllabled couplets, in which Grande Amour instructs the lover how to get the love of Bel Pucell.

1. Early English Literature. By Bernhard ten Brink. Translated from the German by H. M. Kennedy. New York: Henry Holt & Co., 1883.

2. Morris and Skeat's Specimens of Early English. (Clarendon Press Series.) Oxford.

3. Langland's Vision of William concerning Piers the Plowman. Wright's Edition; or Skeat's, in Early English Text Society publications.

4. Chaucer: Canterbury Tales. Tyrwhitt's Edition; or Wright's, in Percy Society publications.

5. Complete Writings. Morris's Edition. 6 vols. (In Aldine Series.)

CHAPTER II.

FROM CHAUCER TO SPENSER.

1400–1599.

THE 15th century was a barren period in Enlish literary history. It was nearly two hundred years after Chaucer's death before any poet came, whose name can be written in the same line with his. He was followed at once by a number of imitators who caught the trick of his language and verse, but lacked the genius to make any fine use of them. The *manner* of a true poet may be learned, but his style, in the high sense of the word, remains his own secret. Some of the poems which have been attributed to Chaucer and printed in editions of his works, as the *Court of Love*, the *Flower and the Leaf*, the *Cuckow and the Nightingale*, are now regarded by many scholars as the work of later writers. If not Chaucer's, they are of Chaucer's school, and the first two, at least, are very pretty poems after the fashion of his minor pieces, such as the *Boke of the Duchesse* and the *Parlament of Foules*.

Among his professed disciples was Thomas Occleve, a dull rhymer, who, in his *Governail of Princes*, a didactic poem translated from the Latin about 1413, drew, or caused to be drawn, on the margin of his MS. a colored portrait of his " maister dere and fader reverent,"

"This londes verray tresour and richesse,
Dethe by thy dethe hath harm irreparable
Unto us done ; hir vengeable duresse
Dispoiled hath this londe of the swetnesse
Of Rhetoryk."

Another versifier of this same generation was John Lydgate, a Benedictine monk, of the Abbey of Bury St. Edmunds, in Suffolk, a very prolix writer, who composed, among other things, the *Story of Thebes*, as an addition to the *Canterbury Tales*. His ballad of *London Lyckpenny*, recounting the adventures of a countryman who goes to the law courts at Westminster in search of justice,

" But for lack of mony I could not speede,"

is of interest for the glimpse that it gives us of London street life.

Chaucer's influence wrought more fruitfully in Scotland, whither it was carried by James I., who had been captured by the English when a boy of eleven, and brought up at Windsor as a prisoner of State. There he wrote during the reign of Henry V. (1413-1422) a poem in six cantos, entitled the *King's Quhair* (King's Book), in Chaucer's seven lined stanza which had been employed by Lydgate in his *Falls of Princes* (from Boccaccio), and which was afterward called

the "rime royal," from its use by King James.
The *King's Quhair* tells how the poet, on a May
morning, looks from the window of his prison
chamber into the castle garden full of alleys, haw-
thorn hedges, and fair arbors set with

> "The sharpē, greenē, sweetē juniper."

He was listening to "the little sweetë nightingale,"
when suddenly casting down his eyes he saw a
lady walking in the garden, and at once his "heart
became her thrall." The incident is precisely
like Palamon's first sight of Emily in Chaucer's
Knight's Tale, and almost in the very words of
Palamon, the poet addresses his lady:

> "Ah, sweet, are ye a worldly crēature
> Or heavenly thing in likeness of natúre?
> Or are ye very Nature, the goddéss,
> That have depainted with your heavenly hand
> This garden full of flowrës as they stand?"

Then, after a vision in the taste of the age, in
which the royal prisoner is transported in turn to
the courts of *Venus*, *Minerva*, and *Fortune*, and
receives their instruction in the duties belonging to Love's service, he wakes from sleep and a
white turtle-dove brings to his window a spray of
red gillyflowers, whose leaves are inscribed, in gold-
en letters, with a message of encouragement.

　　James I. may be reckoned among the English
poets. He mentions Chaucer, Gower, and Lydgate as his masters. His education was English,
and so was the dialect of his poem, although the

unique MS. of it is in the Scotch spelling. The
King's Quhair is somewhat overladen with ornament and with the fashionable allegorical devices,
but it is, upon the whole, a rich and tender love
song, the best specimen of court poetry between
the time of Chaucer and the time of Spenser.
The lady who walked in the garden on that May
morning was Jane Beaufort, niece to Henry IV.
She was married to her poet after his release from
captivity and became Queen of Scotland in 1424.
Twelve years later James was murdered by Sir
Robert Graham and his Highlanders, and his wife,
who strove to defend him, was wounded by the
assassins.　The story of the murder has been told
of late by D. G. Rossetti, in his ballad, *The King's
Tragedy*.

The whole life of this princely singer was, like
his poem, in the very spirit of romance.

The effect of all this imitation of Chaucer was
to fix a standard of literary style, and to confirm
the authority of the East-Midland English in
which he had written.　Though the poets of the
15th century were not overburdened with genius,
they had, at least; a definite model to follow.　As
in the 14th century, metrical romances continued
to be translated from the French, homilies and
saints' legends and rhyming chronicles were still
manufactured.　But the poems of Occleve and
Lydgate and James I. had helped to polish and
refine the tongue and to prolong the Chaucerian
tradition.　The literary English never again slipped

back into the chaos of dialects which had pre-
vailed before Chaucer.

In the history of every literature the development of prose is later than that of verse. The
latter being, by its very form, artificial, is cultivated
as a fine art, and its records preserved in an early
stage of society, when prose is simply the talk of
men, and not thought worthy of being written and
kept. English prose labored under the added
disadvantage of competing with Latin, which was
the cosmopolitan tongue and the medium of com-
munication between scholars of all countries.
Latin was the language of the Church, and in the
Middle Ages churchman and scholar were con-
vertible terms. The word *clerk* meant either priest
or scholar. Two of the *Canterbury Tales* are in
prose, as is also the *Testament of Love*, formerly
ascribed to Chaucer, and the style of all these is so
feeble, wandering, and unformed that it is hard to
believe that they were written by the same man
who wrote the *Knight's Tale* and the story of
Griselda. *The Voiage and Travaile of Sir John
Maundeville*—the forerunner of that great library
of Oriental travel which has enriched our modern
literature—was written, according to its author,
first in Latin, then in French, and, lastly, in the
year 1356, translated into English for the behoof
of "lordes and knyghtes and othere noble and
worthi men, that conne not Latyn but lityle."
The author professed to have spent over thirty
years in Eastern travel, to have penetrated as far

as Farther India and the "iles that ben abouten
Indi," to have been in the service of the Sultan of
Babylon in his wars against the Bedouins, and, at.
another time, in the employ of the Great Khan of
Tartary. But there is no copy of the Latin version of his travels extant; the French seems to be
much later than 1356, and the English MS. to belong to the early years of the fifteenth century, and
to have been made by another hand. Recent inves-
tigations make it probable that Maundeville borrowed his descriptions of the remoter East from
many sources, and particularly from the narrative
of Odoric, a Minorite friar of Lombardy, who wrote
about 1330. Some doubt is even cast upon the
existence of any such person as Maundeville.
Whoever wrote the book that passes under his
name, however, would seem to have visited the
Holy Land, and the part of the "voiage" that describes Palestine and the Levant is fairly close to
the truth. The rest of the work, so far as it is not
taken from the tales of other travelers, is a diverting tissue of fables about gryfouns that fly away with
yokes of oxen, tribes of one-legged Ethiopians who
shelter themselves from the sun by using their
monstrous feet as umbrellas, etc.

During the 15th century English prose was gradually being brought into a shape fitting it for more
serious uses. In the controversy between the
Church and the Lollards Latin was still mainly employed, but Wiclif had written some of his tracts in
English, and, in 1449, Reginald Peacock, Bishop of

St. Asaph, contributed, in English, to the same controversy, *The Repressor of Overmuch Blaming of the
Clergy*. Sir John Fortescue, who was chief-justice
of the king's bench from 1442–1460, wrote during
the reign of Edward IV. a book on the *Difference
between Absolute and Limited Monarchy*, which may
be regarded as the first treatise on political philosophy and constitutional law in the language. But
these works hardly belong to pure literature, and
are remarkable only as early, though not very good,
examples of English prose in a barren time. The
14th century was an era of decay and change. The
Middle Age was dying, Church and State were
slowly disintegrating under the new intellectual
influences that were working secretly under ground.
In England the civil wars of the Red and White
Roses were breaking up the old feudal society by
decimating and impoverishing the baronage, thus
preparing the way for the centralized monarchy of
the Tudors. Toward the close of that century, and
early in the next, happened the four great events,
or series of events, which freed and widened men's
minds, and, in a succession of shocks, overthrew
the mediæval system of life and thought. These
were the invention of printing, the Renascence,
or revival of classical learning, the discovery of
America, and the Protestant Reformation.

William Caxton, the first English printer, learned
the art in Cologne. In 1476 he set up his press
and sign, a red pole, in the Almonry at Westminster.
Just before the introduction of printing the demand

for MS. copies had grown very active, stimulated, perhaps, by the coming into general use of linen paper instead of the more costly parchment. The scriptoria of the monasteries were the places where the transcribing and illuminating of MSS. went on, professional copyists resorting to Westminster Abbey, for example, to make their copies of books belonging to the monastic library. Caxton's choice of a spot was, therefore, significant. His new art for multiplying copies began to supersede the old method of transcription at the very head-quarters of the MS. makers. The first book that bears his Westminster imprint was the *Dictes and Sayings of the Philosophers*, translated from the French by Anthony Woodville, Lord Rivers, a brother-in-law of Edward IV. The list of books printed by Caxton is interesting, as showing the taste of the time, as he naturally selected what was most in demand. The list shows that manuals of devotion and chivalry were still in chief request, books like the *Order of Chivalry*, *Faits of Arms*, and the *Golden Legend*, which last Caxton translated himself, as well as *Reynard the Fox*, and a French version of the *Æneid*. He also printed, with continuations of his own, revisions of several early chronicles, and editions of Chaucer, Gower, and Lydgate. A translation of *Cicero on Friendship*, made directly from the Latin, by Thomas Tiptoft, Earl of Worcester, was printed by Caxton, but no edition of a classical author in the original. The new learning of the Renascence had not, as yet, taken much hold in England. Upon the whole, the productions of Caxton's press were mostly of a kind that may be described as mediæval, and the most important of them, if we except his edition of Chaucer, was that "noble and joyous book," as Caxton called it, *Le Morte Darthur*, written by Sir Thomas Malory in 1469, and printed by Caxton in 1485. This was a compilation from French Arthur romances, and was by far the best English prose that had yet been written. It may be doubted, indeed, whether, for purposes of simple story telling, the picturesque charm of Malory's style has been improved upon. The episode which lends its name to the whole romance, the death of Arthur, is most impressively told, and Tennyson has followed Malory's narrative closely, even to such details of the scene as the little chapel by the sea, the moonlight, and the answer which Sir Bedwere made the wounded king, when bidden to throw Excalibur into the water, "'What saw thou there?' said the king. 'Sir,' he said, 'I saw nothing but the waters wap and the waves wan.'"

> "I heard the ripple washing in the reeds
> And the wild water lapping on the crag."

And very touching and beautiful is the oft-quoted lament of Sir Ector over Launcelot, in Malory's final chapter : "'Ah, Launcelot,' he said, 'thou were head of all Christian knights; and now I dare say,' said Sir Ector, 'thou, Sir Launcelot, there thou liest, that thou were never matched of earthly

knight's hand; and thou were the courtiest knight
that ever bare shield; and thou were the truest
friend to thy lover that ever bestrode horse; and
thou were the truest lover of a sinful man that ever
loved woman; and thou were the kindest man that
ever strake with sword; and thou were the good-
liest person ever came among press of knights;
and thou were the meekest man and the gentlest
that ever ate in hall among ladies; and thou were
the sternest knight to thy mortal foe that ever put
spear in the rest.'"

Equally good, as an example of English prose
narrative, was the translation made by John Bour-
chier, Lord Berners, of that most brilliant of the
French chroniclers, Chaucer's contemporary, Sir
John Froissart. Lord Berners was the English
governor of Calais, and his version of Froissart's
Chronicles was made in 1523–25, at the request of
Henry VIII. In these two books English chivalry
spoke its last genuine word. In Sir Philip Sidney
the character of the knight was merged into that
of the modern gentleman. And although tourna-
ments were still held in the reign of Elizabeth, and
Spenser cast his *Faery Queene* into the form of a
chivalry romance, these were but a ceremonial
survival and literary tradition from an order of
things that had passed away. How antagonistic
the new classical culture was to the vanished ideal
of the Middle Age may be read in *Toxophilus*, a
treatise on archery published in 1545, by Roger
Ascham, a Greek lecturer in Cambridge, and the

tutor of the Princess Elizabeth and of Lady Jane
Grey. "In our forefathers' time, when Papistry
as a standing pool covered and overflowed all England, few books were read in our tongue saving
certain books of chivalry, as they said, for pastime
and pleasure, which, as some say, were made in
monasteries by idle monks or wanton canons: as
one, for example, *Morte Arthure*, the whole pleasure of which book standeth in two special points,
in open manslaughter and bold bawdry. This is
good stuff for wise men to laugh at or honest men
to take pleasure at. Yet I know when God's
Bible was banished the Court, and *Morte Arthure*
received into the prince's chamber."

The fashionable school of courtly allegory, first
introduced into England by the translation of the
Romaunt of the Rose, reached its extremity in Stephen Hawes's *Passetyme of Pleasure*, printed by
Caxton's successor, Wynkyn de Worde, in 1517.
This was a dreary and pedantic poem, in which it
is told how Graunde Amoure, after a long series
of adventures and instructions among such shadowy personages as Verite, Observaunce, Falshed,
and Good Operacion, finally won the love of La
Belle Pucel. Hawes was the last English poet of
note whose culture was exclusively mediæval. His
contemporary, John Skelton, mingled the old
fashions with the new classical learning. In his
Bowge of Courte (Court Entertainment or Dole),
and in others of his earlier pieces, he used, like
Hawes, Chaucer's seven-lined stanza. But his later

poems were mostly written in a verse of his own invention, called after him *Skeltonical*. This was a sort of glorified doggerel, in short, swift, ragged lines, with occasional intermixture of French and Latin.

> " Her beautye to augment.
> Dame Nature hath her lent
> A warte upon her cheke,
> Who so lyst to seke
> In her vyságe a skar,
> That semyth from afar
> Lyke to the radyant star,
> All with favour fret,
> So properly it is set.
> She is the vyolet,
> The daysy delectáble,
> The columbine commendáble,
> The jelofer amyáble ;
> For this most goodly floure,
> This blossom of fressh coloúr,
> So Jupiter me succoúr,
> She florysheth new and new
> In beaute and vertew ;
> *Hac claritate gemina,*
> *O gloriosa femina*, etc."

Skelton was a rude railing rhymer, a singular mixture of a true and original poet with a buffoon ; coarse as Rabelais, whimsical, obscure, but always vivacious. He was the rector of Diss, in Norfolk, but his profane and scurrilous wit seems rather out of keeping with his clerical character. His *Tunnyng of Elynoure Rummyng* is a study of very low life, reminding one slightly of *Burns's Jolly*

4

Beggars. His *Phyllyp Sparowe* is a sportive, pretty, fantastic elegy on the death of a pet bird belonging to Mistress Joanna Scroupe, of Carowe, and has been compared to the Latin poet Catullus's elegy on Lesbia's sparrow. In *Speke, Parrot,* and *Why Come ye not to Courte?* he assailed the powerful Cardinal Wolsey with the most ferocious satire, and was, in consequence, obliged to take sanctuary at Westminster, where he died in 1529. Skelton was a classical scholar, and at one time tutor to Henry VIII. The great humanist, Erasmus, spoke of him as the " one light and ornament of British letters." Caxton asserts that he had read Virgil, Ovid, and Tully, and quaintly adds, " I suppose he hath dronken of Elycon's well."

In refreshing contrast with the artificial court poetry of the 15th and first three quarters of the 16th century, was the folk-poetry, the popular ballad literature which was handed down by oral tradition. The English and Scotch ballads were narrative songs, written in a variety of meters, but chiefly in what is known as the ballad stanza.

" In somer, when the shawes * be sheyne, †
　　And leves be large and longe,
Hit is full merry in feyre forést
　　To here the foulys song.

" To se the dere draw to the dale,
　　And leve the hilles hee, ‡
And shadow them in the leves grene,
　　Under the grene-wode tree."

---

　　* Woods.　　　　† Bright.　　　　‡ High.

It is not possible to assign a definite date to these ballads. They lived on the lips of the people, and were seldom reduced to writing till many years after they were first composed and sung. Meanwhile they underwent repeated changes, so that we have numerous versions of the same story. They belonged to no particular author, but, like all folk-lore, were handled freely by the unknown poets, minstrels, and ballad reciters, who modernized their language, added to them, or corrupted them, and passed them along. Coming out of an uncertain past, based on some dark legend of heart-break or bloodshed, they bear no poet's name, but are *ferae naturae*, and have the flavor of wild game. In the forms in which they are preserved few of them are older than the 17th century, or the latter part of the 16th century, though many, in their original shape, are, doubtless, much older. A very few of the Robin Hood ballads go back to the 15th century, and to the same period is assigned the charming ballad of the *Nut Brown Maid* and the famous border ballad of *Chevy Chase*, which describes a battle between the retainers of the two great houses of Douglas and Percy. It was this song of which Sir Philip Sidney wrote, " I never heard the old song of Percy and Douglas but I found myself more moved than by a trumpet ; and yet it is sung but by some blind crouder,* with no rougher voice than rude style.'' But the style of the ballads was not always rude.

* Fiddler.

In their compressed energy of expression, in the impassioned abrupt, yet indirect way in which they tell their tale of grief and horror, there reside often a tragic power and art superior to any English poetry that had been written since Chaucer, superior even to Chaucer in the quality of intensity. The true home of the ballad literature was " the north country," and especially the Scotch border, where the constant forays of moss-troopers and the raids and private warfare of the lords of the marches supplied many traditions of heroism, like those celebrated in the old poem of the *Battle of Otterbourne*, and in the *Hunting of the Cheviot*, or *Chevy Chase*, already mentioned. Some of these are Scotch and others English ; the dialect of Lowland Scotland did not, in effect, differ much from that of Northumberland and Yorkshire, both descended alike from the old Northumbrian of Anglo-Saxon times. Other ballads were shortened, popular versions of the chivalry romances which were passing out of fashion among educated readers in the 16th century, and now fell into the hands of the ballad makers. Others preserved the memory of local countryside tales, family feuds, and tragic incidents, partly historical and partly legendary, associated often with particular spots. Such are, for example, *The Dowie Dens of Yarrow*, *Fair Helen of Kirkconnell*, *The Forsaken Bride*, and *The Twa Corbies*. Others, again, have a coloring of popular superstition, like the beautiful ballad concerning

Thomas of Ersyldoune, who goes in at Eldon Hill with an Elf queen and spends seven years in fairy land.

But the most popular of all the ballads were those which cluster about the name of that good outlaw, Robin Hood, who, with his merry men, hunted the forest of merry Sherwood, when he killed the king's deer and waylaid rich travelers, but was kind to poor knights and honest workmen. Robin Hood is the true ballad hero, the darling of the common people, as Arthur was of the nobles. The names of his Confessor, Friar Tuck; his mistress, Maid Marian; his companions, Little John, Scathelock, and Much, the Miller's son, were as familiar as household words. Langland, in the 14th century, mentions "rimes of Robin Hood," and efforts have been made to identify him with some actual personage, as with one of the dispossessed barons who had been adherents of Simon de Montfort in his war against Henry III. But there seems to be nothing historical about Robin Hood. He was a creation of the popular fancy. The game laws under the Norman kings were very oppressive, and there were, doubtless, dim memories still cherished among the Saxon masses of Hereward and Edric the Wild, who had defied the power of the Conqueror, as well as of later freebooters, who had taken to the woods and lived by plunder. Robin Hood was a thoroughly national character. He had the English love of fair-play, the English readiness to shake hands and

make up, and keep no malice when worsted in
a square fight.   He beat and plundered the
rich bishops and abbots, who had more than
their share of wealth, but he was generous and
hospitable to the distressed, and lived a free
and careless life in the good green wood. He
was a mighty archer, with those national weap-
ons, the long-bow and the cloth-yard-shaft. He
tricked and baffled legal authority in the person of the proud sheriff of Nottingham, thereby
appealing to that secret sympathy with lawless-
ness and adventure which marked the free-born,
vigorous yeomanry of England.   And finally
the scenery of the forest gives a poetic back-
ground and a never-failing charm to the exploits
of "the old Robin Hood of England" and his
merry men.

The ballads came, in time, to have certain
tricks of style, such as are apt to characterize a body of anonymous folk-poetry. Such is
their use of conventional epithets ; "the red,
red gold," "the good, green wood," "the gray
goose wing." Such are certain recurring terms
of phrase like,

"But out and spak their stepmother."

Such is, finally, a kind of sing-song repetition,
which doubtless helped the ballad singer to mem-
orize his stock, as, for example,

"She had'na pu'd a double rose,
A rose but only twae."

Or again,

> "And mony ane sings o' grass, o' grass,
> And mony ane sings o' corn ;
> An mony ane sings o' Robin Hood,
> Kens little whare he was born.
>
> It was na in the ha', the ha',
> Nor in the painted bower ;
> But it was in the gude green wood,
> Amang the lily flower."

Copies of some of these old ballads were hawked about in the 16th century, printed in black letter, "broad sides," or single sheets. Wynkyn de Worde printed, in 1489, *A Lytell Geste of Robin Hood*, which is a sort of digest of earlier ballads on the subject. In the 17th century a few of the English popular ballads were collected in miscellanies, called *Garlands*. Early in the 18th century the Scotch poet, Allan Ramsay, published a number of Scotch ballads in the *Evergreen* and *Tea-Table Miscellany*. But no large and important collection was put forth until Percy's *Reliques*, 1765, a book which had a powerful influence upon Wordsworth and Walter Scott. In Scotland some excellent ballads in the ancient manner were written in the 18th century, such as Jane Elliott's *Lament for Flodden*, and the fine ballad of *Sir Patrick Spence*. Walter Scott's *Proud Maisie is in the Wood*, is a perfect reproduction of the pregnant, indirect method of the old ballad makers.

In 1453 Constantinople was taken by the Turks,

and many Greek scholars, with their MSS., fled
into Italy, where they began teaching their language and literature, and especially the philosophy of Plato.   There had been little or no
knowledge of Greek in western Europe during
the Middle Ages, and only a very imperfect
knowledge of the Latin classics.   Ovid and
Statius were widely read, and so was the late
Latin poet, Boethius, whose *De Consolatione Phil-
osophiæ* had been translated into English by King
Alfred and by Chaucer.   Little was known of
Vergil at first hand, and he was popularly supposed to have been a mighty wizard, who made
sundry works of enchantment at Rome, such as
a magic mirror and statue.   Caxton's so-called
translation of the *Æneid* was in reality nothing but
a version of a French romance based on Vergil's
epic.   Of the Roman historians, orators, and moral-
ists, such as Livy, Tacitus, Cæsar, Cicero, and Seneca, there was an almost entire ignorance, as
also of poets like Horace, Lucretius, Juvenal, and
Catullus.   The gradual rediscovery of the remains of ancient art and literature which took
place in the 15th century, and largely in Italy,
worked an immense revolution in the mind of
Europe.   MSS. were brought out of their hiding
places, edited by scholars and spread abroad by
means of the printing-press.   Statues were dug
up and placed in museums, and men became ac-
quainted with a civilization far more mature than
that of the Middle Age, and with models of perfect

workmanship in letters and the fine arts. In the
latter years of the 15th century a number of Englishmen learned Greek in Italy and brought it
back with them to England. William Grocyn
and Thomas Linacre, who had studied at Florence
under the refugee, Demetrius Chalcondylas, began teaching Greek, at Oxford, the former as early
as 1491. A little later John Colet, Dean of St.
Paul's and the founder of St. Paul's School, and
his friend, William Lily, the grammarian and first
master of St. Paul's (1500), also studied Greek
abroad, Colet in Italy, and Lily at Rhodes and in
the city of Rome. Thomas More, afterward the
famous chancellor of Henry VIII., was among the
pupils of Grocyn and Linacre at Oxford. Thither
also, in 1497, came in search of the new knowledge, the Dutchman, Erasmus, who became the
foremost scholar of his time. From Oxford the
study spread to the sister university, where the
first English Grecian of his day, Sir Jno. Cheke,
who "taught Cambridge and King Edward
Greek," became the incumbent of the new pro-
fessorship founded about 1540. Among his pupils
was Roger Ascham, already mentioned, in whose
time St. John's College, Cambridge, was the chief
seat of the new learning, of which Thomas Nashe
testifies that it "was as an universitie within itself; having more candles light in it, every winter
morning before four of the clock, than the four of
clock bell gave strokes." Greek was not introduced at the universities without violent opposi-

tion from the conservative element, who were nicknamed Trojans. The opposition came in part from the priests, who feared that the new study would sow seeds of heresy. Yet many of the most devout churchmen were friends of a more liberal culture, among them Thomas More, whose Catholicism was undoubted and who went to the block for his religion. Cardinal Wolsey, whom More succeeded as chancellor, was also a munificent patron of learning and founded Christ Church College, at Oxford. Popular education at once felt the impulse of the new studies, and over twenty endowed grammar schools were established in England in the first twenty years of the 16th century. Greek became a passion even with English ladies. Ascham in his *Schoolmaster*, a treatise on education, published in 1570, says, that Queen Elisabeth "readeth here now at Windsor more Greek every day, than some prebendarie of this Church doth read Latin in a whole week." And in the same book he tells how calling once upon Lady Jane Grey, at Brodegate, in Leicestershire, he "found her in her chamber reading *Phædon Platonis* in Greek, and that with as much delite as some gentlemen would read a merry tale in *Bocase*," and when he asked her why she had not gone hunting with the rest, she answered, "I wisse, all their sport in the park is but a shadow to that pleasure that I find in Plato." Ascham's *Schoolmaster*, as well as his earlier book, *Toxophilus*, a Platonic dialogue on archery, bristles with quotations from the Greek and Latin classics, and with that perpetual reference to the authority of antiquity on every topic that he touches, which remained the fashion in all serious prose down to the time of Dryden.

One speedy result of the new learning was fresh translations of the Scriptures into English, out of the original tongues. In 1525 William Tyndal printed at Cologne and Worms his version of the New Testament from the Greek. Ten years later Miles Coverdale made, at Zurich, a translation of the whole Bible from the German and the Latin. These were the basis of numerous later translations, and the strong beautiful English of Tyndal's *Testament* is preserved for the most part in our Authorized Version (1611). At first it was not safe to make or distribute these early translations in England. * Numbers of copies were brought into the country, however, and did much to promote the cause of the Reformation. After Henry VIII. had broken with the Pope the new English Bible circulated freely among the people. Tyndal and Sir Thomas More carried on a vigorous controversy in English upon some of the questions at issue between the Church and the Protestants. Other important contributions to the literature of the Reformation were the homely sermons preached at Westminster and at Paul's Cross by Bishop Hugh Latimer, who was burned at Oxford in the reign of Bloody Mary. The English Book of Common Prayer was compiled in 1549–52. More was, perhaps, the best representa-

tive of a group of scholars who wished to en-
lighten and reform the Church from inside, but
who refused to follow Henry VIII. in his breach
with Rome. Dean Colet and John Fisher, Bishop
of Rochester, belonged to the same company,
and Fisher was beheaded in the same year (1535)
with More, and for the same offense, namely, re-
fusing to take the oath to maintain the act con-
firming the king's divorce from Catherine of Arra-
gon and his marriage with Anne Boleyn. More's
philosophy is best reflected in his *Utopia*, the description of an ideal commonwealth, modeled on
Plato's *Republic*, and printed in 1516. The name
signifies "no place" (Οὐτόπος), and has furnished
an adjective to the language. The *Utopia* was in
Latin, but More's *History of Edward V. and
Richard III.*, written in 1513, though not printed
till 1557, was in English. It is the first example
in the tongue of a history as distinguished from a
chronicle; that is, it is a reasoned and artistic
presentation of an historic period, and not a mere
chronological narrative of events.

The first three quarters of the 16th century
produced no great original work of literature in
England. It was a season of preparation, of
education. The storms of the Reformation in-
terrupted and delayed the literary renascence
through the reigns of Henry VIII., Edward VI.,
and Queen Mary. When Elizabeth came to the
throne, in 1558, a more settled order of things began, and a period of great national prosperity and

glory. Meanwhile the English mind had been slowly assimilating the new classical culture, which was extended to all classes of readers by the numerous translations of Greek and Latin authors. A fresh poetic impulse came from Italy. In 1557 appeared *Tottel's Miscellany*, containing songs and sonnets by a " new company of courtly makers." Most of the pieces in the volume had been written years before, by gentlemen of Henry VIII.'s court, and circulated in MS. The two chief contributors were Sir Thomas Wiat, at one time English embassador to Spain, and that brilliant noble, Henry Howard, the Earl of Surrey, who was beheaded in 1547 for quartering the king's arms with his own. Both of them were dead long before their work was printed. The pieces in *Tottel's Miscellany* show very clearly the influence of Italian poetry. We have seen that Chaucer took subjects and something more from Boccaccio and Petrarch. But the sonnet, which Petrarch had brought to great perfection, was first introduced into England by Wiat. There was a great revival of sonneteering in Italy in the 16th century, and a number of Wiat's poems were adaptations of the sonnets and *canzoni* of Petrarch and later poets. Others were imitations of Horace's satires and epistles. Surrey introduced the Italian blank verse into English in his translation of two books of the *Æneid*. The love poetry of *Tottel's Miscellany* is polished and artificial, like the models which it followed. Dante's

Beatrice was a child, and so was Petrarch's Laura.
Following their example, Surrey addressed his
love complaints, by way of compliment, to a little
girl of the noble Irish family of Geraldine. The
Amourists, or love sonneters, dwelt on the metaphysics of the passion with a tedious minuteness,
and the conventional nature of their sighs and
complaints may often be guessed by an experienced reader from the titles of their poems:
" Description of the restless state of a lover, with
suit to his lady to rue on his dying heart ; " " Hell
tormenteth not the damned ghosts so sore as un-
kindness the lover; " " The lover prayeth not to
be disdained, refused, mistrusted, nor forsaken,"
etc. The most genuine utterance of Surrey was
his poem written while imprisoned in Windsor—
a cage where so many a song-bird has grown
vocal. And Wiat's little piece of eight lines, " Of
his Return from Spain," is worth reams of his
amatory affectations. Nevertheless the writers in
Tottel's Miscellany were real reformers of English
poetry. They introduced new models of style
and new metrical forms, and they broke away
from the mediæval traditions which had hitherto
obtained. The language had undergone some
changes since Chaucer's time, which made his
scansion obsolete. The accent of many words
of French origin, like *nature, courdge, virtué,
matére*, had shifted to the first syllable, and the *e*
of the final syllables *ĕs, ĕn, ĕd*, and *ĕ*, had largely
disappeared. But the language of poetry tends

to keep up archaisms of this kind, and in Stephen
Hawes, who wrote a century after Chaucer, we
still find such lines as these :

> " But he my strokēs might right well endure,
> He was so great and huge of puissánce." *

Hawes's practice is variable in this respect, and so
is his contemporary, Skelton's. But in Wiat and
Surrey, who wrote only a few years later, the
reader first feels sure that he is reading verse
pronounced quite in the modern fashion.

But Chaucer's example still continued potent.
Spenser revived many of his obsolete words, both
in his pastorals and in his *Faery Queene*, thereby
imparting an antique remoteness to his diction,
but incurring Ben Jonson's censure, that he " writ
no language." A poem that stands midway between Spenser and late mediæval work of Chaucer's school—such as Hawes's *Passetyme of Pleasure*—was the *Induction* contributed by Thomas
Sackville, Lord Buckhurst, in 1563 to a collection
of narrative poems called the *Mirrour for Magis-
trates*. The whole series was the work of many
hands, modeled upon Lydgate's *Falls of Princes*
(taken from Boccaccio), and was designed as a
warning to great men of the fickleness of fortune.
The *Induction* is the only noteworthy part of it.
It was an allegory, written in Chaucer's seven-
lined stanza and described with a somber imaginative power, the figure of Sorrow, her abode

* Trìsyllable—likè *creature, neighbeour*, etc, in Chaucer.

in the " griesly lake " of Avernus and her attend-
ants, Remorse, Dread, Old Age, etc. Sackville
was the author of the first regular English tragedy,
Gorboduc; and it was at his request that Ascham
wrote the *Schoolmaster.*

Italian poetry also fed the genius of Edmund
Spenser (1552–99). While a student at Pembroke Hall, Cambridge, he had translated some
of the *Visions of Petrarch,* and the *Visions of
Bellay,* a French poet, but it was only in 1579 that
the publication of his *Shepheard's Calendar* an-
nounced the coming of a great original poet, the
first since Chaucer. The *Shepheard's Calendar* was
a pastoral in twelve eclogues — one for each
month in the year. There had been a great revival of pastoral poetry in Italy and France, but,
with one or two insignificant exceptions, Spenser's
were the first bucolics in English. Two of his
eclogues were paraphrases from Clement Marot, a
French Protestant poet, whose psalms were greatly
in fashion at the court of Francis I. The pastoral
machinery had been used by Vergil and by his
modern imitators, not merely to portray the loves
of Strephon and Chloe, or the idyllic charms of
rustic life ; but also as a vehicle of compliment,
elegy, satire, and personal allusion of many kinds.
Spenser, accordingly, alluded to his friends, Sidney and Harvey, as the shepherds, Astrophel and
Hobbinol, paid court to Queen Elizabeth as Cynthia,
and introduced, in the form of anagrams, names
of the High-Church Bishop of London, Aylmer,

and the Low-Church Archbishop Grindal. The conventional pastoral is a somewhat delicate exotic in English poetry, and represents a very unreal Arcadia. Before the end of the 17th century the squeak of the oaten pipe had become a burden, and the only piece of the kind which it is easy to read without some impatience is Milton's wonderful *Lycidas*. The *Shepheard's Calendar*, however, though it belonged to an artificial order of literature, had the unmistakable stamp of genius in its style. There was a broad, easy mastery of the resources of language, a grace, fluency, and music which were new to English poetry. It was written while Spenser was in service with the Earl of Leicester, and enjoying the friendship of his nephew, the all-accomplished Sidney, and was, perhaps, composed at the latter's country seat of Penshurst. In the following year Spenser went to Ireland as private secretary to Arthur Lord Grey of Wilton, who had just been appointed Lord Deputy of that kingdom. . After filling several clerkships in the Irish government, Spenser received a grant of the castle and estate of Kilcolman, a part of the forfeited lands of the rebel Earl of Desmond. Here, among landscapes richly wooded, like the scenery of his own fairy land, "under the cooly shades of the green alders by the Mulla's shore," Sir Walter Raleigh found him, in 1589, busy upon his *Faery Queene*. In his poem, *Colin Clout's Come Home Again*, Spenser tells, in pastoral language, how "the shepherd of the

5

ocean "persuaded him to go to London, where he presented him to the Queen, under whose patronage the first three books of his great poem were printed, in 1590. A volume of minor poems, entitled *Complaints*, followed in 1591, and the three remaining books of the *Faery Queene* in 1596. In 1595–96 he published also his *Daphnaida, Prothalamion*, and the four hymns *On Love* and *Beauty*, and *On Heavenly Love* and *Heavenly Beauty*. In 1598, in Tyrone's rebellion, Kilcolman Castle was sacked and burned, and Spenser, with his family, fled to London, where he died in January, 1599.

The *Faery Queene* reflects, perhaps, more fully than any other English work, the many-sided literary influences of the renascence. It was the blossom of a richly composite culture. Its immediate models were Ariosto's *Orlando Furioso*, the first forty cantos of which were published in 1515, and Tasso's *Gerusalemme Liberata*, printed in 1581. Both of these were, in subject, romances of chivalry, the first based upon the old Charlemagne epos — Orlando being identical with the hero of the French *Chanson de Roland*—the second upon the history of the first Crusade, and the recovery of the Holy City from the Saracen. But in both of them there was a splendor of diction and a wealth of coloring quite unknown to the rude mediæval romances. Ariosto and Tasso wrote with the great epics of Homer and Vergil constantly in mind, and all about them was the brilliant light of Italian art, in its early freshness and power. The *Faery Queene*, too, was a tale of knight-errantry. Its hero was King Arthur, and its pages swarm with the familiar adventures and figures of Gothic romance ; distressed ladies and their champions, combats with dragons and giants, enchanted castles, magic rings, charmed wells, forest hermitages, etc. But side by side with these appear the fictions of Greek mythology and the personified abstractions of fashionable allegory. Knights, squires, wizards, hamadryads, satyrs, and river gods, Idleness, Gluttony, and Superstition jostle each other in Spenser's fairy land. Descents to the infernal shades, in the manner of Homer and Vergil, alternate with descriptions of the Palace of Pride in the manner of the *Romaunt of the Rose.* But Spenser's imagination was a powerful spirit, and held all these diverse elements in solution. He removed them to an ideal sphere " apart from place, withholding time," where they seem all alike equally real, the dateless conceptions of the poet's dream.

The poem was to have been " a continued allegory or dark conceit," in twelve books, the hero of each book representing one of the twelve moral virtues. Only six books and the fragment of a seventh were written. By way of complimenting his patrons and securing contemporary interest, Spenser undertook to make his allegory a double one, personal and historical, as well as moral or abstract. Thus Gloriana, the Queen of Faery, stands not only for Glory but for Elizabeth,

to whom the poem was dedicated. Prince Arthur
is Leicester, as well as Magnificence. Duessa is
Falsehood, but also Mary Queen of Scots. Gran-
torto is Philip II. of Spain. Sir Artegal is Jus-
tice, but likewise he is Arthur Grey de Wilton.
Other characters shadow forth Sir Walter Raleigh,
Sir Philip Sidney, Henry IV. of France, etc.; and
such public events as the revolt of the Spanish
Netherlands, the Irish rebellion, the execution of
Mary Stuart, and the rising of the northern Cath-
olic houses against Elizabeth are told in parable.
In this way the poem reflects the spiritual struggle
of the time, the warfare of young England against
Popery and Spain.

The allegory is not always easy to follow. It
is kept up most carefully in the first two books,
but it sat rather lightly on Spenser's conscience,
and is not of the essence of the poem. It is an
ornament put on from the outside and detachable
at pleasure. The "Spenserian stanza," in which
the *Faery Queene* was written, was adapted from
the *ottava rima* of Ariosto. Spenser changed
somewhat the order of the rimes in the first
eight lines and added a ninth line of twelve syllables, thus affording more space to the copious
luxuriance of his style and the long-drawn sweetness of his verse. It was his instinct to dilate and
elaborate every image to the utmost, and his similes, especially—each of which usually fills a whole
stanza—have the pictorial amplitude of Homer's.
Spenser was, in fact, a great painter. His poetry

is almost purely sensuous. The personages in the *Faery Queene* are not characters, but richly colored figures, moving to the accompaniment of delicious music, in an atmosphere of serene remoteness from the earth. Charles Lamb said that he was the poet's poet, that is, he appealed wholly to the artistic sense and to the love of beauty. Not until Keats did another English poet appear so filled with the passion for all outward shapes of beauty, so exquisitely alive to all' impressions of the senses. Spenser was, in some respects, more an Italian than an English poet. It is said that the Venetian gondoliers still sing the stanzas of Tasso's *Gerusalemme Liberata.* It is not easy to imagine the Thames bargees chanting passages from the *Faery Queene.* Those English poets who have taken strongest hold upon their public have done so by their profound interpretation of our common life. But Spenser escaped altogether from reality into a region of pure imagination. His aerial creations resemble the blossoms of the epiphytic orchids, which have no root in the soil, but draw their nourishment from the moisture of the air.

> "*Their* birth was of the womb of morning dew,
> And *their* conception of the glorious prime."

Among the minor poems of Spenser the most delightful were his *Prothalamion* and *Epithalamion.* The first was a " spousal verse," made for the double wedding of the Ladies Catherine and

Elizabeth Somerset, whom the poet figures as two white swans that come swimming down the Thames, whose surface the nymphs strew with lilies, till it appears "like a bride's chamber-floor."

"Sweet Thames, run softly till I end my song,"

is the burden of each stanza. The *Epithalamion* was Spenser's own marriage song, written to crown his series of *Amoretti*, or love sonnets, and is the most splendid hymn of triumphant love in the language. Hardly less beautiful than these was *Muiopotmos ; or, the Fate of the Butterfly*, an addition to the classical myth of Araehne, the spider. The four hymns in praise of *Love* and *Beauty, Heavenly Love* and *Heavenly Beauty*, are also stately and noble poems, but by reason of their abstractness and the Platonic mysticism which they express, are less generally pleasing than the others mentioned. Allegory and mysticism had no natural affiliation with Spenser's genius. He was a seer of visions, of *images* full, brilliant, and distinct, and not like Bunyan, Dante, or Hawthorne, a projector into bodily shapes of *ideas*, typical and emblematic, the shadows which haunt the conscience and the mind.

1. A First Sketch of English Literature. By Henry Morley.

2. English Writers. By the same. Vol. iii. From Chaucer to Dunbar.

3. Skeat's Specimens of English Literature, 1394–1579. Clarendon Press Series.

4. Morte Darthur. Globe Edition.

5. Child's English and Scottish Ballads. 8 vols.

6. Hale's edition of Spenser. Globe.

7. "A Royal Poet." Irving's Sketch-Book.

CHAPTER III.

THE AGE OF SHAKSPERE.

1564–1616.

THE great age of English poetry opened with the publication of Spenser's *Shepheard's Calendar*, in 1579, and closed with the printing of Milton's *Samson Agonistes*, in 1671. Within this period of little less than a century English thought passed through many changes, and there were several successive phases of style in our imaginative literature. Milton, who acknowledged Spenser as his master, and who was a boy of eight years at Shakspere's death, lived long enough to witness the establishment of an entirely new school of poets, in the persons of Dryden and his contemporaries. But, roughly speaking, the dates above given mark the limits of one literary epoch, which may not improperly be called the Elisabethan. In strictness the Elisabethan age ended with the queen's death, in 1603. But the poets of the succeeding reigns inherited much of the glow and splendor which marked the diction of their forerunners; and " the spacious times of great Elisabeth " have been, by courtesy, prolonged to the year of the Restoration (1660). There is a certain likeness

in the intellectual products of the whole period, a
largeness of utterance, and a high imaginative cast
of thought which stamp them all alike with the
queen's seal.

Nor is it by any undue stretch of the royal
prerogative that the name of the monarch has
attached itself to the literature of her reign and
of the reigns succeeding hers. The expression
"Victorian poetry" has a rather absurd sound
when one considers how little Victoria counts for
in the literature of her time. But in Elisabethan
poetry the maiden queen is really the central
figure. She is Cynthia, she is Thetis, great queen
of shepherds and of the sea; she is Spenser's
Gloriana, and even Shakspere, the most impersonal of poets, paid tribute to her in *Henry VIII.*,
and, in a more delicate and indirect way, in the
little allegory introduced into *Midsummer Night's
Dream.*

> " That very time I marked—but thou could'st not—
> Flying between the cold moon and the earth,
> Cupid all armed. A certain aim he took
> At a fair vestal throning in the west,
> And loosed his love-shaft smartly from his bow
> As he would pierce a hundred thousand hearts.
> But I might see young Cupid's fiery dart
> Quenched in the chaste beams of the watery moon,
> And the imperial votaress passed on
> In maiden meditation, fancy free "—

an allusion to Leicester's unsuccessful suit for
Elisabeth's hand.

The praises of the queen, which sound through

all the poetry of her time, seem somewhat overdone
to a modern reader. But they were not merely
the insipid language of courtly compliment. England had never before had a female sovereign,
except in the instance of the gloomy and bigoted
Mary. When she was succeeded by her more
brilliant sister, the gallantry of a gallant and fantastic age was poured at the latter's feet, the sentiment of chivalry mingling itself with loyalty to
the crown. The poets idealized Elisabeth. She
was to Spenser, to Sidney, and to Raleigh, not
merely a woman and a virgin queen, but the
champion of Protestantism, the lady of young England, the heroine of the conflict against popery
and Spain. Moreover Elisabeth was a great
woman. In spite of the vanity, caprice, and in-
gratitude which disfigured her character, and the
vacillating, tortuous policy which often distinguished her government, she was at bottom a
sovereign of large views, strong will, and daunt-
less courage. Like her father, she "loved a *man*,"
and she had the magnificent tastes of the Tudors.
She was a patron of the arts, passionately fond
of shows and spectacles, and sensible to poetic
flattery. In her royal progresses through the
kingdom, the universities and the nobles and the
cities vied with one another in receiving her with
plays, revels, masques, and triumphs, in the mythological taste of the day. "When the queen pa-
raded through a country town," says Warton,
the historian of English poetry, "almost every

pageant was a pantheon. When she paid a visit
at the house of any of her nobility, at entering
the hall she was saluted by the Penates. In the
afternoon, when she condescended to walk in the
garden, the lake was covered with tritons and
nereids; the pages of the family were converted
into wood-nymphs, who peeped from every bower;
and the footmen gamboled over the lawns in the
figure of satyrs. When her majesty hunted in
the park she was met by Diana who, pronouncing
our royal prude to be the brightest paragon of un-
spotted chastity, invited her to groves free from
the intrusions of Acteon." The most elaborate
of these entertainments of which we have any
notice, were, perhaps, the games celebrated in her
honor by the Earl of Leicester, when she visited
him at Kenilworth, in 1575. An account of these
was published by a contemporary poet, George
Gascoigne, *The Princely Pleasures at the Court of
Kenilworth*, and Walter Scott has made them
familiar to modern readers in his novel of *Kenilworth*. Sidney was present on this occasion, and,
perhaps, Shakspere, then a boy of eleven, and living at Stratford, not far off, may have been taken
to see the spectacle, may have seen Neptune, rid-
ing on the back of a huge dolphin in the castle
lake, speak the copy of verses in which he offered
his trident to the empress of the sea, and may have

> " heard a mermaid on a dolphin's back,
> Utter such dulcet and harmonious breath,
> That the rude sea grew civil at the sound."

But in considering the literature of Elisabeth's reign it will be convenient to speak first of the prose. While following up Spenser's career to its close (1599), we have, for the sake of unity of treatment, anticipated somewhat the literary history of the twenty years preceding. In 1579 appeared a book which had a remarkable influence on English prose. This was John Lyly's *Euphues, the Anatomy of Wit.* It was in form a romance, the history of a young Athenian who went to Naples to see the world and get an education; but it is in substance nothing but a series of dialogues on love, friendship, religion, etc., written in language which, from the title of the book, has received the name of *Euphuism.* This new English became very fashionable among the ladies, and " that beauty in court which could not parley Euphuism," says a writer of 1632, " was as little regarded as she which now there speaks not French."

Walter Scott introduced a Euphuist into his novel the *Monastery*, but the peculiar jargon which Sir Piercie Shafton is made to talk is not at all like the real Euphuism. That consisted of antithesis, alliteration, and the profuse illustration of every thought by metaphors borrowed from a kind of fabulous natural history. " Descend into thine own conscience and consider with thyself the great difference between staring and stark-blind, wit and wisdom, love and lust; be merry, but with modesty; be sober, but not too sullen;

be valiant, but not too venturous." "I see now that, as the fish *Scolopidus* in the flood *Araxes* at the waxing of the moon is as white as the driven snow, and at the waning as black as the burnt coal; so Euphues, which at the first increasing of our familiarity was very zealous, is now at the last cast become most faithless." Besides the fish *Scolopidus*, the favorite animals of Lyly's menagerie are such as the chameleon, which, "though he have most guts draweth least breath;" the bird *Piralis*, "which sitting upon white cloth is white, upon green, green;" and the serpent *Porphirius*, which, "though he be full of poison, yet having no teeth, hurteth none but himself."

Lyly's style was pithy and sententious, and his sentences have the air of proverbs or epigrams. The vice of Euphuism was its monotony. On every page of the book there was something pungent, something quotable; but many pages of such writing became tiresome. Yet it did much to form the hitherto loose structure of English prose, by lending it point and polish. His carefully balanced periods were valuable lessons in rhetoric, and his book became a manual of polite conversation and introduced that fashion of witty repartee, which is evident enough in Shakspere's comic dialogue. In 1580 appeared the second part, *Euphues and his England*, and six editions of the whole work were printed before 1598. Lyly had many imitators. In Stephen Gosson's *School of Abuse,* a tract directed against the stage and published about four months later than the first part of *Euphues,* the language is distinctly Euphuistic. The dramatist, Robert Green, published, in 1587, his *Menaphon ; Camilla's Alarum to Slumbering Euphues,* and his *Euphues's Censure to Philautus.* His brother dramatist, Thomas Lodge, published, in 1590, *Rosalynde : Euphues's Golden Legacy,* from which Shakspere took the plot of *As You Like It.* Shakspere and Ben Jonson both quote from *Euphues* in their plays, and Shakspere was really writing Euphuism, when he wrote such a sentence as " 'Tis true, 'tis pity ; pity 'tis 'tis true."

That knightly gentleman, Philip Sidney, was a true type of the lofty aspiration and manifold activity of Elizabethan England. He was scholar, poet, courtier, diplomatist, statesman, soldier, all in one. Educated at Oxford and then introduced at court by his uncle, the Earl of Leicester, he had been sent to France when a lad of eighteen, with the embassy which went to treat of the queen's proposed marriage to the Duke of Alençon, and was in Paris at the time of the Massacre of St. Bartholomew, in 1572. Afterward he had traveled through Germany, Italy, and the Netherlands, had gone as embassador to the Emperor's Court, and every-where won golden opinions. In 1580, while visiting his sister Mary, Countess of Pembroke, at Wilton, he wrote, for her pleasure, the *Countess of Pembroke's Arcadia,* which remained in MS. till 1590. This was a pastoral romance, after the manner of the Italian *Arcadia* of Sanazzaro, and the *Diana Enamorada* of Montemayor, a Portuguese author. It was in prose, but intermixed with songs and sonnets, and Sidney finished only two books and a portion of a third. It describes the adventures of two cousins, Musidorus and Pyrocles, who are wrecked on the coast of Sparta. The plot is very involved and is full of the stock episodes of romance: disguises, surprises, love intrigues, battles, jousts and single combats. Although the insurrection of the Helots against the Spartans forms a part of the story, the Arcadia is not the real Arcadia of the Hellenic Peloponnesus, but the fanciful country of pastoral romance, an unreal clime, like the Faery Land of Spenser.

Sidney was our first writer of poetic prose. The poet Drayton says that he

"did first reduce
Our tongue from Lyly's writing, then in use,
Talking of stones, stars, plants, of fishes, flies,
Playing with words and idle similes."

Sidney was certainly no Euphuist, but his style was as "Italianated" as Lyly's, though in a different way. His English was too pretty for prose. His "Sidneian showers of sweet discourse" sowed every page of the *Arcadia* with those flowers of conceit, those sugared fancies which his contemporaries loved, but which the taste of a severer age finds insipid.   This splendid vice of the Elisabethan writers appears in Sidney, chiefly in the form of an excessive personification. If he describes a field full of roses, he makes " the roses add such a ruddy show unto it, as though the field were bashful at his own beauty." If he describes ladies bathing in a stream, he makes the water break into twenty bubbles, as " not content to have the picture of their face in large upon him, but he would in each of those bubbles set forth the miniature of them."   And even a passage which should be tragic, such as the death of his heroine, Parthenia, he embroiders with conceits like these : " For her exceeding fair eyes having with continued weeping got a little redness about them, her round sweetly swelling lips a little trembling, as though they kissed their neighbor Death; in her cheeks the whiteness striving by little and little to get upon the rosiness of them; her neck, a neck indeed of alabaster, displaying the wound which with most dainty blood labored to drown his own beauties; so as here was a river of purest red, there an island of perfectest white," etc.

The *Arcadia*, like *Euphues*, was a lady's book. It was the favorite court romance of its day, but it surfeits a modern reader with its sweetness, and confuses him with its tangle of adventures.   The lady for whom it was written was the mother of that William Herbert, Earl of Pembroke, to whom Shakspere's sonnets are thought to have been

dedicated.   And she was the subject of Ben
Jonson's famous epitaph.

> " Underneath this sable herse
> Lies the subject of all verse,
> Sidney's sister, Pembroke's mother ;
> Death, ere thou hast slain another
> Learn'd and fair and good as she,
> Time shall throw a dart at thee."

Sidney's *Defense of Poesy*, composed in 1581,
but not printed till 1595, was written in manlier
English than the *Arcadia*, and is one of the very
few books of criticism belonging to a creative and
uncritical time.   He was also the author of a
series of love sonnets, *Astrophel and Stella*, in
which he paid Platonic court to the Lady Penel-
ope Rich (with whom he was not at all in love),
according to the conventional usage of the amourists.

Sidney died in 1586, from a wound received in
a cavalry charge at Zutphen, where he was an
officer in the English contingent, sent to help the
Dutch against Spain.   The story has often been
told of his giving his cup of water to a wounded
soldier with the words, " Thy necessity is yet
greater than mine."   Sidney was England's darling, and there was hardly a poet in the land from
whom his death did not obtain " the meed of some
melodious tear."   Spenser's *Ruins of Time* were
among the number of these funeral songs ; but
the best of them all was by one Matthew Royden,
concerning whom little is known.

6

Another typical Englishman of Elisabeth's reign was Walter Raleigh, who was even more versatile than Sidney, and more representative of the restless spirit of romantic adventure, mixed with cool, practical enterprise that marked the times. He fought against the Queen's enemies by land and sea in many quarters of the globe; in the Netherlands and in Ireland against Spain, with the Huguenot Army against the League in France. Raleigh was from Devonshire, the great nursery of English seamen. He was half-brother to the famous navigator, Sir Humphrey Gilbert, and cousin to another great captain, Sir Richard Grenville. He sailed with Gilbert on one of his voyages against the Spanish treasure fleet, and in 1591 he published a report of the fight, near the Azores, between Grenville's ship, the *Revenge*, and fifteen great ships of Spain, an action, said Francis Bacon, "memorable even beyond credit, and to the height of some heroical fable." Raleigh was active in raising a fleet against the Spanish Armada of 1588. He was present in 1596 at the brilliant action in which the Earl of Essex " singed the Spanish king's beard," in the harbor of Cadiz. The year before he had sailed to Guiana, in search of the fabled El Dorado, destroying on the way the Spanish town of San José, in the West Indies; and on his return he published his *Discovery of the Empire of Guiana*. In 1597 he captured the town of Fayal, in the Azores. He took a prominent part in colonizing

Virginia, and he introduced tobacco and the potato plant into Europe.

America was still a land of wonder and romance, full of rumors, nightmares, and enchantments. In 1580, when Francis Drake, "the Devonshire Skipper," had dropped anchor in Plymouth harbor, after his voyage around the world, the enthusiasm of England had been mightily stirred. These narratives of Raleigh, and the similar accounts of the exploits of the bold sailors, Davis, Hawkins, Frobisher, Gilbert, and Drake; but especially the great cyclopedia of nautical travel, published by Richard Hakluyt, in 1589, *The Principal Navigations, Voyages, and Discoveries made by the English Nation*, worked powerfully on the imaginations of the poets. We see the influence of this literature of travel in the *Tempest*, written undoubtedly after Shakspere had been reading the narrative of Sir George Somers's shipwreck on the Bermudas or "Isles of Devils."

Raleigh was not in favor with Elizabeth's successor, James I. He was sentenced to death on a trumped-up charge of high treason. The sentence hung over him until 1618, when it was revived against him and he was beheaded. Meanwhile, during his twelve years' imprisonment in the Tower, he had written his *magnum opus*, the *History of the World*. This is not a history, in the modern sense, but a series of learned dissertations on law, government, theology, magic, war, etc. A chapter with such a caption as the following

would hardly be found in a universal history nowadays: "Of their opinion which make Paradise
as high as the moon; and of others which make
it higher than the middle region of the air." The
preface and conclusion are noble examples of
Elisabethan prose, and the book ends with an oft-
quoted apostrophe to Death. "O eloquent, just:
and mighty Death! Whom none could advise,
thou has persuaded; what none hath dared, thou
hast done; and whom all the world hath flattered,
thou only hast cast out of the world and despised;
thou hast drawn together all the far-fetched greatness, all the pride, cruelty, and ambition of man,
and covered it all over with these two narrow
words, *hic jacet*."

Although so busy a man, Raleigh found time to
be a poet. Spenser calls him "the summer's
night ingale,"and George Puttenham, in his *Art of
English Poesy* (1589), finds his "vein most lofty,
insolent, and passionate." Puttenham used *insolent* in its old sense, *uncommon ;* but this description is hardly less true, if we accept the word in
its modern meaning. Raleigh's most notable
verses, *The Lie*, are a challenge to the world, inspired by indignant pride and the weariness of
life — the *saeva indignatio* of Swift. The same
grave and caustic melancholy, the same disillusion
marks his quaint poem, *The Pilgrimage*. It is remarkable how many of the verses among his few
poetical remains are asserted in the MSS. or by
tradition to have been "made by Sir Walter

Raleigh the night before he was beheaded." Of
one such poem the assertion is probably true,
namely, the lines " found in his Bible in the gate-
house at Westminster."

> " Even such is Time, that takes in trust,
>   Our youth, our joys, our all we have,
> And pays as but with earth and dust ;
>   Who in the dark and silent grave,
> When we have wandered all our ways,
> Shuts up the story of our days ;
> But from this earth, this grave, this dust,
> My God shall raise me up, I trust ! "

The strictly *literary* prose of the Elisabethan
period bore a small proportion to the verse.
Many entire departments of prose literature were
as yet undeveloped. Fiction was represented—
outside of the *Arcadia* and *Euphues* already mentioned — chiefly by tales translated or imitated
from Italian *novelle*. George Turberville's *Tragical Tales* (1566) was a collection of such stories,
and William Paynter's *Palace of Pleasure* (1576–
1577) a similar collection from Boccaccio's *De-
cameron* and the novels of Bandello. These translations are mainly of interest, as having furnished
plots to the English dramatists. Lodge's *Rosalind*
and Robert Greene's *Pandosto*, the sources respectively of Shakspere's *As You Like It* and *Winter's Tale*, are short pastoral romances, not without prettiness in their artificial way. The satirical
pamphlets of Thomas Nash and his fellows, against
" Martin Marprelate," an anonymous writer, or

company of writers, who attacked the bishops, are
not wanting in wit, but are so cumbered with fantastic whimsicalities, and so bound up with personal quarrels, that oblivion has covered them. The
most noteworthy of them were Nash's *Piers Penni-
less's Supplication to the Devil*, Lyly's *Pap with a
Hatchet*, and Greene's *Groat's Worth of Wit*. Of
books which were not so much literature as the material of literature, mention may be made of the
Chronicle of England, compiled by Ralph Holinshed
in 1577. This was Shakspere's English history, and
its strong Lancastrian bias influenced Shakspere
in his representation of Richard III. and other
characters in his historical plays. In his Roman
tragedies Shakspere followed closely Sir Thomas
North's translation of Plutarch's *Lives*, made in
1579 from the French version of Jacques Amyot.

Of books belonging to other departments than
pure literature, the most important was Richard
Hooker's *Ecclesiastical Polity*, the first four books
of which appeared in 1594. This was a work on
the philosophy of law and a defense, as against
the Presbyterians, of the government of the English Church by bishops. No work of equal
dignity and scope had yet been published in English prose. It was written in sonorous, stately,
and somewhat involved periods, in a Latin rather
than an English idiom, and it influenced strongly
the diction of later writers, such as Milton and Sir
Thomas Browne. Had the *Ecclesiastical Polity*
been written one hundred, or perhaps even fifty,

years earlier, it would doubtless have been written in Latin.

The life of Francis Bacon, "the father of inductive philosophy," as he has been called—better, the founder of inductive logic—belongs to English history, and the bulk of his writings, in Latin and English, to the history of English philosophy. But his volume of *Essays* was a contribution to general literature. In their completed form they belong to the year 1625, but the first edition was printed in 1597 and contained only ten short essays, each of them rather a string of pregnant maxims — the text for an essay — than that developed treatment of a subject which we now understand by the word essay. They were, said their author, "as grains of salt that will rather give you an appetite than offend you with satiety." They were the first essays so-called in the language. "The word," said Bacon, "is late, but the thing is ancient." The word he took from the French *essais* of Montaigne, the first two books of which had been published in 1592. Bacon testified that his essays were the most popular of his writings because they "came home to men's business and bosoms." Their alternate title explains their character: *Counsels Civil and Moral*, that is, pieces of advice touching the conduct of life, "of a nature whereof men shall find much in experience, little in books." The essays contain the quintessence of Bacon's practical wisdom, his wide knowledge of the world of

men. The truth and depth of his sayings, and
the extent of ground which they cover, as well as
the weighty compactness of his style, have given
many of them the currency of proverbs. "Revenge is a kind of wild justice." "He that hath
wife and children hath given hostages to fortune."
"There is no excellent beauty that hath not some
strangeness in the proportion." Bacon's reason
was illuminated by a powerful imagination, and his
noble English rises now and then, as in his essay
On Death, into eloquence—the eloquence of pure
thought, touched gravely and afar off by emotion.
In general, the atmosphere of his intellect is that
lumen siccum which he loved to commend, "not
drenched or bloodied by the affections." Dr.
Johnson said that the wine of Bacon's writings
was a dry wine.

A popular class of books in the 17th century
were "characters" or "witty descriptions of the
properties of sundry persons," such as the Good
Schoolmaster, the Clown, the Country Magistrate;
much as in some modern *Heads of the People*,
where Douglas Jerrold or Leigh Hunt sketches
the Medical Student, the Monthly Nurse, etc.
A still more modern instance of the kind is
George Eliot's *Impressions of Theophrastus Such*,
which derives its title from the Greek philosopher,
Theophrastus, whose character-sketches were the
original models of this kind of literature. The
most popular character-book in Europe in the
17th century was La Bruyère's *Caractères*. But

this was not published till 1588. In England the
fashion had been set in 1614, by the *Characters* of
Sir Thomas Overbury, who died by poison the
year before his book was printed. One of Overbury's sketches — the *Fair and Happy Milkmaid* — is justly celebrated for its old-world
sweetness and quaintness. "Her breath is her
own, which scents all the year long of June, like a
new-made hay-cock. She makes her hand hard
with labor, and her heart soft with pity; and
when winter evenings fall early, sitting at her
merry wheel, she sings defiance to the giddy wheel
of fortune. She bestows her year's wages at next
fair, and, in choosing her garments, counts no
bravery in the world like decency. The garden
and bee-hive are all her physic and surgery, and
she lives the longer for it. She dares go alone
and unfold sheep in the night, and fears no manner of ill, because she means none; yet to say
truth, she is never alone, but is still accompanied
with old songs, honest thoughts and prayers, but
short ones. Thus lives she, and all her care is
she may die in the spring-time, to have store of
flowers stuck upon her winding-sheet."

England was still merry England in the times
of good Queen Bess, and rang with old songs,
such as kept this milkmaid company; songs, said
Bishop Joseph Hall, which were "sung to the
wheel and sung unto the pail." Shakspere loved
their simple minstrelsy; he put some of them into
the mouth of Ophelia, and scattered snatches of

them through his plays, and wrote others like them himself :

> " Now, good Cesario, but that piece of song,
> That old and antique song we heard la:t night,
> Methinks it did relieve my passion much,
> More than light airs and recollected terms
> Of these most brisk and giddy-paced times.
> Mark it, Cesario, it is old and plain.
> The knitters and the spinners in the sun
> And the free maids that weave their threads with bones
> Do use to chant it ; it is silly sooth
> And dallies with the innocence of love
> Like the old age."

Many of these songs, so natural, fresh, and spontaneous, together with sonnets and other more elaborate forms of lyrical verse, were printed in miscellanies, such as the *Passionate Pilgrim*, *England's Helicon*, and Davison's *Poetical Rhapsody*. Some were anonymous, or were by poets of whom little more is known than their names. Others were by well-known writers, and others, again, were strewn through the plays of Lyly, Shakspere, Jonson, Beaumont, Fletcher, and other dramatists. Series of love sonnets, like Spenser's *Amoretti* and Sidney's *Astrophel and Stella*, were written by Shakspere, Daniel, Drayton, Drummond, Constable, Watson, and others, all dedicated to some mistress real or imaginary. Pastorals, too, were written in great number, such as William Browne's *Britannia's Pastorals* and *Shephera's Pipe* (1613–1616) and Marlowe's charmingly rococo little idyl,

The Passionate Shepherd to his Love, which Shakspere quoted in the *Merry Wives of Windsor*, and
to which Sir Walter Raleigh wrote a reply.
There were love stories in verse, like Arthur
Brooke's *Romeo and Juliet* (the source of Shakspere's tragedy), Marlowe's fragment, *Hero and
Leander*, and Shakspere's *Venus and Adonis*, and
Rape of Lucrece, the first of these on an Italian
and the other three on classical subjects, though
handled in any thing but a classical manner.
Wordsworth said finely of Shakspere, that he
" could not have written an epic : he would have
died of a plethora of thought." Shakspere's two
narrative poems, indeed, are by no means models
of their kind. The current of the story is choked
at every turn, though it be with golden sand. It
is significant of his dramatic habit of mind that
dialogue and soliloquy usurp the place of narration,
and that, in the *Rape of Lucrece* especially, the
poet lingers over the analysis of motives and feelings, instead of hastening on with the action, as
Chaucer, or any born story-teller, would have
done.

In Marlowe's poem there is the same spendthrift fancy, although not the same subtlety. In the
first two divisions of the poem the story does, in
some sort, get forward ; but in the continuation, by
George Chapman (who wrote the last four " ses-
tiads "), the path is utterly lost, " with woodbine
and the gadding vine o'ergrown."

One is reminded that modern poetry, if it has

lost in richness, has gained in directness, when one compares any passage in Marlowe and Chapman's *Hero and Leander* with Byron's ringing lines:

> " The wind is high on Helle's wave,
> As on that night of stormy water,
> When Love, who sent, forgot to save
> The young, the beautiful, the brave,
> The lonely hope of Sestos' daughter."

Marlowe's continuator, Chapman, wrote a number of plays, but he is best remembered by his royal translation of Homer, issued in parts from 1598–1615. This was not so much a literal translation of the Greek, as a great Elisabethan poem, inspired by Homer. It has Homer's fire, but not his simplicity; the energy of Chapman's fancy kindling him to run beyond his text into all manner of figures and conceits. It was written, as has been said, as Homer would have written if he had been an Englishman of Chapman's time. Certainly all later versions—Pope's and Cowper's and Lord Derby's and Bryant's — seem pale against the glowing exuberance of Chapman's English. His verse was not the heroic line of ten syllables, chosen by most of the standard translators, but the long fourteen-syllabled measure, which degenerates easily into sing-song in the hands of a feeble metrist. In Chapman it is often harsh, but seldom tame, and in many passages it reproduces wonderfully the ocean-like roll of Homer's hexameters.

" From his bright helm and shield did burn a most unwearied
   fire,
Like rich Autumnus' golden lamp, whose brightness men
   admire,
Past all the other host of stars when, with his cheerful face,
Fresh washed in lofty ocean waves, he doth the sky enchase."

Keats's fine ode, *On First Looking into Chapman's
Homer*, is well-knowñ. Fairfax's version of Tasso's *Jerusalem Delivered* (1600) is one of the best
metrical translations in the language.
The national pride in the achievements of Englishmen, by land and sea, found expression, not
only in prose chronicles and in books, like Stow's
Survey of London, and Harrison's *Description of
England* (prefixed to Holinshed's *Chronicle*), but
in long historical and descriptive poems, like William Warner's *Albion's England*, 1586; Samuel
Daniel's *History of the Civil Wars*, 1595–1602;
Michael Drayton's *Baron's Wars*, 1596, *England's Heroical Epistles*, 1598, and *Polyolbion*,
1613. The very plan of these works was fatal to
their success. It is not easy to digest history and
geography into poetry. Drayton was the most
considerable poet of the three, but his *Polyolbion*
was nothing more than "a gazeteer in rime," a
topographical survey of England and Wales, with
tedious personifications of rivers, mountains, and
valleys, in thirty books and nearly one hundred
thousand lines. It was Drayton who said of Marlowe, that he "had in him those brave translunary
things that the first poets had;" and there are brave

things in Drayton, but they are only occasional passages, oases among dreary wastes of sand. His *Agincourt* is a spirited war-song, and his *Nymphidia ; or, Court of Faery*, is not unworthy, of comparison with Drake's *Culprit Fay*, and is interesting as bringing in Oberon and Robin Goodfellow, and the popular fairy lore of Shakspere's *Midsummer Night's Dream.*

The "well-languaged Daniel," of whom Ben Jonson said that he was "a good honest man, but no poet," wrote, however, one fine meditative piece, his *Epistle to the Countess of Cumberland*, a sermon apparently on the text of the Roman poet Lucretius's famous passage in praise of philosophy,

"Suave mari magno, turbantibus æquora ventis," etc.

But the Elisabethan genius found its fullest and truest expression in the drama. It is a common phenomenon in the history of literature that some old literary form or mold will run along for centuries without having any thing poured into it worth keeping, until the moment comes when the genius of the time seizes it and makes it the vehicle of immortal thought and passion. Such was in England the fortune of the stage play. At a time when Chaucer was writing character-sketches that were really dramatic, the formal drama consisted of rude miracle plays that had no literary quality whatever. These were taken from the Bible and acted at first by the priests as illustrations of Scripture history and additions to the

church service on feasts and saints' days. Afterward the town guilds, or incorporated trades, took
hold of them and produced them annually on
scaffolds in the open air. In some English cities,
as Coventry and Chester, they continued to be
performed almost to the close of the 16th century.
And in the celebrated Passion Play, at Oberam-
mergau, in Bavaria, we have an instance of a
miracle play that has survived to our own day.
These were followed by the moral plays, in which
allegorical characters, such as Clergy, Lusty Ju-
ventus, Riches, Folly, and Good Demeanaunce,
were the persons of the drama. The comic character in the miracle plays had been the Devil, and
he was retained in some of the moralities side by
side with the abstract vice, who became the clown
or fool of Shaksperian comedy. The "formal
Vice, Iniquity," as Shakspere calls him, had it for
his business to belabor the roaring Devil with his
wooden sword

> . . . "with his dagger of lath
> In his rage and his wrath
> Cries 'Aha!' to the Devil,
> 'Pare your nails, Goodman Evil!'"

He survives also in the harlequin of the panto-
mimes, and in Mr. Punch, of the puppet shows,
who kills the Devil and carries him off on his
back, when the latter is sent to fetch him to hell
for his crimes.

Masques and interludes—the latter a species of

short farce—were popular at the Court of Henry VIII. Elisabeth was often entertained at the universities or at the inns of court with Latin plays, or with translations from Seneca, Euripides, and Ariosto. Original comedies and tragedies began to be written, modeled upon Terence, and Seneca, and chronicle histories founded on the annals of English kings. There was a Master of the Revels at court, whose duty it was to select plays to be performed before the queen, and these were acted by the children of the Royal Chapel, or by the choir boys of St. Paul's Cathedral. These early plays are of interest to students of the history of the drama, and throw much light upon the construction of later plays, like Shakspere's; but they are rude and inartistic, and without any literary quality.

There were also private companies of actors maintained by wealthy noblemen, like the Earl of Leicester, and bands of strolling players, who acted in inn-yards and bear-gardens. It was not until stationary theaters were built and stock companies of actors regularly licensed and established, that any plays were produced which deserve the name of literature. In 1576 the first play-house was built in London. This was the *Black Friars*, which was located within the liberties of the dissolved monastery of the Black Friars, in order to be outside of the jurisdiction of the Mayor and Corporation, who were Puritan, and determined in their opposition to the stage. For the same reason the

Theater and the *Curtain* were built in the same
year, outside the city walls in Shoreditch.   Later
the *Rose*, the *Globe*, and the *Swan*, were erected
on the Bankside, across the Thames, and play-
goers resorting to them were accustomed to "take
boat."

These early theaters were of the rudest construction.   The six-penny spectators, or "ground-
lings," stood in the yard, or pit, which had neither
floor nor roof.   The shilling spectators sat on the
stage, where they were accommodated with stools
and tobacco pipes, and whence they chaffed the
actors or the "opposed rascality" in the yard.
There was no scenery, and the female parts were
taken by boys.   Plays were acted in the afternoon.   A placard, with the letters "Venice," or
"Rome," or whatever, indicated the place of the
action.   With such rude appliances must Shakspere bring before his audience the midnight bat-
tlements of Elsinore and the moonlit garden of
the Capulets.   The dramatists had to throw themselves upon the imagination of their public, and it
says much for the imaginative temper of the public of that day, that it responded to the appeal.
It suffered the poet to transport it over wide intervals of space and time, and "with aid of some
few foot and half-foot words, fight over York
and Lancaster's long jars."   Pedantry undertook,
even at the very beginnings of the Elisabethan
drama, to shackle it with the so-called rules of
Aristotle, or classical unities of time and place,

7

to make it keep violent action off the stage and comedy distinct from tragedy. But the play-wrights appealed from the critics to the truer sympathies of the audience, and they decided for freedom and action, rather than restraint and recitation. Hence our national drama is of Shakspere, and not of Racine. By 1603 there were twelve play-houses in London in full blast, although the city then numbered only one hundred and fifty thousand inhabitants.

Fresh plays were produced every year. The theater was more to the Englishman of that time than it has ever been before or since. It was his club, his novel, his newspaper all in one. No great drama has ever flourished apart from a living stage, and it was fortunate that the Elisabethan dramatists were, almost all of them, actors and familiar with stage effect. Even the few exceptions, like Beaumont and Fletcher, who were young men of good birth and fortune, and not dependent on their pens, were probably in-timate with the actors, lived in a theatrical atmos-phere, and knew practically how plays should be put on.

It had now become possible to earn a livelihood as an actor and playwright. Richard Burbage and Edward Alleyn, the leading actors of their generation, made large fortunes. Shakspere him-self made enough from his share in the profits of the *Globe* to retire with a competence, some seven years before his death, and purchase a handsome property in his native Stratford. Accordingly, shortly after 1580, a number of men of real talent began to write for the stage as a career. These were young graduates of the universities, Marlowe, Greene, Peele, Kyd, Lyly, Lodge, and others, who came up to town and led a Bohemian life as actors and playwrights. Most of them were wild and dissipated, and ended in wretchedness. Peele died of a disease brought on by his evil courses; Greene, in extreme destitution, from a surfeit of Rhenish wine and pickled herring; and Marlowe was stabbed in a tavern brawl.

The Euphuist Lyly produced eight plays from 1584 to 1601. They were written for court entertainments, in prose and mostly on mythological subjects. They have little dramatic power, but the dialogue is brisk and vivacious, and there are several pretty songs in them. All the characters talk Euphuism. The best of these was *Alexander and Campaspe*, the plot of which is briefly as follows. Alexander has fallen in love with his beautiful captive, Campaspe, and employs the artist Apelles to paint her portrait. During the sittings, Apelles becomes enamored of his subject and declares his passion, which is returned. Alexander discovers their secret, but magnanimously forgives the treason and joins the lovers' hands. The situation is a good one, and capable of strong treatment in the hands of a real dramatist. But Lyly slips smoothly over the crisis of the action and, in place of passionate scenes, gives us clever discourses and soliloquies, or, at best, a light interchange of question and answer, full of conceits, repartees, and double meanings. For example:

"*Apel.* Whom do you love best in the world?

"*Camp.* He that made me last in the world.

"*Apel.* That was a God.

"*Camp.* I had thought it had been a man," etc.

Lyly's service to the drama consisted in his introduction of an easy and sparkling prose as the language of high comedy, and Shakspere's indebtedness to the fashion thus set is seen in such passages as the wit combats between Benedict and Beatrice in *Much Ado about Nothing*, greatly superior as they are to any thing of the kind in Lyly.

The most important of the dramatists, who were Shakspere's forerunners, or early contemporaries, was Christopher or—as he was familiarly called—Kit Marlowe. Born in the same year with Shakspere (1564), he died in 1593, at which date his great successor is thought to have written no original plays, except the *Comedy of Errors* and *Love's Labour's Lost.* Marlowe first popularized blank verse as the language of tragedy in his *Tamburlaine*, written before 1587, and in subsequent plays he brought it to a degree of strength and flexibility which left little for Shakspere to do but to take it as he found it. Tamburlaine was a crude, violent piece, full of exaggeration and bombast, but with passages here and there of splendid declamation, justifying Ben Jonson's phrase, "Marlowe's mighty line." Jonson, however, ridiculed, in his *Discoveries*, the "scenical strutting and furious vociferation" of Marlowe's hero; and Shakspere put a quotation from Tamburlaine into the mouth of his ranting Pistol. Marlowe's *Edward II.* was the most regularly constructed and evenly written of his plays. It was the best historical drama on the stage before Shakspere, and not undeserving of the comparison which it has provoked with the latter's *Richard II.* But the most interesting of Marlowe's plays, to a modern reader, is the *Tragical History of Doctor Faustus.* The subject is the same as in Goethe's *Faust*, and Goethe, who knew the English play, spoke of it as greatly planned. The opening of Marlowe's *Faustus* is very similiar to Goethe's. His hero, wearied with unprofitable studies, and filled with a mighty lust for knowledge and the enjoyment of life, sells his soul to the Devil in return for a few years of supernatural power. The tragic irony of the story might seem to lie in the frivolous use which Faustus makes of his dearly bought power, wasting it in practical jokes and feats of legerdemain; but of this Marlowe was probably unconscious. The love story of Margaret, which is the central point of Goethe's drama, is entirely wanting in Marlowe's, and so is the subtle conception of Goethe's Mephistophiles. Marlowe's handling of the supernatural is materialistic and downright, as befitted an age which believed in witchcraft. The

greatest part of the English *Faustus* is the last
scene, in which the agony and terror of suspense
with which the magician awaits the stroke of the
clock that signals his doom are powerfully drawn.

> " *O lente, lente currite, noctis equi!*
> The stars move still, time runs, the clock will strike. . .
> O soul, be changed into little water-drops,
> And fall into the ocean, ne'er be found !"

Marlowe's genius was passionate and irregular.
He had no humor, and the comic portions of
Faustus are scenes of low buffoonery.

George Peele's masterpiece, *David and Bethsabe*,
was also, in many respects, a fine play, though its
beauties were poetic rather than dramatic, consisting not in the characterization—which is feeble—
but in the eastern luxuriance of the imagery. There
is one noble chorus—

> " O proud revolt of a presumptuous man," etc.

which reminds one of passages in Milton's *Samson
Agonistes*, and occasionally Peele rises to such
high Aeschylean audacities as this :

> " At him the thunder shall discharge his bolt,
> And his fair spouse, with bright and fiery wings,
> Sit ever burning on his hateful bones."

Robert Greene was a very unequal writer. His
plays are slovenly and careless in construction, and
he puts classical allusions into the mouths of milkmaids and serving boys, with the grotesque pedantry and want of keeping common among the

playwrights of the early stage. He has, notwithstanding, in his comedy parts, more natural lightness and grace than either Marlowe or Peele. In
his *Friar Bacon and Friar Bungay,* and his *Pinner
of Wakefield,* there is a fresh breath, as of the
green English country, in such passages as the de-
. scription of Oxford, the scene at Harleston Fair,
and the picture of the dairy in the keeper's lodge
at merry Fressingfield.

In all these ante-Shaksperian dramatists there
was a defect of art proper to the first comers in a
new literary departure. As compared not only
with Shakspere, but with later writers, who had the
inestimable advantage of his example, their work
was full of imperfection, hesitation, experiment.
Marlowe was probably, in native genius, the equal
at least of Fletcher or Webster, but his plays, as a
whole, are certainly not equal to theirs. They
wrote in a more developed state of the art. But
the work of this early school settled the shape
which the English drama was to take. It fixed the
practice and traditions of the national theater. It
decided that the drama was to deal with the whole
of life, the real and the ideal, tragedy and comedy,
prose and verse, in the same play, without limitations of time, place, and action. It decided that
the English play was to be an action, and not a
dialogue, bringing boldly upon the mimic scene
feasts, dances, processions, hangings, riots, plays
within plays, drunken revels, beatings, battle, murder, and sudden death. It established blank verse,

with occasional riming couplets at the close of a scene or of a long speech, as the language of the tragedy and high comedy parts, and prose as the language of the low comedy and " business " parts. And it introduced songs, a feature of which Shakspere made exquisite use. Shakspere, indeed, like all great poets, invented no new form of literature, but touched old forms to finer purposes, refining every thing, discarding nothing. Even the old chorus and dumb show he employed, though sparingly, as also the old jig, or comic song, which the clown used to give between the acts.

Of the life of William Shakspere, the greatest dramatic poet of the world, so little is known that it has been possible for ingenious persons to construct a theory—and support it with some show of reason—that the plays which pass under his name were really written by Bacon or some one else. There is no danger of this paradox ever making serious headway, for the historical evidence that Shakspere wrote Shakspere's plays, though not overwhelming, is sufficient. But it is startling to think that the greatest creative genius of his day, or perhaps of all time, was suffered to slip out of life so quietly that his title to his own works could even be questioned only two hundred and fifty years after the event. That the single authorship of the Homeric poems should be doubted is not so strange, for Homer is almost prehistoric. But Shakspere was a modern Englishman, and at the time of his death the first English colony in America was already nine years old. The important known facts of his life can be told almost in a sentence. He was born at Stratford-on-Avon in 1564, married when he was eighteen, went to London probably in 1587, and became an actor, playwriter, and stockholder in the company which owned the Blackfriars and the Globe Theaters. He seemingly prospered in his calling and retired about 1609 to Stratford, where he lived in the house that he had bought some years before, and where he died in 1616. His *Venus and Adonis* was printed in 1593, the *Rape of Lucrece* in 1594, and his *Sonnets* in 1609. So far as is known, only eighteen of the thirty-seven plays generally attributed to Shakspere were printed during his life-time. These were printed singly, in quarto shape, and were little more than stage books, or librettos. The first collected edition of his works was the so-called " First Folio " of 1623, published by his fellow-actors, Heming and Condell. No contemporary of Shakspere thought it worth while to write a life of the stage-player. There are a number of references to him in the literature of the time; some generous, as in Ben Jonson's well-known verses; others singularly unappreciative, like Webster's mention of "the right happy and copious industry of Master Shakspere." But all these together do not begin to amount to the sum of what was said about Spenser, or Sidney, or Raleigh, or Ben Jonson. There is, indeed, nothing to show that his contemporaries understood what a man they had

among them in the person of "Our English Terence, Mr. Will Shakespeare!" The age, for the
rest, was not a self-conscious one, nor greatly
given to review writing and literary biography.
Nor is there enough of self-revelation in Shakspere's plays to aid the reader in forming a notion
of the man. He lost his identity completely in the
characters of his plays, as it is the duty of a dramatic writer to do. His sonnets have been ex-
amined carefully in search of internal evidence as
to his character and life, but the speculations
founded upon them have been more ingenious
than convincing.

Shakspere probably began by touching up old
plays. *Henry VI.* and the bloody tragedy of *Titus
Andronicus,* if Shakspere's at all, are doubtless
only his revision of pieces already on the stage.
The *Taming of the Shrew* seems to be an old play
worked over by Shakspere and some other dramatist, and traces of another hand are thought to be
visible in párts of *Henry VIII., Pericles,* and *Timon
of Athens.* Such partnerships were common among
the Elisabethan dramatists, the most illustrious example being the long association of Beaumont and
Fletcher. The plays in the First Folio were divided
into histories, comedies, and tragedies, and it will
be convenient to notice them briefly in that order.

It was a stirring time when the young adventurer
came to London to try his fortune. Elisabeth had
finally thrown down the gage of battle to Catholic
Europe, by the execution of Mary Stuart, in 1587.

The following year saw the destruction of the colossal Armada, which Spain had sent to revenge
Mary's death, and hard upon these events followed
the gallant exploits of Grenville, Essex, and
Raleigh.

That Shakspere shared the exultant patriotism of
the times, and the sense of their aloofness from the
continent of Europe, which was now born in the
breasts of Englishmen, is evident from many a
passage in his plays.

" This happy breed of men, this little world,
This precious stone set in a silver sea,
This blessed plot, this earth, this realm, this England,
This land of such dear souls, this dear, dear land,
England, bound in with the triumphant sea !"

His English histories are ten in number. Of
these *King John* and *Henry VIII.* are isolated
plays. The others form a consecutive series, in
the following order: *Richard III.*, the two parts
of *Henry IV.*, *Henry V.*, the three parts of *Henry
VI.*, and *Richard III.* This series may be divided
into two, each forming a tetralogy, or groups of
four plays. In the first the subject is the rise of
the house of Lancaster. But the power of the Red
Rose was founded in usurpation. In the second
group, accordingly, comes the Nemesis, in the civil
wars of the Roses, reaching their catastrophe in the
downfall of both Lancaster and York, and the
tyranny of Gloucester. The happy conclusion is
finally reached in the last play of the series, when
this new usurper is overthrown in turn, and Henry

VII., the first Tudor sovereign, ascends the throne, and restores the Lancastrian inheritance, purified, by bloody atonement, from the stain of Richard II.'s murder.   These eight plays are, as it were, the eight acts of one great drama; and if such a thing were possible, they should be represented on successive nights, like the parts of a Greek trilogy.   In order of composition, the second group came first. *Henry VI.* is strikingly inferior to the others. *Richard III.* is a good acting play, and its popularity has been sustained by a series of great tragedians, who have taken the part of the king.   But, in a literary sense, it is unequal to *Richard II.*, or the two parts of *Henry IV.*   The latter is unquestionably Shakspere's greatest historical tragedy, and it contains his master-creation in the region of low comedy, the immortal Falstaff.

The constructive art with which Shakspere shaped history into drama is well seen in comparing his *King John* with the two plays on that subject, which were already on the stage.   These, like all the other old "Chronicle histories," such as *Thomas Lord Cromwell* and the *Famous Victories of Henry V.*, follow a merely chronological, or biographical, order, giving events loosely, as they occurred, without any unity of effect, or any reference to their bearing on the catastrophe.   Shakspere's order was logical.   He compressed and selected, disregarding the fact of history oftentimes, in favor of the higher truth of fiction; bringing together a crime and its punishment, as cause and effect, even though they had no such relation in the chronicle, and were separated, perhaps, by many years.

Shakspere's first two comedies were experiments. *Love's Labour's Lost* was a play of manners, with hardly any plot. It brought together a number of *humors*, that is, oddities and affectations of various sorts, and played them off on one another, as Ben Jonson afterward did in his comedies of humor. Shakspere never returned to this type of play, unless, perhaps, in the *Taming of the Shrew*. There the story turned on a single "humor," Katherine's bad temper, just as the story in Jonson's *Silent Woman* turned on Morose's hatred of noise. The *Taming of the Shrew* is, therefore, one of the least Shaksperian of Shakspere's plays; a *bourgeois*, domestic comedy, with a very narrow interest. It belongs to the school of French comedy, like Moliere's *Malade Imaginaire*, not to the romantic comedy of Shakspere and Fletcher.

The *Comedy of Errors* was an experiment of an exactly opposite kind. It was a play, purely of incident ; a farce, in which the main improbability being granted, namely, that the twin Antipholi and twin Dromios are so alike that they cannot be distinguished, all the amusing complications follow naturally enough. There is little character-drawing in the play. Any two pairs of twins, in the same predicament, would be equally droll. The fun lies in the situation. This was a comedy of the Latin school, and resembled the *Menaechmi* of Plautus. Shakspere never returned to this type of

play, though there is an element of "errors" in
Midsummer Night's Dream. In the *Two Gentlemen of Verona* he finally hit upon that species of
romantic comedy which he may be said to have
invented or created out of the scattered materials
at hand in the works of his predecessors. In this
play, as in the *Merchant of Venice, Midsummer
Night's Dream, Much Ado about Nothing, As You
Like It, Twelfth Night, Winter's Tale, All's Well
that Ends Well, Measure for Measure,* and the
Tempest, the plan of construction is as follows.
There is one main intrigue carried out by the high
comedy characters, and a secondary intrigue, or
underplot, by the low comedy characters. The
former is by no means purely comic, but admits
the presentation of the noblest motives, the
strongest passions, and the most delicate graces of
romantic poetry. In some of the plays it has a
prevailing lightness and gayety, as in *As You Like It*
and *Twelfth Night.* In others, like *Measure for
Measure,* it is barely saved from becoming tragedy
by the happy close. Shylock certainly remains a
tragic figure, even to the end, and a play like *Winter's Tale,* in which the painful situation is prolonged for years, is only technically a comedy.
Such dramas, indeed, were called, on many of the
title-pages of the time, "tragi-comedies." The
low comedy interlude, on the other hand, was
broadly comic. It was cunningly interwoven with
the texture of the play, sometimes loosely, and by
way of variety or relief, as in the episode of Touch-

stone and Audrey, in *As You Like It;* sometimes
closely, as in the case of Dogberry and Verges, in
Much Ado about Nothing, where the blunder-
ing of the watch is made to bring about the *denouement* of the main action.   The *Merry Wives
of Windsor* is an exception to this plan of construction.   It is Shakspere's only play of contemporary, middle-class English life, and is written
almost throughout in prose.   It is his only *pure*
comedy, except the *Taming of the Shrew*.

Shakspere did not abandon comedy when writing
tragedy, though he turned it to a new account.   The
two species graded into one another.   Thus *Cymbeline* is, in its fortunate ending, really as much of
a comedy as *Winter's Tale*—to which its plot bears
a resemblance—and is only technically a tragedy,
because it contains a violent death.   In some of
the tragedies, as *Macbeth* and *Julius Cæsar*, the
comedy element is reduced to a minimum.   But in
others, as *Romeo and Juliet*, and *Hamlet*, it heightens
the tragic feeling by the irony of contrast.   Akin
to this is the use to which Shakspere put the old
Vice, or Clown, of the moralities.   The Fool in
Lear, Touchstone in *As You Like It*, and Thersites
in *Troilus and Cressida*, are a sort of parody of the
function of the Greek chorus, commenting the action of the drama with scraps of bitter, or half-
crazy, philosophy, and wonderful gleams of insight
into the depths of man's nature.

The earliest of Shakspere's tragedies, unless
Titus Andronicus be his, was, doubtless, *Romeo and*

Juliet, which is full of the passion and poetry of youth and of first love. It contains a large pro-. portion of riming lines, which is usually a sign in Shakspere of early work. He dropped rime more and more in his later plays, and his blank verse grew freer and more varied in its pauses and the number of its feet. *Romeo and Juliet* is also unique, among his tragedies, in this respect, that the catastrophe is brought about by a fatality, as in the Greek drama. It was Shakspere's habit to work out his tragic conclusions from within, through character, rather than through external chances. This is true of all the great tragedies of his middle life, *Hamlet*, *Othello*, *Lear*, *Macbeth*, in every one of which the catastrophe is involved in the character and actions of the hero. This is so, in a special sense, in *Hamlet*, the subtlest of all Shakspere's plays, and if not his masterpiece, at any rate the one which has most attracted and puzzled the greatest minds. It is observable that in Shakspere's comedies there is no one central figure, but that, in passing into tragedy, he intensified and concentrated the attention upon a single character. This difference is seen, even in the naming of the plays; the tragedies always take their titles from their heroes, the comedies never.

Somewhat later, probably, than the tragedies already mentioned, were the three Roman plays, *Julius Cæsar*, *Coriolanus*, and *Anthony and Cleopatra*. It is characteristic of Shakspere that he invented the plot of none of his plays, but took

material that he found at hand. In these Roman
tragedies, he followed Plutarch closely, and yet,
even in so doing, gave, if possible, a greater evidence of real creative power than when he borrowed a mere outline of a story from some Italian
novelist. It is most instructive to compare *Julius
Cæsar* with Ben Jonson's *Catiline* and *Sejanus*.
Jonson was careful not to go beyond his text. In
Catiline he translates almost literally the whole of
Cicero's first oration against Catiline. Sejanus is
a mosaic of passages, from Tacitus and Suetonius.
There is none of this dead learning in Shakspere's
play. Having grasped the conception of the characters of Brutus, Cassius, and Mark Anthony, as
Plutarch gave them, he pushed them out into their
consequences in every word and act, so independ-
ently of his original, and yet so harmoniously with
it, that the reader knows that he is reading history,
and needs no further warrant for it than Shakspere's
own. *Timon of Athens* is the least agreeable and
most monotonous of Shakspere's undoubted tragedies, and *Troilus and Cressida*, said Coleridge, is
the hardest to characterize. The figures of the old
Homeric world fare but hardly under the glaring
light of modern standards of morality which Shakspere turns upon them. Ajax becomes a stupid
bully, Ulysses a crafty politician, and swift-footed
Achilles a vain and sulky chief of faction. In los-
ing their ideal remoteness, the heroes of the *Iliad*
lose their poetic quality, and the lover of Homer
experiences an unpleasant disenchantment.

8

It was customary in the 18th century to speak
of Shakspere as a rude though prodigious genius.
Even Milton could describe him as "warbling his
native wood-notes wild." But a truer criticism,
beginning in England with Coleridge, has shown
that he was also a profound artist. It is true that
he wrote for his audiences, and that his art is not
every-where and at all points perfect. But a great
artist will contrive, as Shakspere did, to reconcile
practical exigencies, like those of the public stage,
with the finer requirements of his art. Strained in-
terpretations have been put upon this or that item
in Shakspere's plays; and yet it is generally true
that some deeper reason can be assigned for his
method in a given case than that "the audience liked
puns," or, "the audience liked ghosts." Compare,
for example, his delicate management of the supernatural with Marlowe's procedure in *Faustus.*
Shakspere's age believed in witches, elves, and apparitions; and yet there is always something shadowy or allegorical in his use of such machinery.
The ghost in *Hamlet* is merely an embodied suspicion. Banquo's wraith, which is invisible to all but
Macbeth, is the haunting of an evil conscience.
The witches in the same play are but the prompt-
ings of ambition, thrown into a human shape, so as
to become actors in the drama. In the same way,
the fairies in *Midsummer Night's Dream* are the
personified caprices of the lovers, and they are
unseen by the human characters, whose likes and
dislikes they control, save in the instance where

Bottom is "transformed" (that is, becomes mad) and has sight of the invisible world. So in the *Tempest*, Ariel is the spirit of the air and Caliban of the earth, ministering, with more or less of un-willingness, to man's necessities.

Shakspere is the most universal of writers. He touches more men at more points than Homer, or Dante, or Goethe. The deepest wisdom, the sweet-est poetry, the widest range of character, are com-bined in his plays. He made the English language an organ of expression unexcelled in the history of literature. Yet he is not an English poet simply, but a world-poet. Germany has made him her own, and the Latin races, though at first hindered in a true appreciation of him by the canons of clas-sical taste, have at length learned to know him. An ever-growing mass of Shaksperian literature, in the way of comment and interpretation, critical, text-ual, historical, or illustrative, testifies to the dura-bility and growth of his fame. Above all, his plays still keep, and probably always will keep, the stage. It is common to speak of Shakspere and the other Elisabethan dramatists as if they stood, in some sense, on a level. But in truth there is an almost measureless distance between him and all his con-temporaries. The rest shared with him in the mighty influences of the age. Their plays are touched here and there with the power and splen-dor of which they were all joint heirs. But, as a whole, they are obsolete. They live in books, but not in the hearts and on the tongues of men. The most remarkable of the dramatists contemporary with Shakspere was Ben Jonson, whose robust figure is in striking contrast with the other's gracious impersonality. Jonson was nine years younger than Shakspere. He was educated at Westminster School, served as a soldier in the low countries, became an actor in Henslowe's company, and was twice imprisoned—once for killing a fellow-actor in a duel, and once for his part in the comedy of *Eastward Hoe*, which gave offense to King James. He lived down to the times of Charles I. (1635), and became the acknowledged arbiter of English letters and the center of convivial wit combats at the *Mermaid*, the *Devil*, and other famous London taverns.

> "What things have we seen
> Done at the Mermaid ; heard words that have been
> So nimble and so full of subtle flame,
> As if that every one from whom they came
> Had meant to put his whole wit in a jest,
> And had resolved to live a fool the rest
> Of his dull life." *

The inscription on his tomb, in Westminster Abbey, is simply

> "O rare Ben Jonson!"

Jonson's comedies were modeled upon the *vetus comœdia* of Aristophanes, which was satirical in purpose, and they belonged to an entirely different school from Shakspere's. They were classical and not romantic, and were *pure* comedies, admitting

* Francis Beaumont. *Letter to Ben Jonson.*

no admixture of tragic motives. There is hardly one lovely or beautiful character in the entire range of his dramatic creations. They were comedies not of character, in the high sense of the word, but of manners or humors. His design was to lash the follies and vices of the day, and his *dramatis personæ* consisted for the most part of gulls, impostors, fops, cowards, swaggering braggarts, and "Pauls men." In his first play, *Every Man in his Humor* (acted in 1598), in *Every Man Out of his Humor*, *Bartholomew Fair*, and indeed, in all of his comedies, his subject was the "spongy humors of the time," that is, the fashionable affectations, the whims, oddities, and eccentric developments of London life. His procedure was to bring together a number of these fantastic humorists, to play them off upon each other, involve them in all manner of comical misadventures, and render them utterly ridiculous and contemptible. There was thus a perishable element in his art, for manners change; and however effective this exposure of contemporary affectations may have been, before an audience of Jonson's day, it is as hard for a modern reader to detect his points as it will be for a reader two hundred years hence to understand the satire upon the æsthetic craze in such pieces of the present day, as *Patience* or the *Colonel*. Nevertheless, a patient reader, with the help of copious foot-notes, can gradually put together for himself an image of that world of obsolete humors in which Jonson's comedy dwells, and can admire the dramatist's solid good sense, his great learning, his skill in construction, and the astonishing fertility of his invention. His characters are not revealed from within, like Shakspere's, but built up painfully from outside by a succession of minute, laborious particulars. The difference will be plainly manifest if such a character as Slender, in the *Merry Wives of Windsor*, be compared with any one of the inexhaustible variety of idiots in Jonson's plays ; with Master Stephen, for example, in *Every Man in his Humor ;* or, if Falstaff be put side by side with Captain Bobadil, in the same comedy, perhaps Jonson's masterpiece in the way of comic caricature. *Cynthia's Revels* was a satire on the courtiers and the *Poetaster* on Jonson's literary enemies. The *Alchemist* was an exposure of quackery, and is one of his best comedies, but somewhat overweighted with learning. *Volpone* is the most powerful of all his dramas, but is a harsh and disagreeable piece; and the state of society which it depicts is too revolting for comedy. The *Silent Woman* is, perhaps, the easiest of all Jonson's plays for a modern reader to follow and appreciate. There is a distinct plot to it, the situation is extremely ludicrous, and the emphasis is laid upon a single humor or eccentricity, as in some of Moliere's lighter comedies, like *Le Malade Imaginaire*, or *Le Médecin malgré lui.*

In spite of his heaviness in drama, Jonson had a light enough touch in lyric poetry. His songs have not the careless sweetness of Shakspere's, but they have a grace of their own. Such pieces as his

Love's Triumph, Hymn to Diana, The Noble Mind,
and the adaptation from Philostratus,

"Drink to me only with thine eyes,"

and many others entitle their author to rank among
the first English lyrists. Some of these occur in
his two collections of miscellaneous verse, the *Forest* and *Underwoods;* others in the numerous
masques which he composed.   These were a species of entertainment, very popular at the court of
James I., combining dialogue with music, intricate
dances, and costly scenery.   Jonson left an unfinished pastoral drama, the *Sad Shepherd,* which,
though not equal to Fletcher's *Faithful Shepherdess,*
contains passages of great beauty, one, especially,
descriptive of the shepherdess

"Earine,
Who had her very being and her name
With the first buds and breathings of the spring,
Born with the primrose and the violet
And earliest roses blown."

1. Ward's History of English Dramatic Literature.
2. Palgrave's Golden Treasury of Songs and
Lyrics.
3. The Courtly Poets from Raleigh to Montrose.   Edited by J. Hannah.
4. Sir Philip Sidney's Arcadia.   (First and Second Books.)
5. Bacon's Essays.   Edited by W. Aldis Wright.

6. The Cambridge Shakspere. [Clark & Wright.]

7. Charles Lamb's Specimens of English Dramatic Poets.

8. Ben Jonson's Volpone and Silent Woman. (Cunningham's or Gifford's Edition.)

CHAPTER IV.
THE AGE OF MILTON.

1608–1674.

THE Elisabethan age proper closed with the death of the queen, and the accession of James I., in 1603, but the literature of the fifty years following was quite as rich as that of the half-century that had passed since she came to the throne, in 1557. The same qualities of thought and style which had marked the writers of her reign, prolonged themselves in their successors, through the reigns of the first two Stuart kings and the Commonwealth. Yet there was a change in *spirit*. Literature is only one of the many forms in which the national mind expresses itself. In periods of political revolution, literature, leaving the serene air of fine art, partakes the violent agitation of the times. There were seeds of civil and religious discord in Elisabethan England. As between the two parties in the Church there was a compromise and a truce rather than a final settlement. The Anglican doctrine was partly Calvinistic and partly Arminian. The form of government was Episcopal, but there was a large body of Presbyterians in the Church who desired a change. In the ritual and ceremonies many "rags of poperty" had been retained, which the extreme reformers wished to tear away. But Elisabeth was a worldly-minded woman, impatient of theological disputes. Though circumstances had made her the champion of Protestantism in Europe, she kept many Catholic notions, disapproved, for example, of the marriage of priests, and hated sermons. She was jealous of her prerogative in the State, and in the Church she enforced uniformity. The authors of the *Martin Marprelate* pamphlets against the bishops, were punished by death or imprisonment. While the queen lived things were kept well together and England was at one in face of the common foe. Admiral Howard, who commanded the English naval forces against the Armada, was a Catholic.

But during the reigns of James I. (1603–1625) and Charles I. (1625–1649) Puritanism grew stronger through repression. "England," says the historian Green, "became the people of a book, and that book the Bible." The power of the king was used to impose the power of the bishops upon the English and Scotch Churches until religious discontent became also political discontent, and finally overthrew the throne. The writers of this period divided more and more into two hostile camps. On the side of Church and king was the bulk of the learning and genius of the time. But on the side of free religion and the Parliament were the stern conviction, the fiery zeal, the exalted imagination of English Puritanism. The spokesman of this movement was Milton, whose great figure dominates the literary history of his generation, as Shakspere's does of the generation preceding.

The drama went on in the course marked out for it by Shakspere's example, until the theaters were closed by Parliament, in 1642. Of the Stuart dramatists, the most important were Beaumont and Fletcher, all of whose plays were produced during the reign of James I. These were fifty-three in number, but only thirteen of them were joint productions. Francis Beaumont was twenty years younger than Shakspere, and died a few years before him. He was the son of a judge of the Common Pleas. His collaborator, John Fletcher, a son of the bishop of London, was five years older than Beaumont, and survived him nine years. He was much the more prolific of the two and wrote alone some forty plays. Although the life of one of these partners was conterminous with Shakspere's, their works exhibit a later phase of the dramatic art. The Stuart dramatists followed the lead of Shakspere rather than of Ben Jonson. Their plays, like the former's, belong to the romantic drama. They present a poetic and idealized version of life, deal with the highest passions and the wildest buffoonery, and introduced a great variety of those daring situations and incidents which we agree to call romantic. But while Shakspere seldom or never overstepped the modesty of nature, his successors ran into every license. They sought to stimulate the faded appetite of their audience by exhibiting monstrosities of character, unnatural lusts, subtleties of crime, virtues and vices both in excess.

Beaumont and Fletcher's plays are much easier and more agreeable reading than Ben Jonson's. Though often loose in their plots and without that consistency in the development of their characters which distinguished Jonson's more conscientious workmanship, they are full of graceful dialogue and beautiful poetry. Dryden said that after the Restoration two of their plays were acted for one of Shakspere's or Jonson's throughout the year, and he added, that they "understood and imitated the conversation of *gentlemen* much better, whose wild debaucheries and quickness of wit in repartees no poet can ever paint as they have done." Wild debauchery was certainly not the mark of a gentleman in Shakspere, nor was it altogether so in Beaumont and Fletcher. Their gentlemen are gallant and passionate lovers, gay cavaliers, generous, courageous, courteous—according to the fashion of their times—and sensitive on the point of honor. They are far superior to the cold-blooded rakes of Dryden and the Restoration comedy. Still the manners and language in Beaumont and Fletcher's plays are extremely licentious, and it is not hard to sympathize with the objections to the theater expressed by the Puritan writer, William Prynne, who, after denouncing the long hair of the cavaliers in his tract, *The Unlove-*

liness of Lovelocks, attacked the stage, in 1633, with
Histrio-mastix : the Player's Scourge ; an offense
for which he was fined, imprisoned, pilloried, and
had his ears cropped. Coleridge said that Shakspere was coarse, but never gross. He had the
healthy coarseness of nature herself. But Beaumont and Fletcher's pages are corrupt. Even
their chaste women are immodest in language and
thought. They use not merely that frankness of
speech which was a fashion of the times, but a
profusion of obscene imagery which could not pro-
ceed from a pure mind. Chastity with . them is
rather a bodily accident than a virtue of the heart,
says Coleridge.

Among the best of their light comedies are *The
Chances, The Scornful Lady, The Spanish Curate,*
and *Rule a Wife and Have a Wife.* But far
superior to these are their tragedies and tragi-
comedies, *The Maia's Tragedy, Philaster, A King
and No King*—all written jointly—and *Valen-
tinian* and *Thierry and Theodoret*, written by
Fletcher alone, but perhaps, in part, sketched out
by Beaumont. The tragic masterpiece of Beaumont and Fletcher is *The Maid's Tragedy*, a powerful but repulsive play, which sheds a singular
light not only upon its authors' dramatic methods,
but also upon the attitude toward royalty favored
by the doctrine of the divine right of kings, which
grew up under the Stuarts. The heroine, Evadne,
has been in secret a mistress of the king, who mar-
ries her to Amintor, a gentleman of his court, be-

cause, as she explains to her bridegroom, on the
wedding night,

> " I must have one
> To father children, and to bear the name
> Of husband to me, that my sin may be
> More honorable."

This scene is, perhaps, the most affecting and
impressive in the whole range of Beaumont and
Fletcher's drama. Yet when Evadne names the
king as her paramour, Amintor exclaims:

> " O thou hast named a word that wipes away
> All thoughts revengeful. In that sacred name
> ' The king ' there lies a terror. What frail man
> Dares lift his hand against it ? Let the gods
> Speak to him when they please ; till when, let us
> Suffer and wait."

And the play ends with the words

> " On lustful kings,
> Unlooked-for sudden deaths from heaven are sent,
> But cursed is he that is their instrument."

Aspatia, in this tragedy, is a good instance of
Beaumont and Fletcher's pathetic characters. She
is troth-plight wife to Amintor, and after he, by
the king's command, has forsaken her for Evadne,
she disguises herself as a man, provokes her unfaithful lover to a duel, and dies under his sword,
blessing the hand that killed her. This is a common type in Beaumont and Fletcher, and was
drawn originally from Shakspere's *Ophelia*. All
their good women have the instinctive fidelity of
a dog, and a superhuman patience and devotion,

a "gentle forlornness" under wrongs, which is painted with an almost feminine tenderness. In *Philaster, or Love Lies Bleeding*, Euphrasia, conceiving a hopeless passion for Philaster—who is in love with Arethusa—puts on the dress of a page and enters his service. He employs her to carry messages to his lady-love, just as Viola, in *Twelfth Night*, is sent by the Duke to Olivia. Philaster is persuaded by slanderers that his page and his lady have been unfaithful to him, and in his jealous fury he wounds Euphrasia with his sword. Afterward, convinced of the boy's fidelity, he asks forgiveness, whereto Euphrasia replies,

"Alas, my lord, my life is not a thing
Worthy your noble thoughts. 'Tis not a life,
'Tis but a piece of childhood thrown away."

Beaumont and Fletcher's love-lorn maids wear the willow very sweetly, but in all their piteous passages there is nothing equal to the natural pathos— the pathos which arises from the deep springs of character—of that one brief question and answer in *King Lear*.

"*Lear*. So young and so untender?
"*Cordelia*.   So young, my lord, and true."

The disguise of a woman in man's apparel is a common incident in the romantic drama ; and the fact, that on the Elisabethan stage the female parts were taken by boys, made the deception easier. Viola's situation in *Twelfth Night* is precisely similiar to Euphrasia's, but there is a differ-

ence in the handling of the device which is characteristic of a distinction between Shakspere's art
and that of his contemporaries.   The audience in
Twelfth Night is taken into confidence and made
aware of Viola's real nature from the start, while
Euphrasia's *incognito* is preserved till the fifth act,
and then disclosed by an accident.   This kind of
mystification and surprise was a trick below
Shakspere.   In this instance, moreover, it involved
a departure from dramatic probability.   Euphrasia
could, at any moment, by revealing her identity,
have averted the greatest sufferings and dangers
from Philaster, Arethusa, and herself, and the
only motive for her keeping silence is represented
to have been a feeling of maidenly shame at her
position.   Such strained and fantastic motives are
too often made the pivot of the action in Beaumont and Fletcher's tragi-comedies.   Their characters have not the depth and truth of Shakspere's,
nor are they drawn so sharply.   One reads their
plays with pleasure and remembers here and there
a passage of fine poetry, or a noble or lovely trait.
But their characters, as wholes, leave a fading impression.   Who, even after a single reading or
representation, ever forgets Falstaff, or Shylock, or
King Lear?

The moral inferiority of Beaumont and Fletcher
is well seen in such a play as *A King and No King*.
Here Arbaces falls in love with his sister, and, after
a furious conflict in his own mind, finally suc-
cumbs to his guilty passion.   He is rescued from

the consequences of his weakness by the discovery that Panthea is not, in fact, his sister. But
this is to cut the knot and not to untie it. It
leaves the *denouement* to chance, and not to those
moral forces through which Shakspere always
wrought his conclusions. Arbaces has failed, and
the piece of luck which keeps his failure innocent
is rejected by every right-feeling spectator. In
one of John Ford's tragedies, the situation which
in *A King and No King* is only apparent, becomes
real, and incest is boldly made the subject of the
play. Ford pushed the morbid and unnatural in
character and passion into even wilder extremes
than Beaumont and Fletcher. His best play, the
Broken Heart, is a prolonged and unrelieved tort-
ure of the feelings.

Fletcher's *Faithful Shepherdess* is the best English pastoral drama. Its choral songs are richly
and sweetly modulated, and the influence of the
whole poem upon Milton is very apparent in his
Comus. The *Knight of the Burning Pestle*, written by Beaumont and Fletcher jointly, was the
first burlesque comedy in the language, and is excellent fooling. Beaumont and Fletcher's blank
verse is musical, but less masculine than Marlowe's or Shakspere's, by reason of their excessive
use of extra syllables and feminine endings.

In John Webster the fondness for the abnormal
and sensational themes, which beset the Stuart
stage, showed itself in the exaggeration of the terrible into the horrible. Fear, in Shakspere—as in
9

the great murder scene in *Macbeth*—is a pure passion; but in Webster it is mingled with something physically repulsive. Thus his *Duchess of Malfi* is presented in the dark with a dead man's hand, and is told that it is the hand of her murdered husband. She is shown a dance of madmen and, "behind a traverse, the artificial figures of her children, appearing as if dead." Treated in this elaborate fashion, that "terror," which Aristotle said it was one of the objects of tragedy to move, loses half its dignity. Webster's images have the smell of the charnel house about them.

> " She would not after the report keep fresh
> As long as flowers on graves."
> " We are only like dead walls or vaulted graves,
> That, ruined, yield no echo.
>   O this gloomy world !
> In what a shadow or deep pit of darkness
> Doth womanish and fearful mankind live ! "

Webster had an intense and somber genius. In diction he was the most Shaksperian of the Elisabethan dramatists, and there are sudden gleams of beauty among his dark horrors, which light up a whole scene with some abrupt touch of feeling.

> " Cover her face : mine eyes dazzle : she died young,"

says the brother of the Duchess, when he has procured her murder and stands before the corpse. *Vittoria Corombona* is described in the old editions as "a night-piece," and it should, indeed, be acted by the shuddering light of torches, and with the cry of the screech-owl to punctuate the speeches. The scene of Webster's two best tragedies was laid, like many of Ford's, Cyril Tourneur's, and Beaumont and Fletcher's, in Italy—the wicked and splendid Italy of the Renaissance, which had such a fascination for the Elisabethan imagination. It was to them the land of the Borgias and the Cenci; of families of proud nobles, luxurious, cultivated, but full of revenges and ferocious cunning; subtle poisoners, who killed with a perfumed glove or fan; parricides, atheists, committers of unnamable crimes, and inventors of strange and delicate varieties of sin.

But a very few have here been mentioned of the great host of dramatists who kept the theaters busy through the reigns of Elisabeth, James I., and Charles I. The last of the race was James Shirley, who died in 1666, and whose thirty-eight plays were written during the reign of Charles I. and the Commonwealth.

In the miscellaneous prose and poetry of this period there is lacking the free, exulting, creative impulse of the elder generation, but there is a soberer feeling and a certain scholarly choiceness which commend themselves to readers of bookish tastes. Even that quaintness of thought, which is a mark of the Commonwealth writers, is not without its attraction for a nice literary palate. Prose became now of greater relative importance than ever before. Almost every distinguished writer of the time lent his pen to one or the other party in the great theological and political controversy of the time. There were famous theologians, like Hales, Chillingworth, and Baxter; historians and antiquaries, like Selden, Knolles, and Cotton; philosophers, such as Hobbes, Lord Herbert of Cherbury, and More, the Platonist; and writers in natural science—which now entered upon its modern, experimental phase, under the stimulus of Bacon's writings—among whom may be mentioned Wallis, the mathematician; Boyle, the chemist, and Harvey, the discoverer of the circulation of the blood. These are outside of our subject, but in the strictly literary prose of the time, the same spirit of roused inquiry is manifest, and the same disposition to a thorough and exhaustive treatment of a subject which is proper to the scientific attitude of mind. The line between true and false science, however, had not yet been drawn. The age was pedantic, and appealed too much to the authority of antiquity. Hence we have such monuments of perverse and curious erudition as Robert Burton's *Anatomy of Melancholy*, 1621; and Sir Thomas Browne's *Pseudodoxia Epidemica*, or *Inquiries into Vulgar and Common Errors*, 1646. The former of these was the work of an Oxford scholar, an astrologer, who cast his own horoscope, and a victim himself of the atrabilious humor, from which he sought relief in listening to the ribaldry of bargemen, and in compiling this *Anatomy*, in which the causes, symptoms, prognostics, and cures of melan-

choly are considered in numerous partitions, sec-
tions, members, and subsections. The work is a
mosaic of quotations. All literature is ransacked
for anecdotes and instances, and the book has thus
become a mine of out-of-the-way learning, in which
later writers have dug. Lawrence Sterne helped
himself freely to Burton's treasures, and Dr. Johnson said that the *Anatomy* was the only book that
ever took him out of bed two hours sooner than he
wished to rise.

The vulgar and common errors which Sir Thomas
Browne set himself to refute, were such as these :
That dolphins are crooked, that Jews stink, that a
man hath one rib less than a woman, that Xerxes's
army drank up rivers, that cicades are bred out of
cuckoo-spittle, that Hannibal split Alps with vin-
egar, together with many similar fallacies touching
Pope Joan, the Wandering Jew, the decuman or
tenth wave, the blackness of negroes, Friar Bacon's
brazen head, etc. Another book in which great
learning and ingenuity were applied to trifling
ends, was the same author's *Garden of Cyrus; or, the
Quincuncial Lozenge or Network Plantations of the
Ancients*, in which a mystical meaning is sought in
the occurrence throughout nature and art of the
figure of the quincunx or lozenge. Browne was a
physician of Norwich, where his library, museum,
aviary, and botanic garden were thought worthy of
a special visit by the Royal Society. He was an
antiquary and a naturalist, and deeply read in the
schoolmen and the Christian fathers. He was

a mystic, and a writer of a rich and peculiar imagination, whose thoughts have impressed themselves upon many kindred minds, like Coleridge, De Quincey, and Emerson. Two of his
books belong to literature, *Religio Medici*, published
in 1642, and *Hydriotaphia; or, Urn Burial*, 1658,
a discourse upon rites of burial and incremation,
suggested by some Roman funeral urns, dug up in
Norfolk. Browne's style, though too highly Latinized, is a good example of Commonwealth prose,
that stately, cumbrous, brocaded prose, which had
something of the flow and measure of verse, rather
than the quicker, colloquial movement of modern
writing. Browne stood aloof from the disputes of
his time, and in his very subjects there is a calm
and meditative remoteness from the daily interests
of men. His *Religio Medici* is full of a wise toler-
ance and a singular elevation of feeling. " At the
sight of a cross, or crucifix, I can dispense with my
hat, but scarce with the thought or memory of my
Saviour." " They only had the advantage of a
bold and noble faith, who lived before his coming."
" They go the fairest way to heaven, that would
serve God without a hell." " All things are artificial, for Nature is the art of God." The last
chapter of the *Urn Burial* is an almost rithmical
descant on mortality and oblivion. The style
kindles slowly into a somber eloquence. It is the
most impressive and extraordinary passage in the
prose literature of the time. Browne, like Hamlet, loved to " consider too curiously." His subtlety

led him to "pose his apprehension with those involved enigmas and riddles of the Trinity—with in-
carnation and resurrection;" and to start odd inquiries; "what song the Syrens sang, or what name
Achilles assumed when he hid himself among
women;" or whether, after Lazarus was raised
from the dead, "his heir might lawfully detain his
inheritance." The quaintness of his phrase appears at every turn. "Charles the Fifth can never
hope to live within two Methuselahs of Hector."
"Generations pass, while some trees stand, and old
families survive not three oaks." "Mummy is become merchandise; Mizraim cures wounds, and
Pharaoh is sold for balsams."

One of the pleasantest of old English humorists
is Thomas Fuller, who was a chaplain in the royal
army during the civil war, and wrote, among other
things, a *Church History of Britain*, a book of religious meditations; *Good Thoughts in Bad Times*,
and a "character" book, *The Holy and Profane
State*. His most important work, the *Worthies of
England*, was published in 1662, the year after his
death. This was a description of every English
county; its natural commodities, manufactures,
wonders, proverbs, etc., with brief biographies of
its memorable persons. Fuller had a well-stored
memory, sound piety, and excellent common sense.
Wit was his leading intellectual trait, and the
quaintness which he shared with his contemporaries
appears in his writings in a fondness for puns, droll
turns of expressions, and bits of eccentric sugges-

tion. His prose, unlike Browne's, Milton's, and Jeremy Taylor's, is brief, simple, and pithy. His dry vein of humor was imitated by the American Cotton Mather, in his *Magnalia*, and by many of the English and New England divines of the 17th century.

Jeremy Taylor was also a chaplain in the king's army, was several times imprisoned for his opinions, and was afterward made, by Charles II., Bishop of Down and Connor. He is a devotional rather than a theological writer, and his *Holy Living* and *Holy Dying* are religious classics. Taylor, like Sydney, was a "warbler of poetic prose." He has been called the prose Spenser, and his English has the opulence, the gentle elaboration, the "linked sweetness long drawn out" of the poet of the *Faery Queene*. In fullness and resonance, Taylor's diction resembles that of the great orators, though it lacks their nervous energy. His pathos is exquisitely tender, and his numerous similes have Spenser's pictorial amplitude. Some of them have become commonplaces for admiration, notably his description of the flight of the skylark, and the sentence in which he compares the gradual awakening of the human faculties to the sunrise, which "first opens a little eye of heaven, and sends away the spirits of darkness, and gives light to a cock, and calls up the lark to matins, and by and by gilds the fringes of a cloud, and peeps over the eastern hills." Perhaps the most impressive single passage of Taylor's is the concluding chapter in

Holy Dying. From the midst of the sickening para-
phernalia of death which he there accumulates,
rises that delicate image of the fading rose, one of
the most perfect things in its wording, in all our
prose literature: "But so have I seen a rose
newly springing from the clefts of its hood, and at
first it was as fair as the morning, and full with the
dew of heaven as a lamb's fleece; but when a ruder
breath had forced open its virgin modesty, and
dismantled its too youthful and unripe retirements,
it began to put on darkness and to decline to soft-
ness and the symptoms of a sickly age; it bowed
the head and broke its stock; and at night, having
lost some of its leaves and all its beauty, it fell into
the portion of weeds and outworn faces."

With the progress of knowledge and discussion
many kinds of prose literature, which were not ab-
solutely new, now began to receive wider exten-
sion. Of this sort are the *Letters from Italy*, and
other miscellanies included in the *Reliquiæ Wot-
tonianæ*, or remains of Sir Henry Wotton, English
embassador at Venice in the reign of James I., and
subsequently Provost of Eton College. Also the
Table Talk—full of incisive remarks—left by John
Selden, whom Milton pronounced the first scholar
of his age, and who was a distinguished authority
in legal antiquities and international law, furnished
notes to Drayton's *Polyolbion*, and wrote upon
Eastern religions, and upon the Arundel marbles.
Literary biography was represented by the charming little *Lives* of good old Izaak Walton, the first

edition of whose *Compleat Angler* was printed in
1653. The lives were five in number, of Hooker,
Wotton, Donne, Herbert, and Sanderson. Several
of these were personal friends of the author, and
Sir Henry Wotton was a brother of the angle.
The *Compleat Angler*, though not the first piece of
sporting literature in English, is unquestionably
the most popular, and still remains a favorite with
"all that are lovers of virtue, and dare trust in
providence, and be quiet, and go a-angling." As
in Ascham's *Toxophilus*, the instruction is con-
veyed in dialogue form, but the technical part of
the book is relieved by many delightful digressions. *Piscator* and his pupil *Venator* pursue
their talk under a honeysuckle hedge or a syca-
more tree during a passing shower. They repair,
after the day's fishing, to some honest ale-house,
with lavender in the window, and a score of ballads stuck about the wall, where they sing catches
—"old-fashioned poetry but choicely good"—
composed by the author or his friends, drink
barley wine, and eat their trout or chub. They
encounter milkmaids, who sing to them and give
them a draft of the red cow's milk, and they never
cease their praises of the angler's life, of rural contentment among the cowslip meadows, and the
quiet streams of Thames, or Lea, or Shawford
Brook.

The decay of a great literary school is usually
signalized by the exaggeration of its characteristic
traits. The manner of the Elisabethan poets was

pushed into mannerism by their successors. That
manner, at its best, was hardly a simple one, but
in the Stuart and Commonwealth writers it became mere extravagance. Thus Phineas Fletcher
—a cousin of the dramatist—composed a long
Spenserian allegory, the *Purple Island*, descriptive
of the human body. George Herbert and others
made anagrams and verses shaped like an altar, a
cross, or a pair of Easter wings. This group of
poets was named, by Dr. Johnson, in his life of
Cowley, the metaphysical school. Other critics
have preferred to call them the fantastic or conceited school, the later Euphuists, or the English
Marinists and Gongorists, after the poets Marino
and Gongora, who brought this fashion to its ex-
tréme in Italy and in Spain. The English *con-
ceptistas* were mainly clergymen of the established
Church, Donne, Herbert, Vaughan, Quarles, and
Herrick. But Crashaw was a Roman Catholic,
and Cowley—the latest of them—a layman.

The one who set the fashion was Dr. John Donne,
Dean of St. Paul's, whom Dryden pronounced a
great wit, but not a great poet, and whom Ben
Jonson esteemed the best poet in the world for
some things, but likely to be forgotten for want of
being understood. Besides satires and epistles in
verse, he composed amatory poems in his youth,
and divine poems in his age, both kinds distinguished by such subtle obscurity, and far-fetched
ingenuities, that they read like a series of puzzles.
When this poet has occasion to write a valediction

to his mistress upon going into France, he compares their temporary separation to that of a pair of compasses:

> "Such wilt thou be to me, who must,
>   Like the other foot obliquely run ;
> Thy firmness makes my circle just,
>   And makes me end where I begun."

If he would persuade her to marriage he calls her attention to a flea—

> "Me it sucked first and now sucks thee,
> And in this flea our two bloods mingled be."

He says that the flea is their marriage-temple, and bids her forbear to kill it lest she thereby commit murder, suicide, and sacrilege all in one. Donne's figures are scholastic and smell of the lamp. He ransacked cosmography, astrology, alchemy, optics, the canon law, and the divinity of the schoolmen for ink-horn terms and similes. He was in verse what Browne was in prose. He loved to play with distinctions, hyperboles, paradoxes, the very casuistry and dialectics of love or devotion.

> "Thou canst not every day give me thy heart:
> If thou canst give it then thou never gav'st it :
> Love's riddles are that though thy heart depart,
> It stays at home and thou with losing sav'st it."

Donne's verse is usually as uncouth as his thought. But there is a real passion slumbering under these ashy heaps of conceit, and occasion-

ally a pure flame darts up, as in the justly admired
lines:

> " Her pure and eloquent blood
> Spoke in her cheek and so divinely wrought
> That one might almost say her body thought."

This description of Donne is true, with modifications, of all the metaphysical poets. They had
the same forced and unnatural style. The ordinary laws of the association of ideas were re-
versed with them. It was not the nearest, but the
remotest, association that was called up. " Their
attempts," said Johnson, " were always analytic:
they broke every image into fragments." The finest
spirit among them was " holy George Herbert,"
whose *Temple* was published in 1631. The titles
in this volume were such as the following: Christmas, Easter, Good Friday, Holy Baptism, The
Cross, The Church Porch, Church Music, The
Holy Scriptures, Redemption, Faith, Doomsday.
Never since, except, perhaps, in Keble's *Christian
Year*, have the ecclesiastic ideals of the Anglican
Church—the " beauty of holiness "—found such
sweet expression in poetry. The verses entitled
Virtue—

> " Sweet day so cool, so calm, so bright," etc.

are known to most readers, as well as the line,

> " Who sweeps a room, as for thy laws, makes that and the
> action fine."

The quaintly named pieces, the *Elixir*, the *Collar*,
the *Pulley*, are full of deep thought and spiritual

feeling.   But Herbert's poetry is constantly disfigured by bad taste.   Take this passage from
Whitsunday,

> " Listen, sweet dove, unto my song,
>   And spread thy golden wings on me,
> Hatching my tender heart so long,
>   Till it get wing and fly away with thee,"

which is almost as ludicrous as the epitaph, written
by his contemporary, Carew, on the daughter of Sir
Thomas Wentworth, whose soul

> . . . "grew so fast within
> It broke the outward shell of sin,
> And so was hatched a cherubin."

Another of these Church poets was Henry
Vaughan, " the Silurist," or Welshman, whose fine
piece, the *Retreat,* has been often compared
with Wordsworth's *Ode on the Intimations of Immortality.* Francis Quarles' *Divine Emblems* long
remained a favorite book with religious readers,
both in Old and New England.   Emblem books,
in which engravings of a figurative design were
accompanied with explanatory letterpress in verse,
were a popular class of literature in the 17th century.   The most famous of them all were Jacob
Catt's Dutch emblems.

One of the most delightful of English lyric poets
is Robert Herrick, whose *Hesperides,* 1648 has
lately received such sympathetic illustration from
the pencil of an American artist, Mr. E. A. Abbey.
Herrick was a clergyman of the English Church,

and was expelled by the Puritans from his living, the vicarage of Dean Prior, in Devonshire. The most quoted of his religious poems is, *How to Keep a True Lent.* But it may be doubted whether his tastes were prevailingly clerical; his poetry certainly was not. He was a disciple of Ben Jonson and his boon companion at

> . . . " those lyric feasts
>   Made at the Sun,
> The Dog, the Triple Tun ;
> Where we such clusters had
> As made us nobly wild, not mad.
> And yet each verse of thine
> Outdid the meat, outdid the frolic wine."

Herrick's *Noble Numbers* seldom rises above the expression of a cheerful gratitude and contentment. He had not the subtlety and elevation of Herbert, but he surpassed him in the grace, melody, sensuous beauty, and fresh lyrical impulse of his verse. The conceits of the metaphysical school appear in Herrick only in the form of an occasional pretty quaintness. He is the poet of English parish festivals and of English flowers, the primrose, the whitethorn, the daffodil. He sang the praises of the country life, love songs to " Julia," and hymns of thanksgiving for simple blessings. He has been called the English Catullus, but he strikes rather the Horatian note of *Carpe diem,* and regret at the shortness of life and youth in many of his best-known poems, such as

Gather ye Rose-buds while ye may, and *To Corinna, To Go a Maying.*

Abraham Cowley is now less remembered for his poetry than for his pleasant volume of Essays, published after the Restoration; but he was thought in his own time a better poet than Milton. His collection of love songs—the *Mistress*— is a mass of cold conceits, in the metaphysical manner; but his elegies on Crashaw and Harvey have much dignity and natural feeling. He introduced the Pindaric ode into English, and wrote an epic poem on a biblical subject—the *Davideis*—now quite unreadable. Cowley was a royalist and followed the exiled court to France. Side by side with the Church poets were the cavaliers—Carew, Waller, Lovelace, Suckling, L'Estrange, and others—gallant courtiers and officers in the royal army, who mingled love and loyalty in their strains. Colonel Richard Lovelace, who lost every thing in the king's service and was several times imprisoned, wrote two famous songs — *To Lucasta on going to the Wars*—in which occur the lines,

> "I could not love thee, dear, so much,
> Loved I not honor more."

and *To Althæa from Prison*, in which he sings "the sweetness, mercy, majesty, and glories of his king," and declares that "stone walls do not a prison make, nor iron bars a cage." Another of the cavaliers was sir John Suckling, who formed a plot to rescue the Earl of Strafford, raised a troop of horse

for Charles I., was impeached by the Parliament
and fled to France. He was a man of wit and
pleasure, who penned a number of gay trifles, but
has been saved from oblivion chiefly by his exquisite *Ballad upon a Wedding.* Thomas Carew and
Edmund Waller were poets of the same stamp—
graceful and easy, but shallow in feeling. Waller,
who followed the court to Paris, was the author of
two songs, which are still favorites, *Go, Lovely Rose,*
and *On a Girdle,* and he first introduced the smooth
correct manner of writing in couplets, which Dryden
and Pope carried to perfection. Gallantry rather
than love was the inspiration of these courtly sing-
ers. In such verses as Carew's *Encouragements to
a Lover,* and George Wither's *The Manly Heart*—

> "If she be not so to me,
> What care I how fair she be?"

we see the revolt against the high, passionate, Sidneian love of the Elisabethan sonneteers, and the
note of *persiflage* that was to mark the lyrical verse
of the Restoration. But the poetry of the cavaliers
reached its high-water mark in one fiery-hearted
song by the noble and unfortunate James Graham,
Marquis of Montrose, who invaded Scotland in the
interest of Charles II., and was taken prisoner and
put to death at Edinburgh in 1650.

> "My dear and only love, I pray
> That little world of thee
> Be governed by no other sway
> Than purest monarchy."

10

In language borrowed from the politics of the time, he cautions his mistress against *synods* or *committees* in her heart; swears to make her glorious by his pen and famous by his sword; and with that fine recklessness which distinguished the dashing troopers of Prince Rupert, he adds, in words that have been often quoted,

> " He either fears his fate too much,
>   Or his deserts are small,
> That dares not put it to the touch
>   To gain or lose it all."

John Milton, the greatest English poet except Shakspere, was born in London in 1608. His father was a scrivener, an educated man, and a musical composer of some merit. At his home Milton was surrounded with all the influences of a refined and well ordered Puritan household of the better class. He inherited his father's musical tastes, and during the latter part of his life, he spent a part of every afternoon in playing the organ. No poet has written more beautifully of music than Milton. One of his sonnets was addressed to Henry Lawes, the composer, who wrote the airs to the songs in *Comus.* Milton's education was most careful and thorough. He spent seven years at Cambridge where, from his personal beauty and fastidious habits, he was called " The lady of Christ's." At Horton, in Buckinghamshire, where his father had a country seat, he passed five years more, perfecting himself in his studies, and then traveled for fifteen months, main-

ly in Italy, visiting Naples and Rome, but residing
at Florence. Here he saw Galileo, a prisoner of
the Inquisition "for thinking otherwise in astronomy than his Dominican and Franciscan licensers
thought." Milton is the most scholarly and the
most truly classical of English poets. His Latin
verse, for elegance and correctness, ranks with Addison's; and his Italian poems were the admiration
of the Tuscan scholars. But his learning appears
in his poetry only in the form of a fine and chast-
ened result, and not in laborious allusion and pedantic citation, as too often in Ben Jonson, for instance. "My father," he wrote, "destined me,
while yet a little child, for the study of humane letters." He was also destined for the ministry, but,
"coming to some maturity of years and perceiving
what tyranny had invaded the Church, . . . I thought
it better to prefer a blameless silence, before the
sacred office of speaking, bought and begun with
servitude and forswearing." Other hands than
a bishop's were laid upon his head. "He who
would not be frustrate of his hope to write well
hereafter," he says, "ought himself to be a true
poem." And he adds that his "natural haughti-
ness" saved him from all impurity of living. Milton had a sublime self-respect. The dignity and
earnestness of the Puritan gentleman blended in
his training with the culture of the Renaissance.
Born into an age of spiritual conflict, he dedicated
his gift to the service of Heaven, and he became,
like Heine, a valiant soldier in the war for libera-

tion. He was the poet of a cause, and his song was keyed to

> .   " The Dorian mood
> Of flutes and soft recorders such as raised
> To heighth of noblest temper, heroes old
> Arming to battle."

On comparing Milton with Shakspere, with his universal sympathies and receptive imagination, one perceives a loss in breadth, but a gain in intense personal conviction. He introduced a new note into English poetry, the passion for truth and the feeling of religious sublimity. Milton's was an heroic age, and its song must be lyric rather than dramatic; its singer must be in the fight and of it.

Of the verses which he wrote at Cambridge, the most important was his splendid ode *On the Morning of Christ's Nativity*. At Horton he wrote, among other things, the companion pieces, *L'Allegro* and *Il Penseroso*, of a kind quite new in English, giving to the landscape an expression in harmony with two contrasted moods. *Comus*, which belongs to the same period, was the perfection of the Elisabethan court masque, and was presented at Ludlow Castle in 1634, on the occasion of the installation of the Earl of Bridgewater as Lord President of Wales. Under the guise of a skillful addition to the Homeric allegory of Circe, with her cup of enchantment, it was a Puritan song in praise of chastity and temperance. *Lycidas*, in like manner, was the perfection of the Elisabethan pastoral elegy. It was contributed to a volume of memorial verses on the death of Edward King, a Cambridge friend of Milton's, who was drowned in the Irish Channel in 1637. In one stern strain, which is put into the mouth of St. Peter, the author "foretells the ruin of our corrupted clergy, then at their height."

> " But that two-handed engine at the door
> Stands ready to smite once and smite no more."

This was Milton's last utterance in English verse before the outbreak of the civil war, and it sounds the alarm of the impending struggle. In technical quality *Lycidas* is the most wonderful of all Milton's poems. The cunningly intricate harmony of the verse, the pressed and packed language with its fullness of meaning and allusion make it worthy of the minutest study. In these early poems, Milton, merely as a poet, is at his best. Something of the Elisabethan style still clings to them ; but their grave sweetness, their choice wording, their originality in epithet, name, and phrase, were novelties of Milton's own. His English masters were Spenser, Fletcher, and Sylvester, the translator of Du Bartas's *La Semaine*, but nothing of Spenser's prolixity, or Fletcher's effeminacy, or Sylvester's quaintness is found in Milton's pure, energetic diction. He inherited their beauties, but his taste had been tempered to a finer edge by his studies in Greek and Hebrew poetry. He was the last of the Elisabethans, and his style was at once the crown of the old and a departure into the new. In masque, elegy, and sonnet, he set the seal to the Elisabethan poetry, said the last word, and closed one great literary era.

In 1639 the breach between Charles I. and his Parliament brought Milton back from Italy. "I thought it base to be traveling at my ease for amusement, while my fellow-countrymen at home were fighting for liberty." For the next twenty years he threw himself into the contest, and poured forth a succession of tracts, in English and Latin, upon the various public questions at issue. As a political thinker, Milton had what Bacon calls "the humor of a scholar." In a country of endowed grammar schools and universities hardly emerged from a mediæval discipline and curriculum, he wanted to set up Greek gymnasia and philosophical schools, after the fashion of the Porch and the Academy. He would have imposed an Athenian democracy upon a people trained in the traditions of monarchy and episcopacy. At the very moment when England had grown tired of the Protectorate and was preparing to welcome back the Stuarts, he was writing *An Easy and Ready Way to Establish a Free Commonwealth.* Milton acknowledged that in prose he had the use of his left hand only. There are passages of fervid eloquence, where the style swells into a kind of lofty chant, with a rithmical rise and fall to it, as in parts of the English *Book of Common Prayer.* But in gen-

eral his sentences are long and involved, full of
inventions and latinized constructions. Controversy at that day was conducted on scholastic
lines. Each disputant, instead of appealing at
once to the arguments of expediency and common
sense, began with a formidable display of learning,
ransacking Greek and Latin authors and the fathers
of the Church for opinions in support of his own
position. These authorities he deployed at tedious
length and followed them up with heavy scurrilities
and "excusations," by way of attack and defense.
The dispute between Milton and Salmasius over the
execution of Charles I. was like a duel between two
knights in full armor striking at each other with pon-
derous maces. The very titles of these pamphlets
are enough to frighten off a modern reader: *A Con-
futation of the Animadversions upon a Defense of a
Humble Remonstrance against a Treatise, entitled
Of Reformation.* The most interesting of Milton's
prose tracts is his *Areopagitica: A Speech for the
Liberty of Unlicensed Printing,* 1644. The arguments in this are of permanent force; but if the
reader will compare it, or Jeremy Taylor's *Liberty
of Prophesying,* with Locke's *Letters on Toleration,*
he will see how much clearer and more convincing is the modern method of discussion, introduced by writers like Hobbes and Locke and
Dryden. Under the Protectorate Milton was appointed Latin Secretary to the Council of State.
In the diplomatic correspondence which was his
official duty, and in the composition of his tract,

Defensio pro Populo Anglicano, he overtasked his
eyes, and in 1654 became totally blind. The only
poetry of Milton's belonging to the years 1640–1660
are a few sonnets of the pure Italian form, mainly
called forth by public occasions. By the Elisabethans the sonnet had been used mainly in love
poetry. In Milton's hands, said Wordsworth, "the
thing became a trumpet." Some of his were addressed to political leaders, like Fairfax, Cromwell,
and Sir Henry Vane; and of these the best is, perhaps, the sonnet written on the massacre of the
Vaudois Protestants—"a collect in verse," it has
been called—which has the fire of a Hebrew
prophet invoking the divine wrath upon the op-
pressors of Israel. Two were on his own blindness, and in these there is not one selfish repining,
but only a regret that the value of his service is
impaired—

> "Will God exact day labor, light denied?"

After the restoration of the Stuarts, in 1660,
Milton was for a while in peril, by reason of the
part that he had taken against the king. But

> "On evil days though fallen, and evil tongues,
> In darkness and with dangers compassed round
> And solitude,"

he bated no jot of heart or hope. Henceforth he
becomes the most heroic and affecting figure in
English literary history. Years before he had
planned an epic poem on the subject of King

Arthur, and again a sacred tragedy on man's fall and redemption. These experiments finally took shape in *Paradise Lost*, which was given to the world in 1667. This is the epic of English Puritanism and of Protestant Christianity. It was Milton's purpose to

> " assert eternal Providence
> And justify the ways of God to men,"

or, in other words, to embody his theological system in verse. This gives a doctrinal rigidity and even dryness to parts of the *Paradise Lost*, which injure its effect as a poem. His " God the father turns a school divine:" his Christ, as has been wittily said, is " God's good boy:" the discourses of Raphael to Adam are scholastic lectures: Adam himself is too sophisticated for the state of innocence, and Eve is somewhat insipid. The real protagonist of the poem is Satan, upon whose mighty figure Milton unconsciously bestowed something of his own nature, and whose words of defiance might almost have come from some Republican leader when the Good Old Cause went down.

> " What though the field be lost?
> All is not lost, the unconquerable will
> And study of revenge, immortal hate,
> And courage never to submit or yield."

But when all has been said that can be said in disparagement or qualification, *Paradise Lost* remains the foremost of English poems and the sublimest of all epics. Even in those parts where theology encroaches most upon poetry, the diction, though often heavy, is never languid. Milton's blank verse in itself is enough to bear up the most prosaic theme, and so is his epic English, a style more massive and splendid than Shakspere's, and comparable, like Tertullian's Latin, to a river of molten gold. Of the countless single beauties that sow his page

> " Thick as autumnal leaves that strew the brooks
> In Valombrosa,"

there is no room to speak, nor of the astonishing fullness of substance and multitude of thoughts which have caused the *Paradise Lost* to be called the book of universal knowledge. " The heat of Milton's mind," said Dr. Johnson, " might be said to sublimate his learning and throw off into his work the spirit of science, unmingled with its grosser parts." The truth of this remark is clearly seen upon a comparison of Milton's description of the creation, for example, with corresponding passages in Sylvester's *Divine Weeks and Works* (translated from the Huguenot poet, Du Bartas), which was, in some sense, his original. But the most heroic thing in Milton's heroic poem is Milton. There are no strains in *Paradise Lost* so absorbing as those in which the poet breaks the strict epic bounds and speaks directly of himself, as in the majestic lament over his own blindness, and in the invocation to Urania, which open the third and seventh books. Every-where, too, one reads between the lines. We think of the dissolute cavaliers, as Milton himself undoubtedly was thinking of them, when we read of " the sons of Belial flown with insolence and wine," or when the Puritan turns among the sweet landscapes of Eden, to denounce

> " court amours
> Mixed dance, or wanton mask, or midnight ball,
> Or serenade which the starved lover sings
> To his proud fair, best quitted with disdain."

And we think of Milton among the triumphant royalists when we read of the Seraph Abdiel " faithful found among the faithless."

> " Nor number nor example with him wrought
> To swerve from truth or change his constant mind,
> Though single. From amidst them forth he passed,
> Long way through hostile scorn, which he sustained
> Superior, nor of violence feared aught:
> And with retorted scorn his back he turned
> On those proud towers to swift destruction doomed."

Paradise Regained and *Samson Agonistes* were published in 1671. The first of these treated in four books Christ's temptation in the wilderness, a subject that had already been handled in the Spenserian allegorical manner by Giles Fletcher, a brother of the Purple Islander, in his *Christ's Victory and Triumph*, 1610. The superiority of *Paradise Lost* to its sequel is not without significance. The Puritans were Old Testament men. Their God was the Hebrew Jehovah, whose single divinity the Catholic mythology had overlaid with the figures of the Son, the Virgin Mary, and the saints. They identified themselves in thought with his chosen people, with the militant theocracy of the Jews. Their sword was the sword of the Lord and of Gideon. " To your tents, O Israel," was the cry of the London mob when the bishops were committed to the Tower. And when the fog lifted, on the morning of the battle of Dunbar, Cromwell exclaimed, " Let God arise and let his enemies be scattered: like as the sun riseth, so shalt thou drive them away."

Samson Agonistes, though Hebrew in theme and in spirit, was in form a Greek tragedy. It had chorus and semi-chorus, and preserved the so-called dramatic unities; that is, the scene was unchanged, and there were no intervals of time between the acts. In accordance with the rules of the Greek theater, but two speakers appeared upon the stage at once, and there was no violent action. The death of Samson is related by a messenger. Milton's reason for the choice of this subject is obvious. He himself was Samson, shorn of his strength, blind, and alone among enemies; given over

> " to the unjust tribunals, under change of times,
> And condemnation of the ungrateful multitude."

As Milton grew older he discarded more and more the graces of poetry, and relied purely upon the structure and the thought. In *Paradise Lost*, although there is little resemblance to Elisabethan work — such as one notices in *Comus* and the

Christmas hymn—yet the style is rich, especially in the earlier books. But in *Paradise Regained* it is severe to bareness, and in *Samson*, even to ruggedness. Like Michelangelo, with whose genius he had much in common, Milton became impatient of finish or of mere beauty. He blocked out his work in masses, left rough places and surfaces not filled in, and inclined to express his meaning by a symbol, rather than work it out in detail. It was a part of his austerity, his increasing preference for structural over decorative methods, to give up rime for blank verse. His latest poem, *Samson Agonistes*, is a metrical study of the highest interest.

Milton was not quite alone among the poets of his time in espousing the popular cause. Andrew Marvell, who was his assistant in the Latin secretaryship and sat in Parliament for Hull, after the Restoration, was a good Republican, and wrote a fine *Horatian Ode upon Cromwell's Return from Ireland*. There is also a rare imaginative quality in his *Song of the Exiles in Bermuda*, *Thoughts in a Garden*, and *The Girl Describes her Fawn*. George Wither, who was imprisoned for his satires, also took the side of the Parliament, but there is little that is distinctively Puritan in his poetry.

1. Milton's Poetical Works.   Edited by David Masson.   Macmillan.

2. Selections from Milton's Prose.   Edited by F. D. Myers.   (Parchment Series.)

3. England's Antiphon. By George Macdonald.

4. Robert Herrick's Hesperides.

5. Sir Thomas Browne's Religio Medici and Hydriotaphia. Edited by Willis Bund. Sampson Low & Co., 1873.

6. Thomas Fuller's Good Thoughts in Bad Times.

7. Izaak Walton's Compleat Angler.

CHAPTER V.

FROM THE RESTORATION TO THE DEATH OF POPE.

1688–1744.

THE Stuart Restoration was a period of descent from poetry to prose, from passion and imagination to wit and understanding. The serious, exalted mood of the Civil War and the Commonwealth had spent itself and issued in disillusion. There followed a generation of wits, logical, skeptical, and prosaic, without earnestness, as without principle. The characteristic literature of such a time is criticism, satire, and burlesque, and such, indeed, continued to be the course of English literary history for a century after the return of the Stuarts. The age was not a stupid one, but one of active inquiry. The Royal Society, for the cultivation of the natural sciences, was founded in 1662. There were able divines in the pulpit and at the universities—Barrow, Tillotson, Stillingfleet, South, and others: scholars, like Bentley; historians, like Clarendon and Burnet; scientists, like Boyle and Newton; philosophers, like Hobbes and Locke. But of poetry, in any high sense of the word, there was little between the time of Milton and the time of Goldsmith and Gray.

The English writers of this period were strongly influenced by the contemporary literature of France, by the comedies of Molière, the tragedies of Corneille and Racine, and the satires, epistles, and versified essays of Boileau. Many of the Restoration writers—Waller, Cowley, Davenant, Wycherley, Villiers, and others—had been in France during the exile, and brought back with them French tastes. John Dryden (1631–1700), who is the great literary figure of his generation, has been called the first of our moderns. From the reign of Charles II., indeed, we may date the beginnings of modern English life. What we call "society" was forming, the town, the London world. "Coffee, which makes the politician wise," had just been introduced, and the ordinaries of Ben Jonson's time gave way to coffee-houses, like Will's and Button's, which became the head-quarters of literary and political gossip. The two great English parties, as we know them to-day, were organized: the words *Whig* and *Tory* date from this reign. French etiquette and fashions came in and French phrases of convenience—such as *coup de grace, bel esprit*, etc.—began to appear in English prose. Literature became intensely urban and partisan. It reflected city life, the disputes of faction, and the personal quarrels of authors. The politics of the Great Rebellion had been of heroic proportions, and found fitting expression in song. But in the Revolution of 1688 the issues were constitutional and to be settled by the arguments of lawyers. Measures were in ques-

tion rather than principles, and there was little inspiration to the poet in Exclusion Bills and Acts of
Settlement.

Court and society, in the reign of Charles II. and
James II., were shockingly dissolute, and in literature, as in life, the reaction against Puritanism went
to great extremes. The social life of the time is
faithfully reflected in the diary of Samuel Pepys.
He was a simple-minded man, the son of a London
tailor, and became, himself, secretary to the admi-
ralty. His diary was kept in cipher, and published
only in 1825. Being written for his own eye, it is
singularly outspoken; and its naïve, gossipy, con-
fidential tone makes it a most diverting book, as it
is, historically, a most valuable one.

Perhaps the most popular book of its time was
Samuel Butler's *Hudibras* (1663–64), a burlesque romance in ridicule of the Puritans. The king carried a copy of it in his pocket, and Pepys testifies
that it was quoted and praised on all sides. Ridicule of the Puritans was nothing new. Zeal-of-the-
land Busy, in Ben Jonson's *Bartholomew Fair*, is an
early instance of the kind. There was nothing
laughable about the earnestness of men like Cromwell, Milton, Algernon Sidney, and Sir Henry Vane.
But even the French Revolution had its humors;
and as the English Puritan Revolution gathered
head and the extremer sectaries pressed to the
front—Quakers, New Lights, Fifth Monarchy Men,
Ranters, etc.—its grotesque sides came uppermost.
Butler's hero is a Presbyterian Justice of the Peace

11

who sallies forth with his secretary, Ralpho—an Independent and Anabaptist—like Don Quixote with Sancho Panza, to suppress May games and bear-baitings. (Macaulay, it will be remembered, said that the Puritans disapproved of bear-baiting, not because it gave pain to the bear, but because it gave pleasure to the spectators.) The humor of *Hudibras* is not of the finest. The knight and squire are discomfited in broadly comic adventures, hardly removed from the rough, physical drolleries of a pantomime or a circus. The deep heart-laughter of · Cervantes, the pathos on which his humor rests, is, of course, not to be looked for in Butler. But he had wit of a sharp, logical kind, and his style surprises with all manner of verbal antics. He is almost as great a phrase-master as Pope, though in a coarser kind. His verse is a smart doggerel, and his poem has furnished many stock sayings, as, for example,

> " 'Tis strange what difference there can be
> 'Twixt tweedle-dum and tweedle-dee."

Hudibras has had many imitators, not the least successful of whom was the American John Trumbull, in his revolutionary satire *M'Fingal*, some couplets of which are generally quoted as Butler's, as, for example,

> " No man e'er felt the halter draw
> With good opinion of the law."

The rebound against Puritanism is seen no less plainly in the drama of the Restoration, and the

stage now took vengeance for its enforced silence
under the Protectorate. Two theaters were opened
under the patronage, respectively, of the king and
of his brother, the Duke of York. The manager
of the latter, Sir William Davenant—who had fought
on the king's side, been knighted for his services,
escaped to France, and was afterward captured and
imprisoned in England for two years—had managed
to evade the law against stage plays as early as
1656, by presenting his *Siege of Rhodes* as an "opera," with instrumental music and dialogue in reci-
tative, after a fashion newly sprung up in Italy.
This he brought out again in 1661, with the dialogue recast into riming couplets in the French
fashion. Movable painted scenery was now introduced from France, and actresses took the
female parts formerly played by boys. This last
innovation was said to be at the request of the
king, one of whose mistresses, the famous Nell
Gwynne, was the favorite actress at the King's
Theater.

Upon the stage, thus reconstructed, the so-called
"classical" rules of the French theater were followed, at least in theory. The Louis XIV. writers
were not purely creative, like Shakspere and his
contemporaries in England, but critical and self-
conscious. The Academy had been formed in
1636, for the preservation of the purity of the French
language, and discussion abounded on the principles and methods of literary art. Corneille not
only wrote tragedies, but essays on tragedy, and

one in particular on the *Three Unities*. Dryden
followed his example in his *Essay of Dramatic
Poesie* (1667), in which he treated of the unities,
and argued for the use of rime in tragedy in
preference to blank verse.* His own practice
varied. Most of his tragedies were written in
rime, but in the best of them, *All for Love*, 1678,
founded on Shakspere's *Antony and Cleopatra*, he
returned to blank verse. One of the principles of
the classical school was to keep comedy and tragedy distinct. The tragic dramatists of the Restoration, Dryden, Howard, Settle, Crowne, Lee, and
others, composed what they called "heroic plays,"
such as the *Indian Emperor*, the *Conquest of Gra-
nada*, the *Duke of Lerma*, the *Empress of Morocco*,
the *Destruction of Jerusalem*, *Nero*, and the *Rival
Queens*. The titles of these pieces indicate their
character. Their heroes were great historic personages. Subject and treatment were alike remote
from nature and real life. The diction was stilted
and artificial, and pompous declamation took the
place of action and genuine passion. The tragedies of Racine seem chill to an Englishman
brought up on Shakspere, but to see how great an
artist Racine was, in his own somewhat narrow
way, one has but to compare his *Phedre*, or *Iphi-
genie*, with Dryden's ranting tragedy of *Tyrannic
Love*. These bombastic heroic plays were made
the subject of a capital burlesque, the *Rehearsal*,
by George Villiers, Duke of Buckingham, acted in
1671 at the King's Theater. The indebtedness of

the English stage to the French did not stop with a general adoption of its dramatic methods, but extended to direct imitation and translation. Dryden's comedy, *An Evening's Love*, was adapted from Thomas Corneille's *Le Feint Astrologue*, and his *Sir Martin Mar-all*, from Molière's *L'Etourdi*. Shadwell borrowed his *Miser* from Molière, and Otway made versions of Racine's *Bérénice* and Molière's *Fourberies de Scapin*. Wycherley's *Country Wife* and *Plain Dealer*, although not translations, were based, in a sense, upon Molière's *Ecole des Femmes* and *Le 'Misanthrope*. The only one of the tragic dramatists of the Restoration who prolonged the traditions of the Elisabethan stage, was Otway, whose *Venice Preserved*, written in blank verse, still keeps the boards. There are fine passages in Dryden's heroic plays, passages weighty in thought and nobly sonorous in language. There is one great scene (between Antony and Ventidius) in his *All for Love*. And one, at least, of his comedies, the *Spanish Friar*, is skillfully constructed. But his nature was not pliable enough for the drama, and he acknowledged that, in writing for the stage, he "forced his genius."

In sharp contrast with these heroic plays was the comic drama of the Restoration, the plays of Wycherley, Killigrew, Etherege, Farquhar, Van Brugh, Congreve, and others; plays like the *Country Wife*, the *Parson's Wedding*, *She Would if She Could*, the *Beaux' Stratagem*, the *Relapse*, and the *Way of the World*. These were in prose, and represented the gay world and the surface of fashionable life. Amorous intrigue was their constantly recurring theme. Some of them were written expressly in ridicule of the Puritans. Such was the *Committee* of Dryden's brother-in-law, Sir Robert Howard, the hero of which is a distressed gentleman, and the villain a London cit, and president of the committee appointed by Parliament to sit upon the sequestration of the estates of royalists. Such were also the *Roundheads* and the *Banished Cavaliers* of Mrs. Aphra Behn, who was a female spy in the service of Charles II., at Antwerp, and one of the coarsest of the Restoration comedians. The profession of piety had become so disagreeable that a shameless cynicism was now considered the mark of a gentleman. The ideal hero of Wycherley or Etherege was the witty young profligate, who had seen life, and learned to disbelieve in virtue. His highest qualities were a contempt for cant, physical courage, a sort of spendthrift generosity, and a good-natured readiness to back up a friend in a quarrel, or an amour. Virtue was *bourgeois*—reserved for London trades-people. A man must be either a rake or a hypocrite. The gentlemen were rakes, the city people were hypocrites. Their wives, however, were all in love with the gentlemen, and it was the proper thing to seduce them, and to borrow their husbands' money. For the first and last time, perhaps, in the history of the English drama, the sympathy of the audience was deliberately sought for the seducer and the rogue, and the laugh turned against the dishonored husband and the honest man. (Contrast this with Shakspere's *Merry Wives of Windsor*.) The women were represented as worse than the men—scheming, ignorant, and corrupt. The dialogue in the best of these plays was easy, lively, and witty; the situations in some of them audacious almost beyond belief. Under a thin varnish of good breeding, the sentiments and manners were really brutal. The loosest gallants of Beaumont and Fletcher's theater retain a fineness of feeling and that *politesse de coeur*—which marks the gentleman. They are poetic creatures, and own a capacity for romantic passion. But the Manlys and Horners of the Restoration comedy have a prosaic, cold-blooded profligacy that disgusts. Charles Lamb, in his ingenious essay on " The Artificial Comedy of the Last Century," apologized for the Restoration stage, on the ground that it represented a world of whim and unreality in which the ordinary laws of morality had no application.

But Macaulay answered truly, that at no time has the stage been closer in its imitation of real life. The theater of Wycherley and Etherege was but the counterpart of that social condition which we read of in Pepys's *Diary*, and in the *Memoirs* of the Chevalier de Grammont. This prose comedy of manners was not, indeed, " artificial " at all, in the sense in which the contemporary tragedy—the " heroic play "—was artificial. It was, on the contrary, far more natural, and, intellectually, of much higher value.   It 1698 Jeremy Collier, a non-juring Jacobite clergyman, published his *Short View of the Immorality and Profaneness of the English Stage*, which did much toward reforming the practice of the dramatists.   The formal charac-teristics, without the immorality, of the Restoration comedy, re-appeared briefly in Goldsmith's *She Stoops to Conquer*, 1772, and Sheridan's *Rival, School for Scandal*, and *Critic*, 1775–9, our last strictly "classical" comedies.   None of this school of English comedians approached their model, Molière.   He excelled his imitators not only in his French urbanity—the polished wit and delicate grace of his style—but in the dexterous unfolding of his plot, and in the wisdom and truth of his criti-cism of life, and his insight into character.   It is a symptom of the false taste of the age that Shaks-pere's plays were rewritten for the Restoration stage.   Davenant made new versions of *Macbeth* and *Julius Cæsar*, substituting rime for blank verse.   In conjunction with Dryden, he altered the *Tempest*, complicating the intrigue by the intro-duction of a male counterpart to Miranda—a youth who had never seen a woman.   Shadwell " im-proved " *Timon of Athens*, and Nahum Tate fur-nished a new fifth act to *King Lear*, which turned the play into a comedy !   In the prologue to his doctored version of *Troilus and Cressida*, Dry-den made the ghost of Shakspere speak of him-self as

"Untaught, unpracticed in a barbarous age."

Thomas Rymer, whom Pope pronounced a good critic, was very severe upon Shakspere in his *Remarks on the Tragedies of the Last Age;* and in his *Short View of Tragedy,* 1693, he said, " In the neighing of a horse or in the growling of a mastiff, there is more humanity than, many times, in the tragical flights of Shakspere." " To Deptford by water," writes Pepys, in his diary for August 20, 1666, " reading Othello, Moor of Venice; which I ever heretofore esteemed a mighty good play; but, having so lately read the *Adventures of Five Hours,* it seems a mean thing."

In undramatic poetry the new school, both in England and in France, took its point of departure in a reform against the extravagances of the Marinists, or conceited poets, specially represented in England by Donne and Cowley. The new poets, both in their theory and practice, insisted upon correctness, clearness, polish, moderation, and good sense. Boileau's *L' Art Poétique,* 1673, inspired by Horace's *Ars Poetica,* was a treatise in verse upon the rules of correct composition, and it gave the law in criticism for over a century, not only in France, but in Germany and England. It gave English poetry a didactic turn and started the fashion of writing critical essays in riming couplets. The Earl of Mulgrave published two " poems " of this kind, an *Essay on Satire,* and an *Essay on Poetry.* The Earl of Roscommon—who, said Addison, "makes even rules a noble poetry " —made a metrical version of Horace's *Ars Poetica,* and wrote an original *Essay on Translated Verse.* Of the same kind were Addison's epistle to Sacheverel, entitled *An Account of the Greatest English Poets,* and Pope's *Essay on Criticism,* 1711, which was nothing more than versified maxims of rhetoric, put with Pope's usual point and brilliancy. The classicism of the 18th century, it has been said, was a classicism in red heels and a periwig. It was Latin rather than Greek; it turned to the least imaginative side of Latin literature and found its models, not in Vergil, Catullus, and Lucretius, but in the satires, epistles, and didactic pieces of Juvenal, Horace, and Persius.

The chosen medium of the new poetry was the heroic couplet. This had, of course, been used before by English poets as far back as Chaucer. The greater part of the *Canterbury Tales* was written in heroic couplets. But now a new strength and precision were given to the familiar measure by imprisoning the sense within the limit of the couplet, and by treating each line as also a unit in itself. Edmund Waller had written verse of this kind as early as the reign of Charles I. He, said Dryden, "first showed us to conclude the sense most commonly in distichs, which, in the verse of those before him, runs on for so many lines together that the reader is out of breath to overtake it." Sir John Denham, also, in his *Cooper's Hill,* 1643, had written such verse as this:

"O, could I flow like thee, and make thy stream
My great example as it is my theme!

> Though deep yet clear, though gentle yet not dull,
> Strong without rage, without o'erflowing full."

Here we have the regular flow, and the nice balance between the first and second member of each couplet, and the first and second part of each line, which characterized the verse of Dryden and Pope.

> " Waller was smooth, but Dryden taught to join
> The varying verse, the full resounding line,
> The long resounding march and energy divine."

Thus wrote Pope, using for the nonce the triplet and alexandrine by which Dryden frequently varied the couplet. Pope himself added a greater neatness and polish to Dryden's verse and brought the system to such monotonous pefection that he "made poetry a mere mechanic art."

The lyrical poetry of this generation was almost entirely worthless. The dissolute wits of Charles the Second's court, Sedley, Rochester, Sackville, and the " mob of gentlemen who wrote with ease " threw off a few amatory trifles; but the age was not spontaneous or sincere enough for genuine song. Cowley introduced the Pindaric ode, a highly artificial form of the lyric, in which the language was tortured into a kind of spurious grandeur, and the meter teased into a sound and fury, signifying nothing. Cowley's Pindarics were filled with something which passed for fire, but has now utterly gone out. Nevertheless, the fashion spread, and " he who could do nothing else," said Dr. Johnson, "could write like Pindar." The best of these odes was Dryden's famous *Alexander's Feast*, written for a celebration of St. Cecilia's day by a musical club. To this same fashion, also, we owe Gray's two fine odes, the *Progress of Poesy* and the *Bard*, written a half-century later.

Dryden was not so much a great poet, as a solid thinker, with a splendid mastery of expression, who used his energetic verse as a vehicle for political argument and satire. His first noteworthy poem, *Annus Mirabilis*, 1667, was a narrative of the public events of the year 1666, namely: the Dutch war and the great fire of London. The subject of *Absalom and Ahitophel*—the first part of which appeared in 1681 — was the alleged plot of the Whig leader, the Earl of Shaftesbury, to defeat the succession of the Duke of York, afterward James II., by securing the throne to Monmouth, a natural son of Charles II. The parallel afforded by the story of Absalom's revolt against David was wrought out by Dryden with admirable ingenuity and keeping. He was at his best in satirical character-sketches, such as the brilliant portraits in this poem of Shaftesbury, as the false counselor, Ahitophel, and of the Duke of Buckingham as Zimri. The latter was Dryden's reply to the *Rehearsal*. *Absalom and Ahitophel* was followed by the *Medal*, a continuation of the same subject, and *Mac 'Flecknoe*, a personal onslaught on the "true blue Protestant poet," Thomas Shadwell, a political and literary foe of Dryden. Flecknoe, an ob-

scure Irish poetaster, being about to retire from
the throne of duncedom, resolved to settle the succession upon his son, Shadwell, whose claims to the
inheritance are vigorously asserted.

> " The rest to some faint meaning make pretense,
> But Shadwell never deviates into sense. . . .
> The midwife laid her hand on his thick skull
> With this prophetic blessing—*Be thou dull.*"

Dryden is our first great satirist. The formal
satire had been written in the reign of Elisabeth
by Donne, and by Joseph Hall, Bishop of Exe-
ter, and subsequently by Marston, the dramatist, by Wither, Marvell, and others; but all of
these failed through an over violence of language, and a purpose too pronouncedly moral.
They had no lightness of touch, no irony and
mischief. They bore down too hard, imitated
Juvenaland, lashed English society in terms befit-
ting the corruption of Imperial Rome. They
denounced, instructed, preached, did every thing
but satirize. The satirist must raise a laugh.
Donne and Hall abused men in classes: priests
were worldly, lawyers greedy, courtiers obsequious,
etc. But the easy scorn of Dryden and the delightful malice of Pope gave a pungent personal
interest to their sarcasm, infinitely more effective
than these commonplaces of satire. Dryden was
as happy in controversy as in satire, and is unexcelled in the power to reason in verse. His *Religio Laici*, 1682, was a poem in defense of the En-

glish Church. But when James II. came to the throne Dryden turned Catholic and wrote the *Hind and Panther*, 1687, to vindicate his new belief. Dryden had the misfortune to be dependent upon royal patronage and upon a corrupt stage. He sold his pen to the court, and in his comedies he was heavily and deliberately lewd, a sin which he afterward acknowledged and regretted. Milton's "soul was like a star and dwelt apart," but Dryden wrote for the trampling multitude. He had a coarseness of moral fiber, but was not malignant in his satire, being of a large, careless, and forgetting nature. He had that masculine, enduring cast of mind which gathers heat and clearness from motion, and grows better with age. His *Fables* — modernizations from Chaucer and translations from Boccaccio—written the year before he died, are among his best works.

Dryden is also our first critic of any importance. His critical essays were mostly written as prefaces or dedications to his poems and plays. But his *Essay on Dramatic Poesie*, which Dr. Johnson called our "first regular and valuable treatise on the art of writing," was in the shape of a Platonic dialogue. When not misled by the French classicism of his day, Dryden was an admirable critic, full of penetration and sound sense. He was the earliest writer, too, of modern literary prose. If the imitation of French models was an injury to poetry it was a benefit to prose. The best modern prose is French, and it was the essayists of the

Gallicised Restoration age—Cowley, Sir William Temple, and, above all, Dryden—who gave modern English prose that simplicity, directness, and colloquial air, which marks it off from the more artificial diction of Milton, Taylor, and Browne.

A few books whose shaping influences lay in the past belong by their date to this period. John Bunyan, a poor tinker, whose reading was almost wholly in the Bible and Fox's *Book of Martyrs*, imprisoned for twelve years in Bedford jail for preaching at conventicles, wrote and, in 1678, published his *Pilgrim's Progress*, the greatest of religious allegories. Bunyan's spiritual experiences were so real to him that they took visible concrete shape in his imagination as men, women, cities, landscapes. It is the simplest, the most transparent of allegories. Unlike the *Faery Queene*, the story of *Pilgrim's Progress* has no reason for existing apart from its inner meaning, and yet its reality is so vivid that children read of Vanity Fair and the Slough of Despond and Doubting Castle and the Valley of the Shadow of Death with the same belief with which they read of Crusoe's cave or Aladdin's palace.

It is a long step from the Bedford tinker to the cultivated poet of *Paradise Lost*. They represent the poles of the Puritan party. Yet it may admit of a doubt, whether the Puritan epic is, in essentials, as vital and original a work as the Puritan allegory. They both came out quietly and made little noise at first. But the *Pilgrim's Progress* got at once into circulation, and not even a single copy of the first edition remains. Milton, too—who received £10 for the copyright of *Paradise Lost*—seemingly found that "fit audience though few" for which he prayed, as his poem reached its second impression in five years (1672). Dryden visited him in his retirement and asked leave to turn it into rime and put it on the stage as an opera. "Ay," said Milton, good humoredly, "you may tag my verses." And accordingly they appeared, duly tagged, in Dryden's operatic masque, the *State of Innocence*. In this startling conjunction we have the two ages in a nut-shell: the Commonwealth was an epic, the Restoration an opera.

The literary period covered by the life of Pope, 1688–1744, is marked off by no distinct line from the generation before it. Taste continued to be governed by the precepts of Boileau and the French classical school. Poetry remained chiefly didactic and satirical, and satire in Pope's hands was more personal even than in Dryden's, and addressed itself less to public issues. The literature of the "Augustan age" of Queen Anne (1702–1714) was still more a literature of the town and of fashionable society than that of the Restoration had been. It was also closely involved with party struggles of Whig and Tory, and the ablest pens on either side were taken into alliance by the political leaders. Swift was in high favor with the Tory ministers, Oxford and Bolingbroke, and his pamphlets, the *Public Spirit of the Whigs* and the *Con-*

duct of the Allies, were rewarded with the deanery of St. Patrick's, Dublin. Addison became Secretary of State under a Whig government. Prior was in the diplomatic service. Daniel De Foe, the author of *Robinson Crusoe,* 1719, was a prolific political writer, conducted his *Review* in the interest of the Whigs and was imprisoned and pilloried for his ironical pamphlet, *The Shortest Way with the Dissenters.* Steele, who was a violent writer on the Whig side, held various public offices, such as Commissioner of Stamps and Commissioner for Forfeited Estates, and sat in Parliament. After the Revolution of 1688 the manners and morals of English society were somewhat on the mend. The court of William and Mary, and of their successor, Queen Anne, set no such example of open profligacy as that of Charles II. But there was much hard drinking, gambling, dueling, and intrigue in London, and vice was fashionable till Addison partly preached and partly laughed it down in the *Spectator.* The women were mostly frivolous and uneducated, and not unfrequently fast. They are spoken of with systematic disrespect by nearly every writer of the time, except Steele. "Every woman," wrote Pope, "is at heart a rake." The reading public had now become large enough to make letters a profession. Dr. Johnson said that Pope was the first writer in whose case the book-seller took the place of the patron. His translation of Homer, published by subscription, brought him between eight and nine thousand
12

pounds and made him independent. But the activity of the press produced a swarm of poorly-paid hack-writers, penny-a-liners, who lived from hand to mouth and did small literary jobs to order. Many of these inhabited Grub Street, and their lampoons against Pope and others of their more successful rivals called out Pope's *Dunciad,* or epic of the dunces, by way of retaliation. The politics of the time were sordid and consisted mainly of an ignoble scramble for office. The Whigs were fighting to maintain the Act of Succession in favor of the House of Hanover, and the Tories were secretly intriguing with the exiled Stuarts. Many of the leaders, such as the great Whig champion, John Churchill, Duke of Marlborough, were without political principle or even personal honesty. The Church, too, was in a condition of spiritual deadness. Bishoprics and livings were sold and given to political favorites. Clergymen, like Swift and Lawrence Sterne, were worldly in their lives and immoral in their writings, and were practically unbelievers. The growing religious skepticism appeared in the Deist controversy. Numbers of men in high position were Deists; the Earl of Shaftesbury, for example, and Pope's brilliant friend, Henry St. John, Lord Bolingbroke, the head of the Tory ministry, whose political writings had much influence upon his young French acquaintance, Voltaire. Pope was a Roman Catholic, though there is little to show it in his writings, and the underlying thought of his famous *Essay on Man* was furnished him by Bolingbroke. The letters of the cold-hearted Chesterfield to his son were accepted as a manual of conduct, and La Rochefoucauld's cynical maxims were quoted as authority on life and human nature. Said Swift :

> " As Rochefoucauld his maxims drew
> From nature, I believe them true.
> They argue no corrupted mind
> In him; the fault is in mankind."

The succession which Dryden had willed to Congreve was taken up by Alexander Pope. He was a man quite unlike Dryden, sickly, deformed, morbidly precocious, and spiteful; nevertheless he joined on to and continued Dryden. He was more careful in his literary workmanship than his great forerunner, and in his *Moral Essays* and *Satires* he brought the Horatian epistle in verse, the formal satire and that species of didactic poem of which Boileau had given the first example, to an exquisite perfection of finish and verbal art. Dryden had translated Vergil, and so Pope translated Homer. The throne of the dunces, which Dryden had conferred upon Shadwell, Pope, in his *Dunciad*, passed on to two of his own literary foes, Theobald and Colley Cibber. There is a great waste of strength in this elaborate squib, and most of the petty writers, whose names it has preserved, as has been said, like flies in amber, are now quite unknown. But, although we have to read it with notes, to get the point of its allusions, it is easy to see what execution it must have done at the time, and it is impossible to withhold admiration from the wit, the wickedness, the triumphant mischief of the thing. The sketch of Addison—who had offended Pope by praising a rival translation of Homer—as "Atticus," is as brilliant as any thing of the kind in Dryden. Pope's very malignity made his sting sharper than Dryden's. He secreted venom, and worked out his revenges deliberately, bringing all the resources of his art to bear upon the question of how to give the most pain most cleverly.

Pope's masterpiece is, perhaps, the *Rape of the Lock*, a mock heroic poem, a "dwarf Iliad," recounting, in five cantos, a society quarrel, which arose from Lord Petre's cutting a lock of hair from the head of Mrs. Arabella Fermor. Boileau, in his *Lutrin*, had treated, with the same epic dignity, a dispute over the placing of the reading desk in a parish church. Pope was the Homer of the drawing-room, the boudoir, the tea-urn, the omber-party, the sedan-chair, the parrot cage, and the lap-dogs. This poem, in its sparkle and airy grace, is the topmost blossom of a highly artificial society, the quintessence of whatever poetry was possible in those

> "Teacup times of hood and hoop,
> And when the patch was worn,"

with whose decorative features, at least, the recent Queen Anne revival has made this generation familiar. It may be said of it, as Thackeray said of

Gay's pastorals : "It is to poetry what charming little Dresden china figures are to sculpture, graceful, minikin, fantastic, with a certain beauty always accompanying them." The *Rape of the Lock*, perhaps, stops short of beauty, but it attains elegance and prettiness in a supreme degree. In imitation of the gods and goddesses in the Iliad, who intermeddle for or against the human characters, Pope introduced the Sylphs of the Rosicrucian philosophy. We may measure the distance between imagination and fancy, if we will compare these little filagree creatures with Shakspere's elves, whose occupation it was

> " To tread the ooze of the salt deep,
> Or run upon the sharp wind of the north, . . .
> Or on the beached margent of the sea,
> To dance their ringlets to the whispering wind."

Very different were the offices of Pope's fays:

> "Our humble province is to tend the fair ;
> Not a less pleasing, though less glorious, care ;
> To save the powder from too rude a gale,
> Nor let the imprisoned essences exhale. . . .
> Nay oft in dreams invention we bestow
> To change a flounce or add a furbelow."

Pope was not a great poet; it has been doubted whether he was a poet at all. He does not touch the heart, or stimulate the imagination, as the true poet always does. In the poetry of nature, and the poetry of passion, he was altogether impotent.

His *Windsor Forest* and his *Pastorals* are artificial and false, not written with "the eye upon the object." His epistle of *Eloisa to Abelard* is declamatory and academic, and leaves the reader cold. The only one of his poems which is at all possessed with feeling is his pathetic *Elegy to the Memory of an Unfortunate Lady*. But he was a great literary artist. Within the cramped and starched regularity of the heroic couplet, which the fashion of the time and his own habit of mind imposed upon him, he secured the largest variety of modulation and emphasis of which that verse was capable. He used antithesis, periphrasis, and climax with great skill. His example dominated English poetry for nearly a century, and even now, when a poet like Dr. Holmes, for example, would write satire or humorous verse of a dignified kind, he turns instinctively to the measure and manner of Pope. He was not a consecutive thinker, like Dryden, and cared less about the truth of his thought than about the pointedness of its expression. His language was closer-grained than Dryden's. His great art was the art of putting things. He is more quoted than any other English poet, but Shakspere. He struck the average intelligence, the common sense of English readers, and furnished it with neat, portable formulas, so that it no longer needed to "vent its observation in mangled terms," but could pour itself out compactly, artistically, in little, ready-made molds. But his high-wrought brilliancy, this unceasing point, soon fatigue. His poems read like a series of epigrams; and every line has a hit or an effect.

From the reign of Queen Anne date the beginnings of the periodical essay. Newspapers had been published since the time of the Civil War; at first irregularly, and then regularly. But no literature of permanent value appeared in periodical form until Richard Steele started the *Tatler*, in 1709. In this he was soon joined by his friend, Joseph Addison, and in its successor, the *Spectator*, the first number of which was issued March 1, 1711. Addison's contributions outnumbered Steele's. The *Tatler* was published on three, the *Spectator* on six, days of the week. The *Tatler* gave political news, but each number of the *Spectator* consisted of a single essay. The object of these periodicals was to reflect the passing humors of the time, and to satirize the follies and minor immoralities of the town. "I shall endeavor," wrote Addison, in the tenth paper of the *Spectator*, " to enliven morality with wit, and to temper wit with morality. . . . It was said of Socrates that he brought Philosophy down from Heaven to inhabit among men; and I shall be ambitious to have it said of me that I have brought Philosophy out of closets and libraries, schools and colleges, to dwell in clubs and assemblies, at tea-tables and in coffee-houses." Addison's satire was never personal. He was a moderate man, and did what he could to restrain Steele's intemperate party zeal. His character was dignified and pure, and his strongest emotion seems to have

been his religious feeling. One of his contemporaries called him "a parson in a tie wig," and he
wrote several excellent hymns. His mission was
that of censor of the public taste. Sometimes he
lectures and sometimes he preaches, and in his Saturday papers, he brought his wide reading and
nice scholarship into service for the instruction of
his readers. Such was the series of essays, in
which he gave an elaborate review of *Paradise
Lost*. Such also was his famous paper, the *Vision
of Mirza*, an oriental allegory of human life. The
adoption of this slightly pedagogic tone was justi-
fied by the prevalent ignorance and frivolity of the
age. But the lighter portions of the *Spectator* are
those which have worn the best. Their style is
at once correct and easy, and it is as a humorist,
a sly observer of manners, and above all, a delightful talker, that Addison is best known to
posterity. In the personal sketches of the members of the Spectator Club, of Will Honeycomb,
Captain Sentry, Sir Andrew Freeport, and, above
all, Sir Roger de Coverley, the quaint and honest
country gentleman, may be found the nucleus of
the modern prose fiction of character. Addison's
humor is always a trifle grave. There is no whim-
sy, no frolic in it, as in Sterne or Lamb. "He
thinks justly," said Dr. Johnson, "but he thinks
faintly." The *Spectator* had a host of followers,
from the somewhat heavy *Rambler* and *Idler* of
Johnson, down to the *Salmagundi* papers of our
own Irving, who was, perhaps, Addison's latest and

best literary descendant. In his own age Addison made some figure as a poet and dramatist. His *Campaign*, celebrating the victory of Blenheim, had one much-admired couplet, in which Marlborough was likened to the angel of tempest, who

"Pleased the Almighty's orders to perform,
Rides in the whirlwind and directs the storm."

His stately, classical tragedy, *Cato*, which was acted at Drury Lane Theater in 1712, with immense applause, was pronounced by Dr. Johnson "unquestionably the noblest production of Addison's genius." It is, notwithstanding, cold and tedious, as a whole, though it has some fine declamatory passages—in particular the soliloquy of Cato in the fifth act—

"It must be so: Plato, thou reasonest well," etc.

The greatest of the Queen Anne wits, and one of the most savage and powerful satirists that ever lived, was Jonathan Swift. As secretary in the family of Sir William Temple, and domestic chaplain to the Earl of Berkeley, he had known in youth the bitterness of poverty and dependence. Afterward he wrote himself into influence with the Tory ministry, and was promised a bishopric, but was put off with the deanery of St. Patrick's, and retired to Ireland to "die like a poisoned rat in a hole." His life was made tragical by the forecast of the madness which finally overtook him. "The stage darkened," said Scott, "ere the curtain fell." Insanity deepened into idiocy and a hideous silence, and for three years before his death he spoke hardly ever a word. He had directed that his tombstone should bear the inscription, *Ubi saeva indignatio cor ulterius lacerare nequit.* "So great a man he seems to me," wrote Thackeray, "that thinking of him is like thinking of an empire falling." Swift's first noteworthy publication was his *Tale of a Tub*, 1704, a satire on religious differences. But his great work was *Gulliver's Travels*, 1726, the book in which his hate and scorn of mankind, and the long rage of mortified pride and thwarted ambition found their fullest expression. Children read the voyages to Lilliput and Brobdingnag, to the flying island of Laputa and the country of the Houyhnhnms, as they read *Robinson Crusoe*, as stories of wonderful adventure. Swift had all of De Foe's realism, his power of giving veri-similitude to his narrative by the invention of a vast number of small, exact, consistent details. But underneath its fairy tales, *Gulliver's Travels* is a satire, far more radical than any of Dryden's or Pope's, because directed, not against particular parties or persons, but against human nature. In his account of Lilliput and Brobdingnag, Swift tries to show— looking first through one end of the telescope and then through the other — that human greatness, goodness, beauty disappear if the scale be altered a little. If men were six inches high instead of six feet—such is the logic of his tale—their wars, governments, science, religion—all their institutions,

in fine, and all the courage, wisdom, and virtue by
which these have been built up, would appear laughable. On the other hand, if they were sixty feet
high instead of six, they would become disgusting.
The complexion of the finest ladies would show
blotches, hairs, excrescences, and an overpowering
effluvium would breathe from the pores of the
skin. Finally, in his loathsome caricature of mankind, as Yahoos, he contrasts them to their shame
with the beasts, and sets instinct above reason.

The method of Swift's satire was grave irony.
Among his minor writings in this kind are his *Argument against Abolishing Christianity*, his *Modest
Proposal* for utilizing the surplus population of Ireland by eating the babies of the poor, and his *Pre-
dictions of Isaac Bickerstaff*. In the last he predicted the death of one Partridge, an almanac maker,
at a certain day and hour. When the time set was
past, he published a minute account of Partridge's
last moments; and when the subject of this excellent fooling printed an indignant denial of his own
death, Swift answered very temperately, proving
that he was dead and remonstrating with him on
the violence of his language. "To call a man a
fool and villain, an impudent fellow, only for differing from him in a point merely speculative, is, in
my humble opinion, a very improper style for a
person of his education." Swift wrote verses as
well as prose, but their motive was the reverse of poetical. His gross and cynical humor vulgarized
whatever it touched. He leaves us no illusions,

and not only strips his subject, but flays it and shows the raw muscles beneath the skin. He delighted to dwell upon the lowest bodily functions of human nature. "He saw bloodshot," said Thackeray.

1. Macaulay's Essay, The Comic Dramatists of the Restoration.

2. The Poetical Works of John Dryden. Globe Edition. Macmillan & Co.

3. Thackeray's English Humorists of the Last Century.

4. Sir Roger de Coverley. New York: Harper, 1878.

5. Swift's Tale of a Tub, Gulliver's Travels, Directions to Servants, Polite Conversation, The Great Question Debated, Verses on the Death of Dean Swift.

6. The Poetical Works of Alexander Pope. Globe Edition. Macmillan & Co.

CHAPTER VI.
FROM THE DEATH OF POPE TO THE FRENCH REVOLUTION.

1744–1789.

POPE's example continued potent for fifty years after his death. Especially was this so in satiric and didactic poetry. Not only Dr. Johnson's adaptations from Juvenal, *London*, 1738, and the *Vanity of Human Wishes*, 1749, but Gifford's *Baviad*, 1791, and *Maeviad*, 1795, and Byron's *English Bards and Scotch Reviewers*, 1809, were in the verse and manner of Pope. In Johnson's *Lives of the Poets*, 1781, Dryden and Pope are treated as the two greatest English poets. But long before this a revolution in literary taste had begun, a movement which is variously described as The Return to Nature, or The Rise of the New Romantic School.

For nearly a hundred years poetry had dealt with manners and the life of towns, the gay, prosaic life of Congreve or of Pope. The sole concession to the life of nature was the old pastoral, which, in the hands of cockneys, like Pope and Ambrose Philips, who merely repeated stock descriptions at second or third hand, became even more artificial than a *Beggar's Opera* or a *Rape of the*

Lock. These, at least, were true to their environment, and were natural, just *because* they were artificial. But the *Seasons* of James Thomson, published in installments from 1726–30, had opened a
new field. Their theme was the English landscape,
as varied by the changes of the year, and they were
written by a true lover and observer of nature.
Mark Akenside's *Pleasures of Imagination,* 1744,
published the year of Pope's death, was written
like the *Seasons,* in blank verse ; and although its
language had much of the formal, didactic cast of
the Queen Anne poets, it pointed unmistakably in
the new direction. Thomson had painted the soft
beauties of a highly cultivated land—lawns, gardens, forest-preserves, orchards, and sheep-walks.
But now a fresh note was struck in the literature,
not of England alone, but of Germany and France
—romanticism, the chief element in which was a
love of the wild. Poets turned from the tameness
of modern existence to savage nature and the
heroic simplicity of life among primitive tribes. In
France, Rousseau introduced the idea of the natural man, following his instincts in disregard of social conventions. In Germany Bodmer published,
in 1753, the first edition of the old German epic,
the *Nibelungen Lied.* Works of a similar tendency
in England were the odes of William Collins and
Thomas Gray, published between 1747–57, especially Collins's *Ode on the Superstitions of the Highlands,* and Gray's *Bard,* a pindaric, in which the last
survivor of the Welsh bards invokes vengeance on

Edward I., the destroyer of his guild. Gray and Mason, his friend and editor, made translations from the ancient Welsh and Norse poetry. Thomas Percy's *Reliques of Ancient English Poetry*, 1765, aroused a taste for old ballads. Richard Hurd's *Letters on Chivalry and Romance*, Thomas Warton's *History of English Poetry*, 1774–78, Tyrwhitt's critical edition of Chaucer, and Horace Walpole's Gothic romance, the *Castle of Otranto*, 1765, stimulated this awakened interest in the picturesque aspects of feudal life, and contributed to the fondness for supernatural and mediæval subjects. James Beattie's *Minstrel*, 1771, described the educating influence of Scottish mountain scenery upon the genius of a young poet. But the most remarkable instances of this passion for wild nature and the romantic past were the *Poems of Ossian* and Thomas Chatterton's literary forgeries.

In 1762 James Macpherson published the first installment of what professed to be a translation of the poems of Ossian, a Gaelic bard, whom tradition placed in the 3d century. Macpherson said that he made his version — including two complete epics, *Fingal* and *Temora*, from Gaelic MSS., which he had collected in the Scottish Highlands. A fierce controversy at once sprang up over the genuineness of these remains. Macpherson was challenged to produce his originals, and when, many years after, he published the Gaelic text, it was asserted that this was nothing but a translation of his own English into modern Gaelic. Of the MSS. which he professed to have found not a scrap remained: the Gaelic text was printed from transcriptions in Macpherson's handwriting or in that of his secretaries.

But whether these poems were the work of Ossian or of Macpherson, they made a deep impression upon the time.   Napoleon admired them greatly, and Goethe inserted passages from the "Songs of Selma" in his *Sorrows of Werther*. Macpherson composed—or translated—them in an abrupt, rhapsodical prose, resembling the English version of Job or of the prophecies of Isaiah. They filled the minds of their readers with images of vague sublimity and desolation; the mountain torrent, the mist on the hills, the ghosts of heroes half seen by the setting moon, the thistle in the ruined courts of chieftains, the grass whistling on the windy heath, the gray rock by the blue stream of Lutha, and the cliffs of sea-surrounded Gormal.

"A tale of the times of old!"

"Why, thou wanderer unseen!   Thou bender of the thistle of Lora; why, thou breeze of the valley, hast thou left mine ear?   I hear no distant roar of streams!   No sound of the harp from the rock! Come, thou huntress of Lutha, Malvina, call back his soul to the bard.   I look forward to Lochlin of lakes, to the dark billowy bay of U-thorno, where Fingal descends from Ocean, from the roar of winds.   Few are the heroes of Morven in a land unknown."

Thomas Chatterton, who died by his own hand

in 1770, at the age of seventeen, is one of the most
wonderful examples of precocity in the history of
literature.   His father had been sexton of the ancient Church of St. Mary Redcliff, in Bristol, and
the boy's sensitive imagination took the stamp of
his surroundings.   He taught himself to read from
a black-letter Bible.   He drew charcoal sketches
of churches, castles, knightly tombs, and heraldic
blazonry.   When only eleven years old, he began
the fabrication of documents in prose and verse,
which he ascribed to a fictitious Thomas Rowley,
a secular priest at Bristol in the 15th century.
Chatterton pretended to have found these among
the contents of an old chest in the muniment room
of St. Mary Redcliff's.   The Rowley poems included two tragedies, *Aella* and *Goddwyn*, two
cantos of a long poem on the *Battle of Hastings*,
and a number of ballads and minor pieces.   Chatterton had no precise knowledge of early English,
or even of Chaucer.   His method of working was
as follows: He made himself a manuscript glossary
of the words marked as archaic in Bailey's and
Kersey's English dictionaries, composed his poems
first in modern language, and then turned them
into ancient spelling, and substituted here and
there the old words in his glossary for their
modern equivalents.   Naturally he made many
mistakes, and though Horace Walpole, to whom
he sent some of his pieces, was unable to detect
the forgery, his friends, Gray and Mason, to whom
he submitted them, at once pronounced them
12

spurious.   Nevertheless there was a controversy over Rowley, hardly less obstinate than that over Ossian, a controversy made possible only by the then almost universal ignorance of the forms, scansion, and vocabulary of early English poetry. Chatterton's poems are of little value in themselves, but they are the record of an industry and imitative quickness, marvelous in a mere child, and they show how, with the instinct of genius, he threw himself into the main literary current of his time.   Discarding the couplet of Pope, the poets now went back for models to the Elisabethan writers.   Thomas Warton published, in 1753, his *Observations on the Faerie Queene.* Beattie's *Minstrel,* Thomson's *Castle of Indolence,* William Shenstone's *Schoolmistress,* and John Dyer's *Fleece,* were all written in the Spenserian stanza.   Shenstone gave a partly humorous effect to his poem by imitating Spenser's archaisms, and Thomson reproduced in many passages the copious harmony and luxuriant imagery of the *Faerie Queene.* The *Fleece* was a poem on English wool-growing, after the fashion of Vergil's *Georgics.* The subject was unfortunate, for, as Dr. Johnson said, it is impossible to make poetry out of surges and druggets.   Dyer's *Grongar Hill,* which mingles reflection with natural description in the manner of Gray's *Elegy written in a Country Churchyard,* was composed in the octosyllabic verse of Milton's *L'Allegro* and *Il Penseroso.*   Milton's minor poems, which had hitherto been neglected, exercised a great influence on Collins and Gray. Collins's *Ode to Simplicity* was written in the stanza of Milton's *Nativity*, and his exquisite unrimed *Ode to Evening* was a study in versification, after Milton's translation of Horace's *Ode to Pyrrha*, in the original meters. Shakspere began to to be studied more reverently: numerous critical editions of his plays were issued, and Garrick restored his pure text to the stage. Collins was an enthusiastic student of Shakspere, and one of his sweetest poems, the *Dirge in Cymbeline*, was inspired by the tragedy of *Cymbeline*. The verse of Gray, Collins, and the Warton brothers, abounds in verbal reminiscences of Shakspere; but their genius was not allied to his, being exclusively lyrical, and not at all dramatic. The Muse of this romantic school was Fancy rather than Passion. A thoughtful melancholy, a gentle, scholarly pensiveness, the spirit of Milton's *Il Penseroso*, pervades their poetry. Gray was a fastidious scholar, who produced very little, but that little of the finest quality. His famous *Elegy*, expressing a meditative mood in language of the choicest perfection, is the representative poem of the second half of the 18th century, as the *Rape of the Lock* is of the first. The romanticists were quietists, and their scenery is characteristic. They loved solitude and evening, the twilight vale, the mossy hermitage, ruins, glens, and caves. Their style was elegant and academic, retaining a little of the stilted poetic diction of their classical forerunners. Personification and periphrasis were their favorite mannerisms: Collins's Odes were largely addressed to abstractions, such as Fear, Pity, Liberty, Mercy, and Simplicity. A poet in their dialect was always a "bard;" a countryman was "the untutored swain," and a woman was a "nymph" or "the fair," just as in Dryden and Pope. Thomson is perpetually mindful of Vergil, and afraid to speak simply. He uses too many Latin epithets, like *amusive* and *precipitant*, and calls a fish-line

> The floating line snatched from the hoary steed."

They left much for Cowper and Wordsworth to do in the way of infusing the new blood of a strong, racy English into our exhausted poetic diction. Their poetry is impersonal, bookish, literary. It lacks emotional force, except now and then in Gray's immortal *Elegy*, in his *Ode on a Distant Prospect of Eton College*, in Collins's lines, *On the Death of Thomson*, and his little ode beginning, "How sleep the brave?"

The new school did not lack critical expounders of its principles and practice. Joseph Warton published, in 1756, the first volume of his *Essay on the Genius and Writings of Pope*, an elaborate review of Pope's writings *seriatim*, doing him certainly full justice, but ranking him below Shakspere, Spenser, and Milton. "Wit and satire," wrote Warton, "are transitory and perishable, but nature and passion are eternal. . . . He stuck to

describing modern manners; but those manners, because they are familiar, artificial, and polished, are,
in their very nature, unfit for any lofty effort of
the Muse.   Whatever poetical enthusiasm he
actually possessed he withheld and stifled.   Sure-
ly it is no narrow and niggardly encomium to say,
he is the great Poet of Reason, the first of Ethical
authors in verse." Warton illustrated his critical
positions by quoting freely not only from Spenser
and Milton, but from recent poets, like Thomson,
Gray, Collins, and Dyer.   He testified that the
Seasons had "been very instrumental in diffusing
a general taste for the beauties of nature and
landscape." It was symptomatic of the change in
literary taste that the natural or English school of
landscape gardening now began to displace the
French and Dutch fashion of clipped hedges, regular parterres, etc., and that Gothic architecture
came into repute.   Horace Walpole was a vir-
tuoso in Gothic art, and in his castle, at Strawberry
Hill, he made a collection of ancient armor,
illuminated MSS., and bric-a-brac of all kinds.
Gray had been Walpole's traveling companion in
France and Italy, and the two had quarreled and
separated, but were afterward reconciled.   From
Walpole's private printing-press, at Strawberry
Hill, Gray's two "sister odes," the *Bard* and
the *Progress of Poesy*, were first printed, in 1757.
Both Gray and Walpole were good correspond-
ents, and their printed letters are among the most
delightful literature of the kind.

The central figure among the English men of letters of that generation was Samuel Johnson (1709–84), whose memory has been preserved less by his own writings than by James Boswell's famous *Life of Johnson*, published in 1791. Boswell was a Scotch laird and advocate, who first met Johnson in London, when the latter was fifty-four years old. Boswell was not a very wise or witty person, but he reverenced the worth and intellect which shone through his subject's uncouth exterior. He followed him about, note-book in hand, bore all his snubbings patiently, and made the best biography ever written. It is related that the doctor once said that if he thought Boswell meant to write *his* life, he should prevent it by taking *Boswell's*. And yet Johnson's own writings and this biography of him have changed places in relative importance so completely, that Carlyle predicted that the former would soon be reduced to notes on the latter; and Macaulay said that the man who was known to his contemporaries as a great writer was known to posterity as an agreeable companion.

Johnson was one of those rugged, eccentric, self-developed characters, so common among the English. He was the son of a Lichfield book-seller, and after a course at Oxford, which was cut short by poverty, and an unsuccessful career as a school-master, he had come up to London, in 1737, where he supported himself for many years as a book-seller's hack. Gradually his great learning

and abilities, his ready social wit and powers as a
talker, caused his company to be sought at the
tables of those whom he called " the great." He
was a clubbable man, and he drew about him
at the tavern a group of the most distinguished
intellects of the time, Edmund Burke, the orator
and statesman, Oliver Goldsmith, Sir Joshua Rey-
nolds, the portrait painter, and David Garrick, the
great actor, who had been a pupil in Johnson's
school, near Lichfield. Johnson was the typical
John Bull of the last century. His oddities, virtues, and prejudices were thoroughly English.
He hated Frenchmen, Scotchmen, and Americans,
and had a cockneyish attachment to London.
He was a high Tory, and an orthodox churchman;
he loved a lord in the abstract, and yet he asserted a sturdy independence against any lord in
particular. He was deeply religious, but had an
abiding fear of death. •He was burly in person,
and slovenly in dress, his shirt-frill always
covered with snuff. He was a great diner out,
an inordinate tea-drinker, and a voracious and
untidy feeder. An inherited scrofula, which often
took the form of hypochondria and threatened to
affect his brain, deprived him of control over
the muscles of his face. Boswell describes how
his features worked, how he snorted, grunted,
whistled, and rolled about in his chair when get-
ting ready to speak. He records his minutest
traits, such as his habit of pocketing the orange
peels at the club, and his superstitious way of touch-

ing all the posts between his house and the Mitre Tavern, going back to do it, if he skipped one by chance.   Though bearish in his manners and arrogant in dispute, especially when talking "for victory," Johnson had a large and tender heart. He loved his ugly, old wife—twenty-one years his senior—and he had his house full of unfortunates —a blind woman, an invalid surgeon, a destitute widow, a negro servant—whom he supported for many years, and bore with all their ill-humors patiently.

Among Johnson's numerous writings the ones best entitled to remembrance are, perhaps, his *Dictionary of the English Language*, 1755; his moral tale, *Rasselas*, 1759; the introduction to his *Edition of Shakspere*, 1765 ; and his *Lives of the Poets*, 1781.   Johnson wrote a sonorous, cadenced prose, full of big Latin words and balanced clauses.   Here is a sentence, for example, from his *Visit to the Hebrides :* " We were now treading that illustrious island which was once the luminary of the Caledonian regions, whence savage clans and roving barbarians derived the benefits of knowledge and the blessings of religion.   To abstract the mind from all local emotion would be impossible, if it were endeavored, and would be foolish, if it were possible."   The difference between his colloquial style and his book style is well illustrated in the instance cited by Macaulay.   Speaking of Villier's *Rehearsal,* Johnson said, " It has not wit enough to keep it sweet; " then paused and added—translating English into Johnsonese—" it has not vitality sufficient to preserve it from putrefaction." There is more of this in Johnson's *Rambler* and *Idler* papers than in his latest work, the *Lives of the Poets*. In this he showed himself a sound and judicious critic, though with decided limitations. His understanding was solid, but he was a thorough classicist, and his taste in poetry was formed on Pope. He was unjust to Milton and to his own contemporaries, Gray, Collins, Shenstone, and Dyer. He had no sense of the higher and subtler graces of romantic poetry, and he had a comical indifference to the " beauties of nature." When Boswell once ventured to remark that poor Scotland had, at least, some " noble, wild prospects," the doctor replied that the noblest prospect a Scotchman ever saw was the road that led to London.

The English novel of real life had its origin at this time. Books like De Foe's *Robinson Crusoe*, *Captain Singleton*, *Journal of the Plague*, etc., were tales of incident and adventure rather than novels. The novel deals primarily with character and with the interaction of characters upon one another, as developed by a regular plot. The first English novelist, in the modern sense of the word, was Samuel Richardson, a printer, who began authorship in his fiftieth year with his *Pamela*, the story of a young servant girl, who resisted the seductions of her master, and finally, as the reward of her virtue, became his wife. *Clarissa Harlowe*,

1748, was the tragical history of a high spirited young lady, who being driven from home by her family, because she refused to marry the suitor selected for her, fell into the toils of Lovelace, an accomplished rake. After struggling heroically against every form of artifice and violence, she was at last drugged and ruined. She died of a broken heart, and Lovelace, borne down by remorse, was killed in a duel by a cousin of Clarissa. *Sir Charles Grandison*, 1753, was Richardson's portrait of an ideal fine gentleman, whose stately doings fill eight volumes, but who seems to the modern reader a bore and a prig. All of these novels were written in the form of letters passing between the characters, a method which fitted Richardson's subjective cast of mind. He knew little of life, but he identified himself intensely with his principal character and produced a strong effect by minute, accumulated touches. *Clarissa Harlowe* is his masterpiece, though even in that the situation is painfully prolonged, the heroine's virtue is self-conscious and rhetorical, and there is something almost ludicrously unnatural in the copiousness with which she pours herself out in gushing epistles to her female correspondent at the very moment when she is beset with dangers, persecuted, agonized, and driven nearly mad. In Richardson's novels appears, for the first time, that sentimentalism which now began to infect European literature. *Pamela* was translated into French and German, and fell in with that current of popular feeling which found fullest expression in Rousseau's *Nouvelle Heloise*, 1759, and Goethe's *Leiden des Jungen Werther*, which set all the world a-weeping in 1774.

Coleridge said that to pass from Richardson's books to those of Henry Fielding was like going into the fresh air from a close room heated by stoves. Richardson, it has been affirmed, knew *man*, but Fielding knew *men*. The latter's first novel, *Joseph Andrews*, 1742, was begun as a travesty of *Pamela*. The hero, a brother of Pamela, was a young footman in the employ of Lady Booby, from whom his virtue suffered a like assault to that made upon Pamela's by her master. This reversal of the natural situation was in itself full of laughable possibilities, had the book gone on simply as a burlesque. But the exuberance of Fielding's genius led him beyond his original design. This hero, leaving Lady Booby's service, goes traveling with good Parson Adams, and is soon engaged in a series of comical and rather boisterous adventures.

Fielding had seen life, and his characters were painted from the life with a bold, free hand. He was a gentleman by birth, and had made acquaintance with society and the town in 1727, when he was a handsome, stalwart young fellow, with high animal spirits and a great appetite for pleasure. He soon ran himself into debt and began writing for the stage; married, and spent his wife's fortune, living for awhile in much splendor as a

country gentleman, and afterward in a reduced
condition as a rural justice with a salary of £500
of "the dirtiest money on earth." Fielding's masterpiece was *Tom Jones*, 1749, and it remains one
of the best of English novels. Its hero is very
much after Fielding's own heart, wild, spendthrift,
warm-hearted, forgiving, and greatly in need of
forgiveness. The same type of character, with the
lines deepened, re-appears in Captain Booth, in
Amelia, 1751, the heroine of which is a portrait of
Fielding's wife. With Tom Jones is contrasted
Blifil, the embodiment of meanness, hypocrisy, and
cowardice. Sophia Western, the heroine, is one of
Fielding's most admirable creations. For the reg-
ulated morality of Richardson, with its somewhat
old-grannified air, Fielding substituted instinct.
His virtuous characters are virtuous by impulse
only, and his ideal of character is manliness. In
Jonathan Wild the hero is a highwayman. This
novel is ironical, a sort of prose mock-heroic, and
is one of the strongest, though certainly the least
pleasing, of Fielding's writings.

Tobias Smollett was an inferior Fielding with a
difference. He was a Scotch ship-surgeon and
had spent some time in the West Indies. He introduced into fiction the now familiar figure of the
British tar, in the persons of Tom Bowling and
Commodore Trunnion, as Fielding had introduced,
in Squire Western, the equally national type of the
hard-swearing, deep-drinking, fox-hunting Tory
squire. Both Fielding and Smollett were of the

hearty British "beef-and-beer" school; their novels are downright, energetic, coarse, and high-blooded; low life, physical life, runs riot through their pages—tavern brawls, the breaking of pates, and the off-hand courtship of country wenches. Smollett's books, such as *Roderick Random*, 1748, *Peregrine Pickle*, 1751, and *Ferdinand Count Fathom*, 1752, were more purely stories of broadly comic adventure than Fielding's. The latter's view of life was by no means idyllic; but with Smollett this English realism ran into vulgarity and a hard Scotch literalness, and character was pushed to caricature. "The generous wine of Fielding," says Taine, "in Smollett's hands becomes brandy of the dram-shop." A partial exception to this is to be found in his last and best novel, *Humphrey Clinker*, 1770. The influence of Cervantes and of the French novelist, Le Sage, who finished his *Adventures of Gil Blas* in 1735, are very perceptible in Smollett.

A genius of much finer mold was Lawrence Sterne, the author of *Tristram Shandy*, 1759–67, and the *Sentimental Journey*, 1768. *Tristram Shandy* is hardly a novel: the story merely serves to hold together a number of characters, such as Uncle Toby and Corporal Trim, conceived with rare subtlety and originality. Sterne's chosen province was the whimsical, and his great model was Rabelais. His books are full of digressions, breaks, surprises, innuendoes, double meanings, mystifications, and all manner of odd turns.

Coleridge and Carlyle unite in pronouncing him a great humorist. Thackeray says that he was only a great jester. Humor is the laughter of the heart, and Sterne's pathos is closely interwoven with his humor. He was the foremost of English sentimentalists, and he had that taint of insincerity which distinguishes sentimentalism from genuine sentiment, like Goldsmith's, for example. Sterne, in life, was selfish, heartless, and untrue. A clergyman, his worldliness and vanity and the indecency of his writings were a scandal to the Church, though his sermons were both witty and affecting. He enjoyed the titilation of his own emotions, and he had practiced so long at detecting the latent pathos that lies in the expression of dumb things and of poor, patient animals, that he could summon the tear of sensibility at the thought of a discarded postchaise, a dead donkey, a starling in a cage, or of Uncle Toby putting a house fly out of the window, and saying, "There is room enough in the world for thee and me." It is a high proof of his cleverness that he generally succeeds in raising the desired feeling in his readers even from such trivial occasions. He was a minute philosopher, his philosophy was kindly, and he taught the delicate art of making much out of little. Less coarse than Fielding, he is far more corrupt. Fielding goes bluntly to the point; Sterne lingers among the temptations and suspends the expectation to tease and excite it. Forbidden fruit had a relish for him, and his pages

seduce. He is full of good sayings, both tender
and witty. It was Sterne, for example, who wrote,
"God tempers the wind to the shorn lamb."
A very different writer was Oliver Goldsmith,
whose *Vicar of Wakefield*, 1766, was the earliest,
and is still one of the best, novels of domestic and
rural life. The book, like its author, was thoroughly Irish, full of bulls and inconsistencies.
Very improbable things happened in it with a
cheerful defiance of logic. But its characters
are true to nature, drawn with an idyllic sweetness and purity, and with touches of a most loving
humor. Its hero, Dr. Primrose, was painted after
Goldsmith's father, a poor clergyman of the English Church in Ireland, and the original, likewise,
of the country parson in Goldsmith's *Deserted
Village*, 1770, who was "passing rich on forty
pounds a year." This poem, though written in
the fashionable couplet of Pope, and even containing a few verses contributed by Dr. Johnson
—so that it was not at all in line with the work of
the romanticists—did, perhaps, as much as any
thing of Gray or of Collins to recall English poetry
to the simplicity and freshness of country life.
Except for the comedies of Sheridan and Goldsmith, and, perhaps, a few other plays, the stage
had now utterly declined. The novel, which is
dramatic in essence, though not in form, began to
take its place, and to represent life, though less intensely, yet more minutely, than the theater could
do. In the novelists of the 18th century, the life

of the people, as distinguished from "society" or
the upper classes, began to invade literature.
Richardson was distinctly a *bourgeois* writer, and
his contemporaries—Fielding, Smollett, Sterne, and
Goldsmith—ranged over a wide variety of ranks
and conditions. This is one thing which distinguishes the literature of the second half of the 18th
century from that of the first, as well as in some
degree from that of all previous centuries. Among
the authors of this generation whose writings belonged to other departments of thought than pure
literature may be mentioned, in passing, the great
historian, Edward Gibbon, whose *Decline and Fall
of the Roman Empire* was published from 1776–88,
and Edmund Burke, whose political speeches and
pamphlets possess a true literary quality. The romantic poets had addressed the imagination rather
than the heart. It was reserved for two men—a
contrast to one another in almost every respect—
to bring once more into British song a strong individual feeling, and with it a new warmth and directness of speech. These were William Cowper
(1731–1800) and Robert Burns (1759–96). Cowper
spoke out of his own life experience, his agony, his
love, his worship and despair; and straightway the
varnish that had glittered over all our poetry since
the time of Dryden melted away. Cowper had
scribbled verses when he was a young law student
at the Middle Temple in London, and he had contributed to the *Olney Hymns*, published in 1779 by
his friend and pastor, the Rev. John Newton; but

he only began to write poetry in earnest when he
was nearly fifty years old.   In 1782, the date of his
first volume, he said, in a letter to a friend, that he
had read but one English poet during the past
twenty years. .Perhaps, therefore, of all English
poets of equal culture, Cowper owed the least impulse to books and the most to the need of utter-
ing his inmost thoughts and feelings.   Cowper had
a most unhappy life.   As a child, he was shy, sensitive, and sickly, and suffered much from bullying
and fagging at a school whither he was sent after
his mother's death.   This happened when he was
six years old; and in his affecting lines written *On
Receipt of My Mother's Picture*, he speaks of himself as a

"Wretch even then, life's journey just begun."

In 1763 he became insane and was sent to an asylum, where he spent a year.   Judicious treatment
restored him to sanity, but he came out a broken
man and remained for the rest of his life an invalid, unfitted for any active occupation.   His disease took the form of religious melancholy.   He
had two recurrences of madness, and both times
made attempts upon his life.   At Huntingdon, and
afterward at Olney, in Buckinghamshire, he found
a home with the Unwin family, whose kindness did
all which the most soothing and delicate care could
do to heal his wounded spirit.   His two poems *To
Mary Unwin*, together with the lines on his mother's picture, were almost the first examples of deep
14

and tender sentiment in the lyrical poetry of the
last century. Cowper found relief from the black
thoughts that beset him only in an ordered round
of quiet household occupations. He corresponded
indefatigably, took long walks through the neigh-
borhood, read, sang, and conversed with Mrs. Unwin and his friend, Lady Austin; and amused himself with carpentry, gardening, and raising pets, especially hares, of which gentle animals he grew very
fond. All these simple tastes, in which he found
for a time a refuge and a sheltered happiness, are
reflected in his best poem, *The Task*, 1785. Cowper is the poet of the family affections, of domestic
life, and rural retirement; the laureate of the fire-
side, the tea-table, the evening lamp, the garden, the
green-house, and the rabbit-coop. He draws with
elegance and precision a chair, a clock, a harpsi-
chord, a barometer, a piece of needle-work. But
Cowper was an out-door as well as an in-door man.
The Olney landscape was tame, a fat, agricultural
region, where the sluggish Ouse wound between
plowed fields and the horizon was bounded by
low hills. Nevertheless Cowper's natural descriptions are at once more distinct and more imaginative than Thomson's. *The Task* reflects, also, the
new philanthropic spirit, the enthusiasm of humanity, the feeling of the brotherhood of men to which
Rousseau had given expression in France and which
issued in the French Revolution. In England this
was the time of Wilberforce, the antislavery agi-
tator; of Whitefield, the eloquent revival preacher;

of 'John and Charles Wesley, and of the Evangel-
ical and Methodist movements which gave new life
to the English Church.   John Newton, the curate
of Olney and the keeper of Cowper's conscience,
was one of the leaders of the Evangelicals; and
Cowper's first volume of *Table Talk* and other poems, 1782, written under Newton's inspiration, was
a series of sermons in verse, somewhat intolerant of
all worldly enjoyments, such as hunting, dancing,
and theaters.   "God made the country and man
made the town," he wrote.   He was a moralizing
poet, and his morality was sometimes that of the
invalid and the recluse.   Byron called him a "cod-
dled poet."   And, indeed, there is a suspicion of
gruel and dressing-gowns about him.   He lived
much among women, and his sufferings had refined
him to a feminine delicacy.   But there is no sick-
liness in his poetry, and he retained a charming,
playful humor—displayed in his excellent comic
ballad, *John Gilpin ;* and Mrs. Browning has sung
of him,

" How when one by one sweet sounds and wandering lights
    departed
He bore no less a loving face, because so broken-hearted."

At the close of the year 1786 a young Scotchman, named Samuel Rose, called upon Cowper at
Olney, and left with him a small volume, which had
appeared at Edinburgh during the past summer,
entitled *Poems chiefly in the Scottish Dialect, by
Robert Burns.*   Cowper read the book through

twice, and, though somewhat bothered by the dialect, pronounced it a "very extraordinary production." This momentary flash, as of an electric spark, marks the contact not only of the two chief British poets of their generation, but of two literatures. Scotch poets, like Thomson and Beattie, had written in Southern English, and, as Carlyle said, *in vacuo*, that is, with nothing specially national in their work. Burns's sweet though rugged Doric first secured the vernacular poetry of his country a hearing beyond the border. He had, to be sure, a whole literature of popular songs and ballads behind him, and his immediate models were Allan Ramsay and Robert Ferguson; but these remained provincial, while Burns became universal.

He was born in Ayrshire, on the banks of "bonny Doon," in a clay biggin not far from " Alloway's auld haunted kirk," the scene of the witch dance in *Tam O'Shanter*. His father was a hard-headed, God-fearing tenant farmer, whose life and that of his sons was a harsh struggle with poverty. The crops failed; the landlord pressed for his rent; for weeks at a time the family tasted no meat; yet this life of toil was lightened by love and homely pleasures. In the *Cotter's Saturday Night*, Burns has drawn a beautiful picture of his parents' household, the rest that came at the week's end, and the family worship about the "wee bit ingle, blinkin' bonnily." Robert was handsome, wild, and witty. He was universally susceptible, and his first songs, like his last, were of "the lasses." His head had been

stuffed, in boyhood, with "tales and songs concerning devils, ghosts, fairies, brownies, witches, war-
locks, spunkies, kelpies, elf-candles, dead-lights,"
etc., told him by one Jenny Wilson, an old woman
who lived in the family. His ear was full of ancient Scottish tunes, and as soon as he fell in love
he began to make poetry as naturally as a bird
sings. He composed his verses while following the
plow or working in the stack-yard; or, at evening, balancing on two legs of his chair and watch-
ing the light of a peat fire play over the reeky walls
of the cottage. Burns's love songs are in many
keys, ranging from strains of the most pure and
exalted passion, like *Ae Fond Kiss* and *To Mary in
Heaven*, to such loose ditties as *When Januar
Winds* and *Green Grow the Rashes O.*

Burns liked a glass almost as well as a lass, and
at Mauchline, where he carried on a farm with his
brother Gilbert, after their father's death, he began to seek a questionable relief from the pressure
of daily toil and unkind fates, in the convivialities
of the tavern. There, among the wits of the
Mauchline Club, farmers' sons, shepherds from the
uplands, and the smugglers who swarmed over the
west coast, he would discuss politics and farming,
recite his verses, and join in the singing and ranting, while

"Bousin o'er the nappy,
And gettin' fou and unco happy."

To these experiences we owe not only those excellent drinking songs, *John Barleycorn* and *Willie*

Brewed a Peck o' Maut, but the headlong fun of *Tam O'Shanter,* and the visions, grotesquely terrible, of *Death and Dr. Hornbook,* and the dramatic humor of the *Jolly Beggars.* Cowper had celebrated " the cup which cheers but not inebriates." Burns sang the praises of *Scotch Drink.* Cowper was a stranger to Burns's high animal spirits, and his robust enjoyment of life. He had affections, but no passions. At Mauchline, Burns, whose irregularities did not escape the censure of the kirk, became involved, through his friendship with Gavin Hamilton, in the controversy between the Old Light and New Light clergy. His *Holy Fair, Holy Tulzie, Twa Herds, Holy Willie's Prayer,* and *Address to the Unco Gude,* are satires against bigotry and hypocrisy. But in spite of the rollicking profanity of his language, and the violence of his rebound against the austere religion of Scotland, Burns was at bottom deeply impressible by religious ideas, as may be seen from his *Prayer under the Pressure of Violent Anguish,* and *Prayer in Prospect of Death.*

His farm turned out a failure, and he was on the eve of sailing for Jamaica, when the favor with which his volume of poems was received, stayed his departure, and turned his steps to Edinburgh. There the peasant poet was lionized for a winter season by the learned and polite society of the Scotch capital, with results in the end not altogether favorable to Burns's best interests. For when society finally turned the cold shoulder on

him, he had to go back to farming again, carrying
with him a bitter sense of injustice and neglect.
He leased a farm in Ellisland, in 1788, and some
friends procured his appointment as exciseman
for his district. But poverty, disappointment, irregular habits, and broken health clouded his last
years, and brought him to an untimely death at the
age of thirty-seven. He continued, however, to
pour forth songs of unequaled sweetness and
force. "The man sank," said Coleridge, "but the
poet was bright to the last."

Burns is the best of British song-writers. His
songs are singable; they are not merely lyrical
poems. They were meant to be sung, and they are
sung. They were mostly set to old Scottish airs,
and sometimes they were built up from ancient
fragments of anonymous, popular poetry, a chorus,
or stanza, or even a single line. Such are, for example, *Auld Lang Syne*, *My Heart's in the Highlands*, and *Landlady, Count the Lawin*. Burns had
a great, warm heart. His sins were sins of passion,
and sprang from the same generous soil that nour-
ished his impulsive virtues. His elementary qualities as a poet were sincerity, a healthy openness to
all impressions of the beautiful, and a sympathy
which embraced men, animals, and the dumb objects of nature. His tenderness toward flowers
and the brute creation may be read in his lines
To a Mountain Daisy, *To a Mouse*, and *The Auld
Farmer's New Year's Morning Salutation to his
Auld Mare Maggie*. Next after love and good fel-

lowship, patriotism is the most frequent motive of his song. Of his national anthem, *Scots wha hae wi' Wallace bled,* Carlyle said: "So long as there is warm blood in the heart of Scotchman, or man, it will move in fierce thrills under this war ode,"

Burns's politics were a singular mixture of sentimental toryism with practical democracy. A romantic glamour was thrown over the fortunes of the exiled Stuarts, and to have been "out" in '45 with the Young Pretender was a popular thing in parts of Scotland. To this purely poetic loyalty may be attributed such Jacobite ballads of Burns as *Over the Water to Charlie.* But his sober convictions were on the side of liberty and human brotherhood, and are expressed in the *Twa Dogs,* the *First Epistle to Davie,* and *A Man's a Man for a' that.* His sympathy with the Revolution led him to send four pieces of ordnance, taken from a captured smuggler, as a present to the French Convention, a piece of bravado which got him into difficulties with his superiors in the excise. The poetry which Burns wrote, not in dialect, but in the classical English, is in the stilted manner of his century, and his prose correspondence betrays his lack of culture by his constant lapse into rhetorical affectation and fine writing.

1. T. S. Perry's English Literature in the Eighteenth Century.

2. James Thomson. The Castle of Indolence.

3. The Poems of Thomas Gray.

4. William Collins.   Odes.

5. The Six Chief Lives from Johnson's Lives of the Poets.   Edited by Matthew Arnold.   Macmillan, 1878.

6. Boswell's Life of Johnson [abridged].   Henry Holt & Co., 1878.

7. Samuel Richardson.   Clarissa Harlowe.

8. Henry Fielding.   Tom Jones.

9. Tobias Smollett.   Humphrey Clinker.

10. Lawrence Sterne.   Tristram Shandy.

11. Oliver Goldsmith.   Vicar of Wakefield and Deserted Village.

12. William Cowper.   The Task and John Gilpin.

13. The Poems and Songs of Robert Burns.

CHAPTER VII.

FROM THE FRENCH REVOLUTION
TO THE DEATH OF SCOTT.

1789-1832.

THE burst of creative activity at the opening of
the 19th century has but one parallel in English
literary history, namely, the somewhat similar flow-
ering out of the national genius in the time of Elisabeth and the first two Stuart kings.   The later age
gave birth to no supreme poets, like Shakspere and
Milton.   It produced no *Hamlet* and no *Paradise
Lost ;* but it offers a greater number of important
writers, a higher average of excellence, and a wider
range and variety of literary work than any preceding era. Wordsworth, Coleridge, Scott, Byron, Shelley, and Keats are all great names; while Southey,
Landor, Moore, Lamb, and De Quincey would be
noteworthy figures at any period, and deserve a
fuller mention than can be here accorded them.
But in so crowded a generation, selection becomes
increasingly needful, and in the present chapter,
accordingly, the emphasis will be laid upon the first-
named group as not only the most important, but
the most representative of the various tendencies
of their time.

The conditions of literary work in this century have been almost unduly stimulating. The rapid advance in population, wealth, education, and the means of comunication have vastly increased the number of readers. Every one who has any thing to say can say it in print, and is sure of some sort of a hearing. A special feature of the time is the multiplication of periodicals. The great London dailies, like the *Times* and the *Morning Post,* which were started during the last quarter of the 18th century, were something quite new in journalism. The first of the modern reviews, the *Edinburgh,* was established in 1802, as the organ of the Whig party in Scotland. This was followed by the London *Quarterly,* in 1808, and by *Blackwood's Magazine,* in 1817, both in the Tory interest. The first editor of the *Edinburgh* was Francis Jeffrey, who assembled about him a distinguished corps of contributors, including the versatile Henry Brougham, afterward a great parliamentary orator and lord-chancellor of England, and the Rev. Sydney Smith, whose witty sayings are still current. The first editor of the *Quarterly* was William Gifford, a satirist, who wrote the *Baviad* and *Mæviad* in ridicule of literary affectations. He was succeeded in 1824 by James Gibson Lockhart, the son-in-law of Walter Scott, and the author of an excellent *Life of Scott. Blackwood's* was edited by John Wilson, Professor of Moral Philosophy in the University of Edinburgh, who, under the pen-name of "Christopher North," contributed to his magazine a series of brilliant, imaginary dialogues between famous characters of the day, entitled *Noctes Ambrosianæ*, because they were supposed to take place at Ambrose's tavern in Edinburgh. These papers were full of a profuse, headlong eloquence, of humor, literary criticism, and personalities interspersed with songs expressive of a roystering and convivial Toryism and an uproarious contempt for Whigs and cockneys. These reviews and magazines, and others which sprang up beside them, became the *nuclei* about which the wit and scholarship of both parties gathered. Political controversy under the Regency and the reign of George IV. was thus carried on more regularly by permanent organs, and no longer so largely by privateering, in the shape of pamphlets, like Swift's *Public Spirit of the Allies*, Johnson's *Taxation No Tyranny*, and Burke's *Reflections on the Revolution in France*. Nor did politics by any means usurp the columns of the reviews. Literature, art, science, the whole circle of human effort and achievement passed under review. *Blackwood's*, *Fraser's*, and the other monthlies, published stories, poetry, criticism, and correspondence — every thing, in short, which enters into the make-up of our magazines to-day, except illustrations.

Two main influences, of foreign origin, have left their trace in the English writers of the first thirty years of the 19th century, the one communicated by contact with the new German literature of the latter half of the 18th century, and in particular

with the writings of Goethe, Schiller, and Kant;
the other springing from the events of the French
Revolution. The influence of German upon English literature in the 19th century was more intellectual and less formal than that of the Italian
in the 16th and of the French in the 18th. In oth-
er·words, the German writers furnished the English
with ideas and ways of feeling rather than with
models of style. Goethe and Schiller did not become subjects for literary imitation as Moliere,
Racine, and Boileau had become in Pope's time.
It was reserved for a later generation and for
·Thomas Carlyle to domesticate the diction of German prose. But the nature and extent of this influence can, perhaps, best be noted when we come to
take up the authors of the time one by one.

The excitement caused by the French Revolution was something more obvious and immediate.
When the Bastile fell, in 1789, the enthusiasm among
the friends of liberty and human progress in England was hardly less intense than in France. It
was the dawn of a new day: the shackles were
stricken from the slave; all men were free and all
men were brothers, and radical young England sent
up a shout that echoed the roar of the Paris mob.
Wordsworth's lines on the *Fall of the Bastile*, Coleridge's *Fall of Robespierre* and *Ode to France*,
and Southey's revolutionary drama, *Wat Tyler*,
gave expression to the hopes and aspirations of the
English democracy. In after life Wordsworth,
looking back regretfully to those years of promise,

wrote his poem on the *French Revolution as it Appeared to Enthusiasts at its Commencement.*

> "Bliss was it in that dawn to be alive,
> But to be young was very heaven. Oh times
> In which the meager, stale, forbidding ways
> Of custom, law, and statute took at once
> The attraction of a country in romance."

Those were the days in which Wordsworth, then an under-graduate at Cambridge, spent a college vacation in tramping through France, landing at Calais on the eve of the very day (July 14, 1790) on which Louis XVI. signalized the anniversary of the fall of the Bastile by taking the oath of fidelity to the new Constitution. In the following year Wordsworth revisited France, where he spent thirteen months, forming an intimacy with the republican general, Beaupuis, at Orleans, and reaching Paris not long after the September massacres of 1792. Those were the days, too, in which young Southey and young Coleridge, having married sisters at Bristol, were planning a "Pantisocracy," or ideal community, on the banks of the Susquehannah, and denouncing the British government for going to war with the French Republic. This group of poets, who had met one another first in the south of England, came afterward to be called the Lake Poets, from their residence in the mountainous lake country of Westmoreland and Cumberland, with which their names, and that of Wordsworth, especially, are forever associated. The so-called " Lakers " did not, properly speaking, constitute a school of poetry. They differed greatly from one another in mind and art. But they were connected by social ties and by religious and political sympathies. The excesses of the French Revolution, and the usurpation of Napoleon disappointed them, as it did many other English liberals, and drove them into the ranks of the reactionaries. Advancing years brought conservatism, and they became in time loyal Tories and orthodox Churchmen.

William Wordsworth (1770–1850), the chief of the three, and, perhaps, on the whole, the greatest English poet since Milton, published his *Lyrical Ballads* in 1798. The volume contained a few pieces by his friend Coleridge—among them the *Ancient Mariner*—and its appearance may fairly be said to mark an epoch in the history of English poetry. Wordsworth regarded himself as a reformer of poetry; and in the preface to the second volume of *Lyrical Ballads*, he defended the theory on which they were composed. His innovations were twofold, in subject-matter and in diction. " The principal object which I proposed to myself in these poems," he said, "was to choose incidents and situations from common life. Low and rustic life was generally chosen, because, in that condition, the essential passions of the heart find a better soil in which they can attain their maturity . . . and are incorporated with the beautiful and permanent forms of nature." Wordsworth discarded, in theory, the poetic diction of his predecessors, and professed to use "a selection of the real language of men in a state of vivid sensation." He adopted, he said, the language of men in rustic life, "because such men hourly communicate with the best objects from which the best part of language is originally derived."

In the matter of poetic diction Wordsworth did not, in his practice, adhere to the doctrine of this preface. Many of his most admired poems, such as the *Lines written near Tintern Abbey*, the great *Ode on the Intimations of Immortality*, the *Sonnets*, and many parts of his longest poems, *The Excursion* and *The Prelude*, deal with philosophic thought and highly intellectualized emotions. In all of these and in many others the language is rich, stately, involved, and as remote from the "real language" of Westmoreland shepherds, as is the epic blank verse of Milton. On the other hand, in those of his poems which were consciously written in illustration of his theory, the affectation of simplicity, coupled with a defective sense of humor, sometimes led him to the selection of vulgar and trivial themes, and the use of language which is bald, childish, or even ludicrous. His simplicity is too often the simplicity of Mother Goose rather than of Chaucer. Instances of this occur in such poems as *Peter Bell*, the *Idiot Boy*, *Goody Blake and Harry Gill*, *Simon Lee*, and the *Wagoner*. But there are multitudes of Wordsworth's ballads and lyrics which are simple without being silly, and which, in their homeliness and clear profundity, in their production of the strongest effects by the fewest strokes, are among the choicest modern examples of *pure*, as distinguished from decorated, art. Such are (out of many) *Ruth, Lucy, A Portrait, To a Highland Girl, The Reverie of Poor Susan, To the Cuckoo, The Reaper, We Are Seven, The Pet Lamb, The Fountain, The Two April Mornings, The Leech Gatherer, The Thorn,* and *Yarrow Unvisited.*

Wordsworth was something of a Quaker in poetry, and loved the sober drabs and grays of life. Quietism was his literary religion, and the sensational was to him not merely vulgar, but almost wicked. "The human mind," he wrote, "is capable of being excited without the application of gross and violent stimulants." He disliked the far-fetched themes and high-colored style of Scott and Byron. He once told Landor that all of Scott's poetry together was not worth sixpence. From action and passion he turned away to sing the inward life of the soul and the outward life of Nature. He said:

"To me the meanest flower that blows can give
Thoughts that do often lie too deep for tears."

And again:

"Long have I loved what I behold,
The night that calms, the day that cheers;
The common growth of mother earth
Suffices me—her tears, her mirth,
Her humblest mirth and tears."

Wordsworth's life was outwardly uneventful. The companionship of the mountains and of his

15

own thoughts; the sympathy of his household; the lives of the dalesmen and cottagers about him furnished him with all the stimulus that he required.

> " Love had he found in huts where poor men lie :
>   His only teachers had been woods and rills,
> The silence that is in the starry sky,
>   The sleep that is among the lonely hills."

He read little, but reflected much, and made poetry daily, composing, by preference, out of doors, and dictating his verses to some member of his family. His favorite amanuensis was his sister Dorothy, a woman of fine gifts, to whom Wordsworth was indebted for some of his happiest inspirations. She was the subject of the poem beginning " Her eyes are wild," and her charming *Memorials of a Tour in the Scottish Highlands* records the origin of many of her brother's best poems.   Throughout life Wordsworth was remarkably self-centered. The ridicule of the reviewers, against which he gradually made his way to public recognition, never disturbed his serene belief in himself, or in the divine message which he felt himself com- missioned to deliver.   He was a slow and serious person, a preacher as well as a poet, with a cer- tain rigidity, not to say narrowness, of character. That plastic temperament which we associate with poetic genius Wordsworth either did not possess, or it hardened early.   Whole sides of life were beyond the range of his sympathies.   He touched life at fewer points than Byron and Scott, but touched it more profoundly. It is to him that we owe the phrase "plain living and high thinking," as also a most noble illustration of it in his own practice. His was the wisest and deepest spirit among the English poets of his generation, though hardly the most poetic. He wrote too much, and, attempting to make every petty incident or reflection the occasion of a poem, he finally reached the point of composing verses *On Seeing a Harp in the shape of a Needle Case*, and on other themes more worthy of Mrs. Sigourney. In parts of his long blank-verse poems, *The Excursion*, 1814, and *The Prelude* — which was printed after his death in 1850, though finished as early as 1806—the poetry wears very thin and its place is taken by prosaic, tedious didacticism. These two poems were designed as portions of a still more extended work, *The Recluse*, which was never completed. *The Excursion* consists mainly of philosophical discussions on nature and human life between a school-master, a solitary, and an itinerant peddler. *The Prelude* describes the development of Wordsworth's own genius. In parts of *The Excursion* the diction is fairly Shaksperian.

> " The good die first,
> And they whose hearts are dry as summer dust
> Burn to the socket."

A passage not only beautiful in itself, but dramatically true, in the mouth of the bereaved mother

who utters it, to that human instinct which gen-
eralizes a private sorrow into a universal law.
Much of *The Prelude* can hardly be called poetry
at all, yet some of Wordsworth's loftiest poetry is
buried among its dreary wastes, and now and then,
in the midst of commonplaces, comes a flash of
Miltonic splendor—like

> "Golden cities ten months' journey deep
> Among Tartarian wilds."

Wordsworth is, above all things, the poet of Nature. In this province he was not without forerunners. To say nothing of Burns and Cowper,
there was George Crabbe, who had published his
Village in 1783—fifteen years before the *Lyrical Ballads*—and whose last poem, *Tales of the Hall*, came
out in 1819, five years after *The Excursion*. Byron
called Crabbe " Nature's sternest painter, and her
best." He was a minutely accurate delineator of the
harsher aspects of rural life. He photographs a
Gypsy camp; a common, with its geese and donkey; a salt marsh, a shabby village street, or tumble-
down manse. But neither Crabbe nor Cowper
has the imaginative lift of Wordsworth,

> " The light that never was on sea or land
> The consecration and the poet's dream."

In a note on a couplet in one of his earliest
poems, descriptive of an oak tree standing dark
against the sunset, Wordsworth says: " I recollect
distinctly the very spot where this struck me.

The moment was important in my poetical history, for I date from it my consciousness of the infinite variety of natural appearances which had been unnoticed by the poets of any age or country, and I made a resolution to supply, in some degree, the deficiency." In later life he is said to have been impatient of any thing spoken or written by another about mountains, conceiving himself to have a monopoly of " the power of hills." But Wordsworth did not stop with natural description. Matthew Arnold has said that the office of modern poetry is the " moral interpretation of Nature." Such, at any rate, was Wordsworth's office. To him Nature was alive and divine. He felt, under the veil of phenomena,

> " A presence that disturbs me with the joy
> Of elevated thought: a sense sublime
> Of something far more deeply interfused."

He approached, if he did not actually reach, the view of Pantheism, which identifies God with Nature; and the mysticism of the Idealists, who identify Nature with the soul of man. This tendency was not inspired in Wordsworth by German philosophy. He was no metaphysician. In his rambles with Coleridge about Nether Stowey and Alfoxden, when both were young, they had, indeed, discussed Spinoza. And in the autumn of 1798, after the publication of the *Lyrical Ballads*, the two friends went together to Germany, where Wordsworth spent half a year. But the literature and philosophy of Germany made little direct impression upon Wordsworth. He disliked Goethe, and he quoted with approval the saying of the poet Klopstock, whom he met at Hamburg, that he placed the romanticist Bürger above both Goethe and Schiller.

It was through Samuel Taylor Coleridge (1772-1834), who was pre-eminently the *thinker* among the literary men of his generation, that the new German thought found its way into England. During the fourteen months which he spent in Germany—chiefly at Ratzburg and Göttingen—he had familiarized himself with the transcendental philosophy of Immanuel Kant and of his continuators, Fichte and Schelling, as well as with the general literature of Germany. On his return to England, he published, in 1800, a free translation of Schiller's *Wallenstein*, and through his writings, and more especially through his conversations, he became the conductor by which German philosophic ideas reached the English literary class.

Coleridge described himself as being from boyhood a book-worm and a day-dreamer. He remained through life an omnivorous, though unsystematic, reader. He was helpless in practical affairs, and his native indolence and procrastination were increased by his indulgence in the opium habit. On his return to England, in 1800, he went to reside at Keswick, in the Lake Country, with his brother-in-law, Southey, whose industry supported both families. During his last nineteen years Coleridge found an asylum under the roof of Mr. James Gilman, of Highgate, near London, whither many of the best young men in England were accustomed to resort to listen to Coleridge's wonderful talk. Talk, indeed, was the medium through which he mainly influenced his generation. It cost him an effort to put his thoughts on paper. His *Table Talk*—crowded with pregnant paragraphs—was taken down from his lips by his nephew, Henry Coleridge. His criticisms of Shakspere are nothing but notes, made here and there, from a course of lectures delivered before the Royal Institute, and never fully written out. Though only hints and suggestions, they are, perhaps, the most penetrative and helpful Shaksperian criticism in English. He was always forming projects and abandoning them. He projected a great work on Christian philosophy, which was to have been his *magnum opus*, but he never wrote it. He projected an epic poem on the fall of Jerusalem. " I schemed it at twenty-five," he said, " but, alas! *venturum expectat.*" What bade fair to be his best poem, *Christabel*, is a fragment. Another strangely beautiful poem, *Kubla Khan*—which came to him, he said, in sleep—is even more fragmentary. And the most important of his prose remains, his *Biographia Literaria*, 1817, a history of his own opinions, breaks off abruptly.

It was in his suggestiveness that Coleridge's great service to posterity resided. He was what J. S. Mill called a " seminal mind," and his thought had that power of stimulating thought in others, which is the mark and the privilege of original genius.   Many a man has owed to some sentence of Coleridge's, if not the awakening in himself of a new intellectual life, at least the starting of fruitful trains of reflection which have modified his whole view of certain great subjects.   On every thing that he left is set the stamp of high mental authority.   He was not, perhaps, primarily, he certainly was not exclusively, a poet.   In theology, in philosophy, in political thought, and literary criticism, he set currents flowing which are flowing yet. The terminology of criticism, for example, is in his debt for many of those convenient distinctions— such as that between genius and talent, between wit and humor, between fancy and imagination— which are familiar enough now, but which he first introduced, or enforced.   His definitions and apothegms we meet every-where.   Such are, for example, the sayings: "Every man is born an Aristotelian or a Platonist."   "Prose is words in their best order; poetry, the best words in the best order."   And among the bits of subtle interpretation, that abound in his writings, may be mentioned his estimate of Wordsworth, in the *Biographia Literaria*, and his sketch of Hamlet's character— one with which he was personally in strong sympathy—in the *Lectures on Shakspere*.   ·

The Broad-Church party, in the English Church, among whose most eminent exponents have been Frederic Robertson, Arnold of Rugby, F. D.

Maurice, Charles Kingsley, and the late Dean
Stanley, traces its intellectual origin to Coleridge's *Aids to Reflection ;* to his writings and
conversations in general, and particularly to his
ideal of a national Clerisy, as set forth in his
essay on *Church and State.* In politics, as in religion, Coleridge's conservatism represents the reaction against the destructive spirit of the eighteenth century and the French revolution. To
this root-and-branch democracy he opposed the
view, that every old belief, or institution, such as
the throne or the Church, had served some need,
and had a rational idea at the bottom of it, to
which it might be again recalled, and made once
more a benefit to society, instead of a curse and an
anachronism.

As a poet, Coleridge has a sure, though slender,
hold upon immortal fame. No English poet has
"sung so wildly well " as the singer of *Christabel* and
the *Ancient Mariner.* The former of these is, in form,
a romance in a variety of meters, and in substance,
a tale of supernatural possession, by which a lovely
and innocent maiden is brought under the control
of a witch. Though unfinished and obscure in in-
tention, it haunts the imagination with a mystic
power. Byron had seen *Christabel* in MS., and
urged Coleridge to publish it. He hated all the
" Lakers," but when, on parting from Lady Byron,
he wrote his song,

> " Fare thee well, and if forever,
> Still forever fare thee well,"

he prefixed to it the noble lines from Coleridge's poem, beginning

"Alas ! they had been friends in youth."

In that weird ballad, the *Ancient Mariner*, the supernatural is handled with even greater subtlety than in *Christabel*. The reader is led to feel that amid the loneliness of the tropic sea, the line between the earthly and the unearthly vanishes, and the poet leaves him to discover for himself whether the spectral shapes that the mariner saw were merely the visions of the calenture, or a glimpse of the world of spirits. Coleridge is one of our most perfect metrists. The poet Swinburne—than whom there can be no higher authority on this point (though he is rather given to exaggeration)—pronounces *Kubla Khan*, "for absolute melody and splendor, the first poem in the language."

Robert Southey, the third member of this group, was a diligent worker and one of the most voluminous of English writers. As a poet, he was lacking in inspiration, and his big Oriental epics, *Thalaba*, 1801, and the *Curse of Kehama*, 1810, are little better than wax-work. Of his numerous works in prose, the *Life of Nelson* is, perhaps, the best, and is an excellent biography.

Several other authors were more or less closely associated with the Lake Poets by residence or social affiliation. John Wilson, the editor of *Blackwood's*, lived for some time, when a young man, at Elleray, on the banks of Windermere. He was an athletic man of out-door habits, an enthusiastic sportsman, and a lover of natural scenery. His admiration of Wordsworth was thought to have led him to imitation of the latter, in his *Isle of Palms*, 1812, and his other poetry.

One of Wilson's companions, in his mountain walks, was Thomas De Quincey, who had been led by his reverence for Wordsworth and Coleridge to take up his residence, in 1808, at Grasmere, where he occupied for many years the cottage from which Wordsworth had removed to Allan Bank. De Quincey was a shy, bookish little man, of erratic, nocturnal habits, who impresses one, personally, as a child of genius, with a child's helplessness and a child's sharp observation. He was, above all things, a magazinist. All his writings, with one exception, appeared first in the shape of contributions to periodicals; and his essays, literary criticisms, and miscellaneous papers are exceedingly rich and varied. The most famous of them was his *Confessions of an English Opium Eater*, published as a serial in the *London Magazine*, in 1821. He had begun to take opium, as a cure for the toothache, when a student at Oxford, where he resided from 1803 to 1808. By 1816 he had risen to eight thousand drops of laudanum a day. For several years after this he experienced the acutest misery, and his will suffered an entire paralysis. In 1821 he succeeded in reducing his dose to a comparatively small allowance, and in shaking off his torpor so as to become capable of literary work.

The most impressive effect of the opium habit was seen in his dreams, in the unnatural expansion of space and time, and the infinite repetition of the same objects. His sleep was filled with dim, vast images ; measureless cavalcades deploying to the sound of orchestral music; an endless succession of vaulted halls, with staircases climbing to heaven, up which toiled eternally the same solitary figure. "Then came sudden alarms, hurrying to and fro; trepidations of innumerable fugitives; darkness and light; tempest and human faces." Many of De Quincey's papers were autobiographical, but there is always something baffling in these reminiscences. In the interminable wanderings of his pen—for which, perhaps, opium was responsible—he appears to lose all trace of facts or of any continuous story. Every actual experience of his life seems to have been taken up into a realm of dream, and there distorted till the reader sees not the real figures, but the enormous, grotesque shadows of them, executing wild dances on a screen. An instance of this process is described by himself in his *Vision of Sudden Death*. But his unworldliness and faculty of vision-seeing were not inconsistent with the keenness of judgment and the justness and delicacy of perception displayed in his *Biographical Sketches* of Wordsworth, Coleridge, and other contemporaries: in his critical papers on *Pope, Milton, Lessing, Homer and the Homeridæ*: his essay on *Style ;* and his *Brief Appraisal of the Greek Literature*. His curious scholarship is seen in his articles on the *Toilet of a He-*

brew Lady, and the *Casuistry of Roman Meals ;* his
ironical and somewhat elaborate humor in his essay
on *Murder Considered as One of the Fine Arts.* Of
his narrative pieces the most remarkable is his *Revolt of the Tartars,* describing the flight of a Kal-
muck tribe of six hundred thousand souls from
Russia to the Chinese frontier: a great hegira or
anabasis, which extended for four thousand miles
over desert steppes infested with foes; occupied six
months' time, and left nearly half of the tribe dead
upon the way. The subject was suited to De Quincey's imagination. It was like one of his own opium visions, and he handled it with a dignity and
force which make the history not altogether unworthy of comparison with Thucydides's great chapter
on the Sicilian Expedition.

An intimate friend of Southey was Walter Savage Landor, a man of kingly nature, of a leonine
presence, with a most stormy and unreasonable
temper, and yet with the courtliest graces of manner and with—said Emerson—a "wonderful brain,
despotic, violent, and inexhaustible." He inherited wealth, and lived a great part of his life at Florence, where he died, in 1864, in his ninetieth year.
Dickens, who knew him at Bath, in the latter part
of his life, made a kindly caricature of him as Lawrence Boythom, in *Bleak House,* whose "combination of superficial ferocity and inherent tenderness,"
testifies Henry Crabb Robinson, in his *Diary,* was
true to the life. Landor is the most purely classical of English writers. Not merely his themes,

but his whole way of thinking was pagan and antique. He composed, indifferently, in English or
Latin, preferring the latter, if any thing, in obedience to his instinct for compression and exclusive-
ness. Thus portions of his narrative poem, *Gebir*,
1798, were written originally in Latin, and he added
a Latin version, *Gebirius*, to the English edition.
In like manner his *Hellenics*, 1847, were mainly
translations from his Latin *Idyllia Heroica*, written
years before. The Hellenic clearness and repose
which were absent from his life, Landor sought in his
art. His poems, in their restraint, their objectivity,
their aloofness from modern feeling, have something
chill and artificial. The verse of poets like Byron
and Wordsworth is alive ; the blood runs in it. But
Landor's polished, clean-cut *intaglios* have been
well described as "written in marble." He was
a master of fine and solid prose. His *Pericles
and Aspasia* consists of a series of letters passing
between the great Athenian demagogue, the hetaira,
Aspasia, her friend, Cleone of Miletus, Anaxagorus,
the philosopher, and Pericles's nephew, Alcibiades.
In this masterpiece the intellectual life of Athens,
at its period of highest refinement, is brought before
the reader with singular vividness, and he is made
to breathe an atmosphere of high-bred grace, delicate wit, and thoughtful sentiment, expressed in
English "of Attic choice." The *Imaginary Conversations*, 1824–1846, were Platonic dialogues between a great variety of historical characters ; between, for example, Dante and Beatrice, Washing-

ton and Franklin, Queen Elisabeth and Cecil,
Xenophon and Cyrus the Younger, Bonaparte and
the President of the Senate. Landor's writings
have never been popular; they address an aristoc-
racy of scholars; and Byron—whom Landor disliked and considered vulgar — sneered at the
latter as a writer who "cultivated much private
renown in the shape of Latin verses." He said of
himself that he "never contended with a contemporary, but walked alone on the far eastern uplands, meditating and remembering."

A schoolmate of Coleridge, at Christ's Hospital,
and his friend and correspondent through life, was
Charles Lamb, one of the most charming of English essayists. He was an old bachelor, who lived
alone with his sister Mary a lovable and intellectual woman, but subject to recurring attacks of madness. Lamb was "a notched and cropped scrivener, a votary of the desk," a clerk, that is, in the
employ of the East India Company. He was of
antiquarian tastes, an ardent play-goer, a lover of
whist and of the London streets; and these tastes
are reflected in his *Essays of Elia*, contributed to
the *London Magazine* and reprinted in book form
in 1823. From his mousing among the Elisabethan dramatists and such old humorists as Burton
and Fuller, his own style imbibed a peculiar quaintness and pungency. His *Specimens of English
Dramatic Poets*, 1808, is admirable for its critical
insight. In 1802 he paid a visit to Coleridge at
Keswick, in the Lake Country; but he felt or af-

fected a whimsical horror of the mountains, and said, "Fleet Street and the Strand are better places to live in." Among the best of his essays are *Dream Children, Poor Relations, The Artificial Comedy of the Last Century, Old China, Roast Pig, A Defense of Chimney-sweeps, A Complaint of the Decay of Beggars in the Metropolis,* and *The Old Benchers of the Inner Temple.*

The romantic movement, preluded by Gray, Collins, Chatterton, Macpherson, and others, culminated in Walter Scott (1771–1832). His passion for the medieval was first excited by reading Percy's *Reliques,* when he was a boy; and in one of his school themes he maintained that Ariosto was a greater poet than Homer. He began early to collect manuscript ballads, suits of armor, pieces of old plate, border-horns, and similar relics. He learned Italian in order to read the romancers— Ariosto, Tasso, Pulei, and Boiardo, preferring them to Dante. He studied Gothic architecture, heraldry, and the art of fortification, and made drawings of famous ruins and battle-fields. In particular he read eagerly every thing that he could lay hands on relating to the history, legends, and antiquities of the Scottish border—the vale of Tweed, Teviotdale, Ettrick Forest, and the Yarrow, of all which land he became the laureate, as Burns had been of Ayrshire and the "West Country." Scott, like Wordsworth, was an out-door poet. He spent much time in the saddle, and was fond of horses, dogs, hunting, and salmon-fishing. He had a keen

eye for the beauties of natural scenery, though
"more especially," he admits, "when combined with
ancient ruins or remains of our forefathers' piety or
splendor." He had the historic imagination, and,
in creating the historical novel, he was the first to
throw a poetic glamour over European annals. In
1803 Wordsworth visited Scott at Lasswade, near
Edinburgh ; and Scott afterward returned the visit at Grasmere. Wordsworth noted that his guest
was "full of anecdote and averse from disquisition." The Englishman was a moralist and much
given to "disquisition," while the Scotchman was,
above all things, a *raconteur*, and, perhaps, on the
whole, the foremost of British story-tellers. Scott's
Toryism, too, was of a different stripe from Wordsworth's, being rather the result of sentiment and
imagination than of philosophy and reflection. His
mind struck deep root in the past ; his local at-
tachments and family pride were intense. Abbots-
ford was his darling, and the expenses of this do-
main and of the baronial hospitality which he there
extended to all comers were among the causes of
his bankruptcy. The enormous toil which he ex-
acted of himself, to pay off the debt of £117,000,
contracted by the failure of his publishers, cost
him his life. It is said that he was more grat-
ified when the Prince Regent created him a bar-
onet, in 1820, than by all the public recognition
that he acquired as the author of the Waverley
Novels.

Scott was attracted by the romantic side of Ger-
16

man literature.   His first published poem was a
translation made in 1796 from Bürger's wild ballad, *Leonora*.   He followed this up with versions
of the same poet's *Wilde Jäger*, of Goethe's violent drama of feudal life, *Götz Von Berlichingen*, and
with other translations from the German, of a
similar class.   On his horseback trips through the
border, where he studied the primitive manners of
the Liddlesdale people, and took down old ballads
from the recitation of ancient dames and cottagers,
he amassed the materials for his *Minstrelsy of the
Scottish Border*, 1802.   But the first of his original
poems was the *Lay of the Last Minstrel*, published
in 1805, and followed, in quick succession, by
Marmion, the *Lady of the Lake*, *Rokeby*, the *Lord
of the Isles*, and a volume of ballads and lyrical
pieces, all issued during the years 1806–1814.   The
popularity won by this series of metrical romances
was immediate and wide-spread.   Nothing so fresh,
or so brilliant, had appeared in English poetry for
nearly two centuries.   The reader was hurried
along through scenes of rapid action, whose effect
was heightened by wild landscapes and picturesque manners.   The pleasure was a passive one.
There was no deep thinking to perplex, no subtler
beauties to pause upon; the feelings were stirred
pleasantly, but not deeply; the effect was on the
surface.   The spell employed was novelty—or, at
most, wonder—and the chief emotion aroused was
breathless interest in the progress of the story.
Carlyle said that Scott's genius was *in extenso*,

rather than *in intenso*, and that its great praise was
its healthiness. This is true of his verse, but not
altogether so of his prose, which exhibits deeper
qualities. Some of Scott's most perfect poems,
too, are his shorter ballads, like *Jock o' Hazeldean*,
and *Proud Maisie is in the Wood*, which have a
greater intensity and compression than his metrical tales.

From 1814 to 1831 Scott wrote and published
the *Waverley* novels, some thirty in number; if we
consider the amount of work done, the speed with
which it was done, and the general average of excellence maintained, perhaps the most marvelous
literary feat on record. The series was issued
anonymously, and takes its name from the first ,
number, *Waverley, or 'Tis Sixty Years Since*. This
was founded upon the rising of the clans, in 1745,
in support of the Young Pretender, Charles Edward
Stuart, and it revealed to the English public that
almost foreign country which lay just across their
threshold, the Scottish Highlands. The *Waverley*
novels remain, as a whole, unequaled as historical
fiction, although, here and there a single novel,
like George Eliot's *Romola*, or Thackeray's *Henry
Esmond*, or Kingsley's *Hypatia*, may have attained
a place beside the best of them. They were a
novelty when they appeared. English prose fiction
had somewhat declined since the time of Fielding
and Goldsmith. There were truthful, though
rather tame, delineations of provincial life, like
Jane Austen's *Sense and Sensibility*, 1811, and

Pride and Prejudice, 1813; or Maria Edgeworth's *Popular Tales*, 1804. On the other hand, there were Gothic romances, like the *Monk* of Matthew Gregory Lewis, to whose *Tales of Wonder* some of Scott's translations from the German had been contributed; or like Anne Radcliffe's *Mysteries of Udolpho.* The great original of this school of fiction was Horace Walpole's *Castle of Otranto*, 1765, an absurd tale of secret trap-doors, subterranean vaults, apparitions of monstrous mailed figures and colossal helmets, pictures that descend from their frames, and hollow voices that proclaim the ruin of ancient families.

Scott used the machinery of romance, but he was not merely a romancer, or a historical novelist even, and it is not, as Carlyle implies, the buff-belts and jerkins which principally interest us in his heroes. *Ivanhoe* and *Kenilworth* and the *Talisman* are, indeed, romances pure and simple, and very good romances at that. But, in novels such as *Rob Roy*, the *Antiquary*, the *Heart of Midlothian*, and the *Bride of Lammermoor*, Scott drew from contemporary life, and from his intimate knowledge of Scotch character. The story is there, with its entanglement of plot and its exciting adventures, but there are also, as truly as in Shakspere, though not in the same degree, the observation of life, the knowledge of men, the power of dramatic creation. No writer awakens in his readers a warmer personal affection than Walter Scott, the brave, honest, kindly gentleman, the noblest

figure among the literary men of his generation.

Another Scotch poet was Thomas Campbell,
whose *Pleasures of Hope*, 1799, was written in
Pope's couplet, and in the stilted diction of the
eighteenth century. *Gertrude of Wyoming*, 1809,
a long narrative poem in Spenserian stanza, is
untrue to the scenery and life of Pennsylvania,
where its scene is laid. But Campbell turned
his rhetorical manner and his clanking, martial
verse to fine advantage in such pieces as *Hohen-
linden*, *Ye Mariners of England*, and the *Battle
of the Baltic*. These have the true lyric, fire, and
rank among the best English war-songs.

When Scott was asked why he had left off writing poetry, he answered, " Byron *bet* me." George
Gordon Byron (1788–1824) was a young man of
twenty-four, when, on his return from a two years'
sauntering through Portugal, Spain, Albania,
Greece, and the Levant, he published, in the first
two cantos of *Childe Harold*, 1812, a sort of poetic
itinerary of his experiences and impressions. The
poem took, rather to its author's surprise, who said
that he woke one morning and found himself
famous. *Childe Harold* opened a new field to
poetry, the romance of travel, the picturesque
aspects of foreign scenery, manners, and costumes.
It is instructive of the difference between the two
ages, in poetic sensibility to such things, to compare Byron's glowing imagery with Addison's tame
Letter from Italy, written a century before. *Childe*

Harold was followed by a series of metrical tales, the *Giaour*, the *Bride of Abydos*, the *Corsair*, *Lara*, the *Siege of Corinth*, *Parasina*, and the *Prisoner of Chillon*, all written in the years 1813–1816. These poems at once took the place of Scott's in popular interest, dazzling a public that had begun to weary of chivalry romances, with pictures of Eastern life, with incidents as exciting as Scott's, descriptions as highly colored, and a much greater intensity of passion. So far as they depended for this interest upon the novelty of their accessories, the effect was a temporary one. Seraglios, divans, bulbuls, Gulistans, Zuleikas, and other Oriental properties, deluged English poetry for a time, and then subsided; even as the tide of moss-troopers, sorcerers, hermits, and feudal castles had already had its rise and fall.

But there was a deeper reason for the impression made by Byron's poetry upon his contemporaries. He laid his finger right on the sore spot in modern life. He had the disease with which the time was sick, the world-weariness, the desperation which proceeded from " passion incapable of being converted into action." We find this tone in much of the literature which followed the failure of the French Revolution and the Napoleonic wars. From the irritations of that period, the disappointment of high hopes for the future of the race, the growing religious disbelief, and the revolt of democracy and free thought against conservative reaction, sprang what Southey called the "Satanic school," which spoke its loudest word in Byron. Titanic is the better word, for the rebellion was not against God, but Jupiter, that is, against the State, Church, and society of Byron's day; against George III., the Tory cabinet of Lord Castlereigh, the Duke of Wellington, the bench of Bishops, London gossip, the British Constitution, and British cant. In these poems of Byron, and in his dramatic experiments, *Manfred* and *Cain*, there is a single figure—the figure of Byron under various masks—and one pervading mood, a restless and sardonic gloom, a weariness of life, a love of solitude, and a melancholy exaltation in the presence of the wilderness and the sea. Byron's hero is always represented as a man originally noble, whom some great wrong, by others, or some mysterious crime of his own, has blasted and embittered, and who carries about the world a seared heart and a somber brow. Harold—who may stand as a type of all his heroes—has run " through sin's labyrinth " and feeling the "fullness of satiety," is drawn abroad to roam, " the wandering exile of his own dark mind." The loss of a capacity for pure, unjaded emotion is the constant burden of Byron's lament.

> " No more, no more, O never more on me
> The freshness of the heart shall fall like dew."

and again,

> " O could I feel as I have felt—or be what I have been,
> Or weep as I could once have wept, o'er many a vanished
> scene ;

As springs in deserts found seem sweet, all brackish tho' they
    be,
So, midst the withered waste of life, those tears would flow
    to me."

This mood was sincere in Byron ; but by cultiva-
ting it, and posing too long in one attitude, he became self-conscious and theatrical, and much of
his serious poetry has a false ring. His example
infected the minor poetry of the time, and it was
quite natural that Thackeray—who represented a
generation that had a very different ideal of the heroic—should be provoked into describing Byron as
"a big, sulky dandy."

Byron was well fitted by birth and temperament
to be the spokesman of this fierce discontent. He
inherited from his mother a haughty and violent
temper, and profligate tendencies from his father.
He was through life a spoiled child, whose main
characteristic was willfulness. He liked to shock
people by exaggerating his wickedness, or by per-
versely maintaining the wrong side of a dispute.
But he had traits of bravery and generosity. Wom-
en loved him, and he made strong friends. There
was a careless charm about him which fascinated
natures as unlike each other as Shelley and Scott.
By the death of the fifth Lord Byron without issue,
Byron came into a title and estates at the age of
ten. Though a liberal in politics he had aristo-
cratic feelings, and was vain of his rank as he was
of his beauty. He was educated at Harrow and at
Trinity College, Cambridge, where he was idle and

dissipated, but did a great deal of miscellaneous reading. He took some of his Cambridge set— Hobhouse, Matthews, and others — to Newstead Abbey, his ancestral seat, where they filled the ancient cloisters with eccentric orgies. Byron was strikingly handsome. His face had a spiritual paleness and a classic regularity, and his dark hair curled closely to his head. A deformity in one of his feet was a mortification to him, though it did not greatly impair his activity, and he prided himself upon his powers as a swimmer.

In 1815, when at the height of his literary and social *éclat* in London, he married. In February of the following year he was separated from Lady Byron, and left England forever, pursued by the execrations of outraged respectability. In this chorus of abuse there was mingled a share of cant ; but Byron got, on the whole, what he deserved. From Switzerland, where he spent a summer by Lake Leman, with the Shelleys ; from Venice, Ravenna, Pisa, and Rome, scandalous reports of his intrigues and his wild debaucheries were wafted back to England, and with these came poem after poem, full of burning genius, pride, scorn, and anguish, and all hurling defiance at English public opinion. The third and fourth cantos of *Childe Harold*, 1816–1818, were a great advance upon the first two, and contain the best of Byron's serious poetry. He has written his name all over the continent of Europe, and on a hundred memorable spots has made the scenery his own. On the field of Waterloo, on "the castled crag of Drachenfels," "by the blue rushing of the arrowy Rhone," in Venice, on the Bridge of Sighs, in the Coliseum at Rome, and among the "Isles of Greece," the tourist is compelled to see with Byron's eyes and under the associations of his pilgrimage. In his later poems, such as *Beppo*, 1818, and *Don Juan*, 1819–1823, he passed into his second manner, a mocking cynicism gaining ground upon the somewhat stagy gloom of his early poetry—Mephistophiles gradually elbowing out Satan. *Don Juan*, though morally the worst, is intellectually the most vital and representative of Byron's poems. It takes up into itself most fully the life of the time ; exhibits most thoroughly the characteristic alternations of Byron's moods and the prodigal resources of wit, passion, and understanding, which— rather than imagination—were his prominent qualities as a poet. The hero, a graceless, amorous, stripling, goes wandering from Spain to the Greek islands and Constantinople, thence to St. Petersburg, and finally to England. Every-where his seductions are successful, and Byron uses him as a means of exposing the weakness of the human heart and the rottenness of society in all countries. In 1823, breaking away from his life of selfish indulgence in Italy, Byron threw himself into the cause of Grecian liberty, which he had sung so gloriously in the *Isles of Greece*. He died at Missolonghi, in the following year, of a fever contracted by exposure and overwork.

Byron was a great poet but not a great literary

artist. He wrote negligently and with the ease of assured strength, his mind gathering heat as it moved, and pouring itself forth in reckless profusion. His work is diffuse and imperfect ; much of it is melodrama or speech-making rather than true poetry. But, on the other hand, much, very much of it, is unexcelled as the direct, strong, sincere utterance of personal feeling. Such is the quality of his best lyrics, like *When We Two Parted*, the *Elegy on Thyrza*, *Stanzas to Augusta*, *She Walks in Beauty*, and of innumerable passages, lyrical and descriptive, in his longer poems. He had not the wisdom of Wordsworth, nor the rich and subtle imagination of Coleridge, Shelley, and Keats when they were at their best. But he had greater body and motive force than any of them. He is the strongest personality among English poets since Milton, though his strength was wasted by want of restraint and self-culture. In Milton the passion was there, but it was held in check by the will and the artistic conscience, made subordinate to good ends, ripened by long reflection, and finally uttered in forms of perfect and harmonious beauty. Byron's love of Nature was quite different in kind from Wordsworth's. Of all English poets he has sung most lyrically of that national theme, the sea, as witness among many other passages, the famous apostrophe to the ocean, which closes *Childe Harold*, and the opening of the third canto in the same poem,

"Once more upon the waters," etc.

He had a passion for night and storm, because
they made him forget himself.

> " Most glorious night !
> Thou wert not sent for slumber !   Let me be
> A sharer in thy fierce and far delight,
> A portion of the tempest and of thee ! "

Byron's literary executor and biographer was the
Irish poet, Thomas Moore, a born song-writer,
whose *Irish Melodies*, set to old native airs, are,
like Burns's, genuine, spontaneous, singing, and run
naturally to music.   Songs such as the *Meeting of
the Waters*, *The Harp of Tara*, *Those Evening Bells*,
the *Light of Other Days*, *Araby's Daughter*, and the
Last Rose of Summer were, and still are, popular
favorites.   Moore's Oriental romance, *Lalla Rookh*,
1817, is overladen with ornament and with a sugary
sentiment that clogs the palate.   He had the quick
Irish wit, sensibility rather than passion, and fancy
rather than imagination.

Byron's friend, Percy Bysshe Shelley (1792–
1822), was also in fiery revolt against all conventions and institutions, though his revolt proceeded
not, as in Byron's case, from the turbulence of passions which brooked no restraint, but rather from
an intellectual impatience of any kind of control.
He was not, like Byron, a sensual man, but temper-
ate and chaste.   He was, indeed, in his life and in
his poetry, as nearly a disembodied spirit as a human creature can be.   The German poet, Heine,
said that liberty was the religion of this century,

and of this religion Shelley was a worshiper. His rebellion against authority began early. He refused to fag at Eton, and was expelled from Oxford for publishing a tract on the *Necessity of Atheism*. At nineteen, he ran away with Harriet Westbrook, and was married to her in Scotland. Three years later he deserted her for Mary Godwin, with whom he eloped to Switzerland. Two years after this his first wife drowned herself in the Serpentine, and Shelley was then formally wedded to Mary Godwin. All this is rather startling, in the bare statement of it, yet it is not inconsistent with the many testimonies that exist, to Shelley's singular purity and beauty of character, testimonies borne out by the evidence of his own writings. Impulse with him took the place of conscience. Moral law, accompanied by the sanction of power, and imposed by outside authority, he rejected as a form of tyranny. His nature lacked robustness and ballast. Byron, who was at bottom intensely practical, said that Shelley's philosophy was too spiritual and romantic. Hazlitt, himself a Radical, wrote of Shelley: " He has a fire in his eye, a fever in his blood, a maggot in his brain, a hectic flutter in his speech, which mark out the philosophic fanatic. He is sanguine complexioned and shrill voiced." It was, perhaps, with some recollection of this last-mentioned trait of Shelley the man, that Carlyle wrote of Shelley the poet, that " the sound of him was shrieky," and that he had " filled the earth with an inarticulate wailing."

His career as a poet began characteristically enough, with the publication, while at Oxford, of a volume of political rimes, entitled *Margaret Nicholson's Remains*, Margaret Nicholson being the crazy woman who tried to stab George III. His boyish poem, *Queen Mab*, was published in 1813; *Alastor* in 1816, and the *Revolt of Islam*—his longest —in 1818, all before he was twenty-one. These were filled with splendid, though unsubstantial, imagery, but they were abstract in subject, and had the faults of incoherence and formlessness which make Shelley's longer poems wearisome and confusing. They sought to embody his social creed of Perfectionism, as well as a certain vague Pantheistic system of belief in a spirit of love in nature and man, whose presence is a constant source of obscurity in Shelley's verse. In 1818 he went to Italy, where the last four years of his life were passed, and where, under the influences of Italian art and poetry, his writing became deeper and stronger. He was fond of yachting, and spent much of his time upon the Mediterranean. In the summer of 1822, his boat was swamped in a squall off the Gulf of Spezzia, and Shelley's drowned body was washed ashore, and burned in the presence of Byron and Leigh Hunt The ashes were entombed in the Protestant cemetery at Rome, with the epitaph, *Cor cordium.*

Shelley's best and maturest work, nearly all of which was done in Italy, includes his tragedy, *The Cenci*, 1819, and his lyrical drama, *Prometheus Un-*

bound, 1821. The first of these has a unity and a definiteness of contour unusual with Shelley, and is, with the exception of some of Robert Browning's, the best English tragedy since Otway. Prometheus represented to Shelley's mind the human spirit fighting against divine oppression, and in his portrayal of this figure, he kept in mind not only the *Prometheus* of Æschylus, but the Satan of *Paradise Lost.* Indeed, in this poem, Shelley came nearer to the sublime than any English poet since Milton. Yet it is in lyrical, rather than in dramatic, quality that *Prometheus Unbound* is great. If Shelley be not, as his latest editor, Mr. Forman, claims him to be, the foremost of English lyrical poets, he is at least the most lyrical of them. He had, in a supreme degree, the "lyric cry." His vibrant nature trembled to every breath of emotion, and his nerves craved ever newer shocks; to pant, to quiver, to thrill, to grow faint in the spasm of intense sensation. The feminine cast observable in Shelley's portrait is borne out by this tremulous sensibility in his verse. It is curious how often he uses the metaphor of wings: of the winged spirit, soaring, like his skylark, till lost in music, rapture, light, and then falling back to earth. Three successive moods — longing, ecstasy, and the revulsion of despair—are expressed in many of his lyrics; as in the *Hymn to the Spirit of Nature*, in *Prometheus*, in the ode *To a Skylark*, and in the *Lines to an Indian Air* — Edgar Poe's favorite. His passionate desire to lose himself in Nature, to become one with that spirit of love and beauty in the universe, which was to him in place of God, is expressed in the *Ode to the West Wind*, his most perfect poem:

> " Make me thy lyre, even as the forest is ;
>   What if my leaves are falling like its own !
> The tumult of thy mighty harmonies
>   Will take from both a deep autumnal tone.
> Sweet, though in sadness, be thou, Spirit fierce,
>   My spirit ! be thou me, impetuous one !"

In the lyrical pieces already mentioned, together with *Adonais*, the lines *Written in the Euganean Hills, Epipsychidion, Stanzas Written in Dejection near Naples, A Dream of the Unknown*, and many others, Shelley's lyrical genius reaches a rarer loveliness and a more faultless art than Byron's ever attained, though it lacks the directness and momentum of Byron.

In Shelley's longer poems, intoxicated with the music of his own singing, he abandons himself wholly to the guidance of his imagination, and the verse seems to go on of itself, like the enchanted boat in *Alastor*, with no one at the helm. Vision succeeds vision in glorious but bewildering profusion; ideal landscapes and cities of cloud " pinnacled dim in the intense inane." These poems are like the water-falls in the Yosemite, which, tumbling from a height of several thousand feet, are shattered into foam by the air, and waved about over the valley. Very beautiful is this descending spray, and the rainbow dwells in its bosom; but there is no longer any stream, nothing but an irridescent mist. The word *etherial* best expresses the quality of Shelley's genius. His poetry is full of atmospheric effects; of the tricks which light plays with the fluid elements of water and air; of stars, clouds, rain, dew, mist, frost, wind, the foam of seas, the phases of the moon, the green shadows of waves, the shapes of flames, the " golden lightning of the setting sun." Nature, in Shelley, wants homeliness and relief. While poets like Wordsworth and Burns let in an ideal light upon the rough fields of earth, Shelley escapes into a " moonlight-colored " realm of shadows and dreams, among whose abstractions the heart turns cold. One bit of Wordsworth's mountain turf is worth them all.

By the death of John Keats (1796–1821), whose elegy Shelley sang in *Adonais*, English poetry suffered an irreparable loss. His *Endymion*, 1818, though disfigured by mawkishness and by some affectations of manner, was rich in promise. Its faults were those of youth, the faults of exuberance and of a tremulous sensibility, which time corrects. *Hyperion*, 1820, promised to be his masterpiece, but he left it unfinished—" a Titanic torso "—because, as he said, " there were too many Miltonic inversions in it." The subject was the displacement, by Phœbus Apollo, of the ancient sun-god, Hyperion, the last of the Titans who retained his dominion. It was a theme of great capabilities, and the poem was begun by Keats,

17

with a strength of conception which leads to the belief that here was once more a really epic genius, had fate suffered it to mature. The fragment, as it stands—"that inlet to severe magnificence"— proves how rapidly Keats's diction was clarifying. He had learned to string up his looser chords. There is nothing maudlin in *Hyperion;* all there is in whole tones and in the grand manner, "as sublime as Æschylus," said Byron, with the grave, antique simplicity, and something of modern sweetness interfused.

Keats's father was a groom in a London livery-stable. The poet was apprenticed at fifteen to a surgeon. At school he had studied Latin, but not Greek. He, who of all English poets had the most purely Hellenic spirit, made acquaintance with Greek literature and art only through the medium of classical dictionaries, translations, and popular mythologies; and later through the marbles and casts in the British Museum. His friend, the artist Haydon, lent him a copy of Chapman's Homer, and the impression that it made upon him he recorded in his sonnet, *On First Looking into Chapman's Homer.* Other poems of the same inspiration are his three sonnets, *To Homer, On Seeing the Elgin Marbles, On a Picture of Leander, Lamia,* and the beautiful *Ode on a Grecian Urn.* But Keats's art was retrospective and eclectic, the blossom of a double root; and "golden-tongued Romance with serene lute" had her part in him, as well as the classics. In his seventeenth year he had read the *Faery Queene*, and from Spenser he went on to a study of Chaucer, Shakspere, and Milton. Then he took up Italian and read Ariosto. The influence of these studies is seen in his poem, *Isabella, or the Pot of Basil*, taken from a story of Boccaccio; in his wild ballad, *La Belle Dame sans Merci;* and in his love tale, the *Eve of Saint Agnes*, with its wealth of medieval adornment. In the *Ode to Autumn*, and *Ode to a Nightingale*, the Hellenic choiceness is found touched with the warmer hues of romance.

There is something deeply tragic in the short story of Keats's life. The seeds of consumption were in him; he felt the stirrings of a potent genius, but knew that he could not wait for it to unfold, but must die

> " Before high-piled books, in charactry
> Hold like rich garners the full-ripened grain."

His disease was aggravated, possibly, by the stupid brutality with which the reviewers had treated *Endymion;* and certainly by the hopeless love which devoured him. "The very thing which I want to live most for," he wrote, "will be a great occasion of my death. If I had any chance of recovery, this passion would kill me." In the autumn of 1820, his disease gaining apace, he went on a sailing vessel to Italy, accompanied by a single friend, a young artist named Severn. The change was of no avail, and he died at Rome a few weeks after, in his twenty-sixth year.

Keats was, above all things, the *artist*, with that love of the beautiful and that instinct for its reproduction which are the artist's divinest gifts. He cared little about the politics and philosophy of his day, and he did not make his poetry the vehicle of ideas. It was sensuous poetry, the poetry of youth and gladness. But if he had lived, and if, with wider knowledge of men and deeper experience of life, he had attained to Wordsworth's spiritual insight and to Byron's power of passion and understanding, he would have become a greater poet than either. For he had a style—a "natural magic"—which only needed the chastening touch of a finer culture to make it superior to any thing in modern English poetry and to force us back to Milton or Shakspere for a comparison. His tombstone, not far from Shelley's, bears the inscription of his own choosing: "Here lies one whose name was writ in water." But it would be within the limits of truth to say that it is written in large characters on most of our contemporary poetry. "Wordsworth," says Lowell, "has influenced most the ideas of succeeding poets; Keats their forms." And he has influenced these out of all proportion to the amount which he left, or to his intellectual range, by virtue of the exquisite quality of his *technique*.

1. Wordsworth's Poems. Chosen and edited by Matthew Arnold. London, 1879.
2. Poetry of Byron. Chosen and arranged by Matthew Arnold. London, 1881.

3. Shelley. Julian and Maddalo, Prometheus Unbound, The Cenci, Lyrical Pieces.

4. Landor. Pericles and Aspasia.

5. Coleridge. Table Talk, Notes on Shakspere, The Ancient Mariner, Christabel, Love, Ode to France, Ode to the Departing Year, Kubla Khan, Hymn before Sunrise in the Vale of Chamouni, Youth and Age, Frost at Midnight.

6. De Quincey. Confessions of an English Opium Eater, Flight of a Tartar Tribe, Biographical Sketches.

7. Scott. Waverley, Heart of Midlothian, Bride of Lammermoor, Rob Roy, Antiquary, Marmion, Lady of the Lake.

8. Keats. Hyperion, Eve of St. Agnes, Lyrical Pieces.

9. Mrs. Oliphant's Literary History of England, 18th–19th Centuries.

CHAPTER VIII.

FROM THE DEATH OF SCOTT TO THE PRESENT TIME.

1832-1886.

THE literature of the past fifty years is too close to our eyes to enable the critic to pronounce a final judgment, or the literary historian to get a true perspective. Many of the principal writers of the time are still living, and many others have been dead but a few years. This concluding chapter, therefore, will be devoted to the consideration of the few who stand forth, incontestably, as the leaders of literary thought, and who seem likely, under all future changes of fashion and taste, to remain representative of their generation. As regards *form*, the most striking fact in the history of the period under review is the immense preponderance in its imaginative literature of prose fiction, of the novel of real life. The novel has become to the solitary reader of to-day what the stage play was to the audiences of Elisabeth's reign, or the periodical essay, like the *Tatlers* and *Spectators*, to the clubs and breakfast-tables of Queen Anne's. And, if its criticism of life is less concentrated and brilliant than the drama gives, it is far

more searching and minute. No period has ever
left in its literary records so complete a picture of
its whole society as the period which is just clos-
ing.   At any other time than the present, the
names of authors like Charlotte Brontë, Charles
Kingsley, and Charles Reade—names which are
here merely mentioned in passing—besides many
others which want of space forbids us even to
mention—would be of capital importance. As it is,
we must limit our review to the three acknowledged
masters of modern English fiction, Charles Dickens
(1812–1870), William Makepeace Thackeray (1811
–1863), and "George Eliot " (Mary Ann Evans,
1819–1880).

It is sometimes helpful to reduce a great writer
to his lowest terms, in order to see what the prevailing bent of his genius is.   This lowest term
may often be found in his early work, before experience of the world has overlaid his original impulse with foreign accretions.   Dickens was much
more than a humorist, Thackeray than a satirist, and
George Eliot than a moralist; but they had their
starting-points respectively in humor, in burlesque,
and in strong ethical and religious feeling.   Dickens began with a broadly comic series of papers,
contributed to the *Old Magazine* and the *Evening
Chronicle*, and reprinted in book form, in 1836, as
Sketches by Boz.   The success of these suggested
to a firm of publishers the preparation of a number of similar sketches of the misadventures of
cockney sportsmen, to accompany plates by the

comic draughtsman, Mr. R. Seymour. This suggestion resulted in the *Pickwick Papers*, published
in monthly installments, in 1836–1837. The series
grew, under Dickens's hand, into a continuous,
though rather loosely strung narrative of the doings of a set of characters, conceived with such
exuberant and novel humor that it took the public
by storm, and raised its author at once to fame.
Pickwick is by no means Dickens's best, but it is his
most characteristic, and most popular, book. At
the time that he wrote these early sketches he was
a reporter for the *Morning Chronicle*. His naturally acute powers of observation had been trained
in this pursuit to the utmost efficiency, and there
always continued to be about his descriptive writing a reportorial and newspaper air. He had the
eye for effect, the sharp fidelity to detail, the
instinct for rapidly seizing upon and exaggerating
the salient point, which are developed by the requirements of modern journalism. Dickens knew
London as no one else has ever known it, and, in
particular, he knew its hideous and grotesque re-
cesses, with the strange developments of human
nature that abide there; slums like Tom-all-Alone's,
in *Bleak House;* the river-side haunts of Roger Rid-
erhood, in *Our Mutual Friend ;* as well as the old
inns, like the "White Hart," and the "dusky pur-
lieus of the law." As a man, his favorité occupation was walking the streets, where, as a child, he
had picked up the most valuable part of his education. His tramps about London—often after night-

fall—sometimes extended to fifteen miles in a day. He knew, too, the shifts of poverty. His father— some traits of whom are preserved in Mr. Micawber—was imprisoned for debt in the Marshalsea prison, where his wife took lodging with him, while Charles, then a boy of ten, was employed at six shillings a week to cover blacking-pots in Warner's blacking warehouse. The hardships and loneliness of this part of his life are told under a thin disguise in Dickens's masterpiece, *David Copperfield*, the most autobiographical of his novels. From these young experiences he gained that insight into the lives of the lower classes, and that sympathy with children and with the poor which shine out in his pathetic sketches of Little Nell, in *The Old Curiosity Shop*, of Paul Dombey, of Poor Jo, in *Bleak House*, of " the Marchioness," and a hundred other figures.

In *Oliver Twist*, contributed, during 1837–1838, to *Bentley's Miscellany*, a monthly magazine of which Dickens was editor, he produced his first regular novel. In this story of the criminal classes the author showed a tragic power which he had not hitherto exhibited. Thenceforward his career was a series of dazzling successes. It is impossible here to particularize his numerous novels, sketches, short tales, and " Christmas Stories "—the latter a fashion which he inaugurated, and which has produced a whole literature in itself. In *Nicholas Nickleby*, 1839; *Master Humphrey's Clock*, 1840; *Martin Chuzzlewit*, 1844; *Dombey and Son*, 1848;

David Copperfield, 1850; and *Bleak House*, 1853, there is no falling off in strength. The last named was, in some respects, and especially in the skillful construction of the plot, his best novel. In some of his latest books, as *Great Expectations*, 1861, and *Our Mutual Friend*, 1865, there are signs of a decline. This showed itself in an unnatural exaggeration of characters and motives, and a painful straining after humorous effects, faults; indeed, from which Dickens was never wholly free. There was a histrionic side to him, which came out in his fondness for private theatricals, in which he exhibited remarkable talent, and in the dramatic action which he introduced into the delightful public readings from his works that he gave before vast audiences all over the United Kingdom, and in his two visits to America. It is not surprising, either, to learn that upon the stage his preference was for melodrama and farce. His own serious writing was always dangerously close to the melodramatic, and his humor to the farcical. There is much false art, bad taste, and even vulgarity in Dickens. He was never quite a gentleman, and never succeeded well in drawing gentlemen or ladies. In the region of low comedy he is easily the most original, the most inexhaustible, the most wonderful of modern humorists. Creations such as Mrs. Nickleby, Mr. Micawber, Sam Weller, Sairy Gamp, take rank with Falstaff and Dogberry; while many others, like Dick Swiveller, Stiggins, Chadband, Mrs. Jellyby, and Julia Mills are almost equally good. In the innumerable swarm of minor characters with which he has enriched our comic literature, there is no indistinctness. Indeed, the objection that has been made to him is that his characters are too distinct—that he puts labels on them ; that they are often mere personifications of a single trick of speech or manner, which becomes tedious and unnatural by repetition; thus, Grandfather Smallweed is always settling down into his cushion, and having to be shaken up; Mr. Jellyby is always sitting with his head against the wall; Peggotty is always bursting her buttons off, etc., etc. As Dickens's humorous characters tend perpetually to run into caricatures and grotesques, so his sentiment, from the same excess, slops over too frequently into " gush," and into a too deliberate and protracted attack upon the pity. A favorite humorous device in his style is a stately and roundabout way of telling a trivial incident, as where, for example, Mr. Roker " muttered certain unpleasant invocations concerning his own eyes, limbs, and circulating fluids;" or where the drunken man who is singing comic songs in the Fleet received from Mr. Smangle " a gentle intimation, through the medium of the water-jug, that his audience were not musically disposed." This manner was original with Dickens, though he may have taken a hint of it from the mock heroic language of *Jonathan Wild;* but as practiced by a thousand imitators, ever since, it has gradually become a burden.

It would not be the whole truth to say that the

difference between the humor of Thackeray and
Dickens is the same as between that of Shakspere
and Ben Jonson. ` Yet it is true that the "humors"
of Ben Jonson have an analogy with the extremer
instances of Dickens's character sketches in this
respect, namely : that they are both studies of the
eccentric, the abnormal, the whimsical, rather than
of the typical and universal—studies of manners,
rather than of whole characters. And it is easily
conceivable that, at no distant day, the oddities of
Captain Cuttle, Deportment Turveydrop, Mark
Tapley, and Newman Noggs will seem as far-fetched
and impossible as those of Captain Otter, Fastidious Brisk, and Sir Amorous La-Foole.

When Dickens was looking about for some one
to take Seymour's place as illustrator of *Pickwick*,
Thackeray applied for the job, but without success. He was then a young man of twenty-five, and
still hesitating between art and literature. He had
begun to draw caricatures with his pencil when a
school-boy at the Charter House, and to scribble
them with his pen when a student at Cambridge,
editing *The Snob*, a weekly under-graduate paper,
and parodying the prize poem *Timbuctoo* of his
contemporary at the university, Alfred Tennyson.
Then he went abroad to study art, passing a season at Weimar, where he met Goethe and filled the
albums of the young Saxon ladies with caricatures; afterward living, in the Latin Quarter at
Paris, a Bohemian existence, studying art in a des-
ultory way, and seeing men and cities; accumu-

lating portfolios full of sketches, but laying up stores of material to be used afterward to greater advantage when he should settle upon his true medium of expression. By 1837, having lost his fortune of £500 a year in speculation and gambling, he began to contribute to *Fraser's*, and thereafter to the *New Monthly*, Cruikshank's *Comic Almanac*, *Punch*, and other periodicals, clever burlesques, art criticisms by "Michael Angelo Titmarsh," *Yellow Plush Papers*, and all manner of skits, satirical character sketches, and humorous tales, like the *Great Hoggarty Diamond* and the *Luck of Barry Lyndon*. Some of these were collected in the *Paris Sketch-Book*, 1840, and the *Irish Sketch-Book*, 1843; but Thackeray was slow in winning recognition, and it was not until the publication of his first great novel, *Vanity Fair*, in monthly parts, during 1846–1848, that he achieved any thing like the general reputation which Dickens had reached at a bound. *Vanity Fair* described itself, on its title-page, as "a novel without a hero." It was also a novel without a plot—in the sense in which *Bleak House* or *Nicholas Nickleby* had a plot—and in that respect it set the fashion for the latest school of realistic fiction, being a transcript of life, without necessary beginning or end. Indeed, one of the pleasantest things to a reader of Thackeray is the way which his characters have of re-appearing, as old acquaintances, in his different books; just as, in real life, people drop out of mind and then turn up again in other years and places. *Vanity Fair* is Thackeray's masterpiece, but it is not the best introduction to his writings. There are no illusions in it, and, to a young reader fresh from Scott's romances or Dickens's sympathetic extravagances, it will seem hard and repellant. But men who, like Thackeray, have seen life and tasted its bitterness and felt its hollowness, know how to prize it. Thackeray does not merely expose the cant, the emptiness, the self-seeking, the false pretenses, flunkeyism, and snobbery—the " mean admiration of mean things "—in the great world of London society : his keen, unsparing vision detects the base alloy in the purest natures. There are no " heroes " in his books, no perfect characters. Even his good women, such as Helen and Laura Pendennis, are capable of cruel injustice toward less fortunate sisters, like little Fanny ; and Amelia Sedley is led, by blind feminine instinct, to snub and tyrannize over poor Dobbin. The shabby miseries of life, the numbing and belittling influences of failure and poverty upon the most generous natures, are the tragic themes which Thackeray handles by preference. He has been called a cynic, but the boyish playfulness of his humor and his kindly spirit are incompatible with cynicism. Charlotte Bronté said that Fielding was the vulture and Thackeray the eagle. The comparison would have been truer if made between Swift and Thackeray. Swift was a cynic ; his pen was driven by hate, but Thackeray's by love, and it was not in bitterness but in sadness that the latter laid bare the wickedness of the world. He was himself a thorough man of the world, and he had that dislike for a display of feeling which characterizes the modern Englishman. But behind his satiric mask he concealed the manliest tenderness, and a reverence for every thing in human nature that is good and true. Thackeray's other great novels are *Pendennis*, 1849; *Henry Esmond*, 1852; and *The Newcomes*, 1855—the last of which contains his most lovable character, the pathetic and immortal figure of Colonel Newcome, a creation worthy to stand, in its dignity and its sublime weakness, by the side of Don Quixote. It was alleged against Thackeray that he made all his good characters, like Major Dobbin and Amelia Sedley and Colonel Newcome, intellectually feeble, and his brilliant characters, like Becky Sharp and Lord Steyne and Blanche Amory, morally bad. This is not entirely true, but the other complaint —that his women are inferior to his men—is true in a general way. Somewhat inferior to his other novels were *The Virginians*, 1858, and *The Adventures of Philip*, 1862. All of these were stories of contemporary life, except *Henry Esmond* and its sequel, *The Virginians*, which, though not precisely historical fictions, introduced historical figures, such as Washington and the Earl of Peterborough. Their period of action was the 18th century, and the dialogue was a cunning imitation of the language of that time. Thackeray was strongly

attracted by the 18th century.   His literary teach-
ers were Addison, Swift, Steele, Gay, Johnson,
Richardson, Goldsmith, Fielding, Smollett, and
Sterne, and his special master and model was
Fielding,   He projected a history of the century,
and his studies in this kind took shape in his two
charming series of lectures on *The English Humorists* and *The Four Georges.* These he delivered
in England and in America, to which country he,
like Dickens, made two several visits.

Thackeray's genius was, perhaps, less astonishing than Dickens's, less fertile, spontaneous, and
inventive ; but his art is sounder, and his delinea-
tion of character more truthful.   After one has
formed a taste for his books, Dickens's sentiment
will seem overdone, and much of his humor will
have the air of buffoonery.   Thackeray had the
advantage in another particular : he described the
life of the upper classes, and Dickens of the lower.
It may be true that the latter offers richer material to the novelist, in the play of elementary passions and in strong, native developments of character.   It is true, also, that Thackeray approached
" society " rather to satirize it than to set forth its
agreeableness.   Yet, after all, it is " the great
world " which he describes, that world upon which
the broadening and refining processes of a high
civilization have done their utmost, and which,
consequently, must possess an intellectual interest
superior to any thing in the life of London thieves,
traveling showmen, and coachees.   Thackeray is

the equal of Swift as a satirist, of Dickens as a humorist, and of Scott as a novelist. The one element lacking in him—and which Scott had in a high degree—is the poetic imagination. " I have no brains above my eyes," he said ; " I describe what I see." Hence there is wanting in his creations that final charm which Shakspere's have. For what the eyes see is not all.

The great woman who wrote under the pen-name of George Eliot was a humorist, too. She had a rich, deep humor of her own, and a wit that crystallized into sayings which are not epigrams, only because their wisdom strikes more than their smartness. But humor was not, as with Thackeray and Dickens, her point of view. A country girl, the daughter of a land agent and surveyor at Nuneaton, in Warwickshire, her early letters and journals exhibit a Calvinistic gravity and moral severity. Later, when her truth to her convictions led her to renounce the Christian belief, she carried into Positivism the same religious earnestness, and wrote the one English hymn of the religion of humanity:

"O, let me join the choir invisible," etc.

Her first published work was a translation of Strauss's *Leben Jesu*, 1846. In 1851 she went to London and became one of the editors of the Radical organ, the *Westminster Review*. Here she formed a connection—a marriage in all but the name—with George Henry Lewes, who was, like

18

herself, a freethinker, and who published, among
other things, a *Biographical History of Philosophy*.
Lewes had also written fiction, and it was at his
suggestion that his wife undertook story writing.
Her *Scenes of Clerical Life* were contributed to
Blackwood's Magazine for 1857, and published in
book form in the following year. *Adam Bede* followed in 1859, the *Mill on the Floss* in 1860, *Silas
Marner* in 1861, *Romola* in 1863, *Felix Holt* in
1866, and *Middlemarch* in 1872. All of these, except *Romola*, are tales of provincial, and largely of
domestic, life in the midland counties. *Romola* is
a historical novel, the scene of which is Florence,
in the 15th century, the Florence of Macchia-
velli and of Savonarola. George Eliot's method
was very different from that of Thackeray or
Dickens. She did not crowd her canvas with the
swarming life of cities. Her figures are comparatively few, and they are selected from the middle-
class families of rural parishes or small towns, amid
that atmosphere of "fine old leisure," whose dis-
appearance she lamented. Her drama is a still
life drama, intensely and profoundly inward.
Character is the stuff that she works in, and she
deals with it more subtly than Thackeray. With
him the tragedy is produced by the pressure of society and its false standards upon the individual;
with her, by the malign influence of individuals
upon one another. She watches "the stealthy con-
vergence of human fates," the intersection at various angles of the planes of character, the power

that the lower nature has to thwart, stupefy, or corrupt the higher, which has become entangled with it in the mesh of destiny. At the bottom of every one of her stories, there is a problem of the conscience or the intellect. In this respect she resembles Hawthorne, though she is not, like him, a romancer, but a realist.

There is a melancholy philosophy in her books, most of which are tales of failure or frustration. The *Mill on the Floss* contains a large element of autobiography, and its heroine, Maggie Tulliver, is, perhaps, her idealized self. Her aspirations after a fuller and nobler existence are condemned to struggle against the resistance of a narrow, provincial environment, and the pressure of untoward fates. She is tempted to seek an escape even through a desperate throwing off of moral obligations, and is driven back to her duty only to die by a sudden stroke of destiny. "Life is a bad business," wrote George Eliot, in a letter to a friend, "and we must make the most of it." *Adam Bede* is, in construction, the most perfect of her novels, and *Silas Marner* of her shorter stories. Her analytic habit gained more and more upon her as she wrote. *Middlemarch*, in some respects her greatest book, lacks the unity of her earlier novels, and the story tends to become subordinate to the working out of character stories and social problems. The philosophic speculations, which she shared with her husband, were seemingly unfavorable to her artistic growth, a circumstance which becomes apparent in her last novel, *Daniel Deronda*, 1877. Finally in the *Impressions of Theophrastus Such*, 1879, she abandoned narrative altogether, and recurred to that type of "character" books which we have met, as a flourishing department of literature in the 17th century, represented by such works as Earle's *Microcosmographie* and Fuller's *Holy and Profane State.* The moral of George Eliot's writings is not obtruded. She never made the artistic mistake of writing a novel of purpose, or what the Germans call a *tendenz-roman;* as Dickens did, for example, when he attacked imprisonment for debt, in *Pickwick;* the poor laws, in *Oliver Twist;* the Court of Chancery, in *Bleak House;* and the Circumlocution office, in *Little Dorrit.*

Next to the novel, the essay has been the most overflowing literary form used by the writers of this generation—a form, characteristic, it may be, of an age which "lectures, not creates." It is not the essay of Bacon, nor yet of Addison, nor of Lamb, but attempts a complete treatment. Indeed, many longish books, like Carlyle's *Heroes and Hero Worship* and Ruskin's *Modern Painters*, are, in spirit, rather literary essays than formal treatises. The most popular essayist and historian of his time was Thomas Babington Macaulay (1800–1859), an active and versatile man, who won splendid success in many fields of labor. He was prominent in public life as one of the leading orators and writers of the Whig party. He sat many times in the House of Commons, as member for Calne, for Leeds, and for Edinburgh, and took a distinguished part in the debates on the Reform bill of 1832. He held office in several Whig governments, and during his four years' service in British India, as member of the Supreme Council of Calcutta, he did valuable work in promoting education in that province, and in codifying the Indian penal law. After his return to England, and especially after the publication of his *History of England from The Accession of James II.*, honors and appointments of all kinds were showered upon him. In 1857 he was raised to the peerage as Baron Macaulay of Rothley.

Macaulay's equipment, as a writer on historical and biographical subjects, was, in some points, unique. His reading was prodigious, and his memory so tenacious, that it was said, with but little exaggeration, that he never forgot any thing that he had read. He could repeat the whole of *Paradise Lost* by heart, and thought it probable that he could rewrite *Sir Charles Grandison* from memory. In his books, in his speeches in the House of Commons, and in private conversation— for he was an eager and fluent talker, running on often for hours at a stretch—he was never at a loss to fortify and illustrate his positions by citation after citation of dates, names, facts of all kinds, and passages quoted *verbatim* from his multifarious reading. The first of Macaulay's writings to attract general notice was his article on *Milton*, printed in the August number of the *Edinburgh Review*, for 1825. The editor, Lord Jeffrey, in

acknowledging the receipt of the MS., wrote to his
new contributor, "The more I think, the less I
can conceive where you picked up that style."
That celebrated style—about which so much has
since been written—was an index to the mental
character of its owner. Macaulay was of a confi-
dent, sanguine, impetuous nature. He had great
common sense, and he saw what he saw quickly
and clearly, but he did not see very far below the
surface. He wrote with the conviction of an advocate, and the easy omniscience of a man whose
learning is really nothing more than "general in-
formation," raised to a very high power, rather
than with the subtle penetration of an original or
truly philosophic intellect, like Coleridge's or De
Quincey's. He always had at hand explanations of
events or of characters, which were admirably easy
and simple—too simple, indeed, for the complicated phenomena which they professed to explain.
His style was clear, animated, showy, and even its
faults were of an exciting kind. It was his habit
to give piquancy to his writing by putting things
concretely. Thus, instead of saying, in general
terms—as Hume or Gibbon might have done—
that the Normans and Saxons began to mingle about
1200, he says: "The great grandsons of those who
had fought under William and the great grandsons
of those who had fought under Harold began to draw
near to each other." Macaulay was a great scene
painter, who neglected delicate truths of detail for
exaggerated distemper effects. He used the rhe-

torical machinery of climax and hyperbole for all that it was worth, and he "made points "—as in his essay on *Bacon*—by creating antithesis. In his *History of England*, he inaugurated the picturesque method of historical writing. The book was as fascinating as any novel. Macaulay, like Scott, had the historic imagination, though his method of turning history into romance was very different from Scott's. Among his essays, the best are those which, like the ones on *Lord Clive*, *Warren Hastings*, and *Frederick the Great*, deal with historical subjects; or those which deal with literary subjects under their public historic relations, such as the essays on *Addison, Bunyan*, and *The Comic Dramatists of the Restoration*. "I have never written a page of criticism on poetry, or the fine arts," wrote Macaulay, "which I would not burn if I had the power." Nevertheless his own *Lays of Ancient Rome*, 1842, are good, stirring verse of the emphatic and declamatory kind, though their quality may be rather rhetorical than poetic.

Our critical time has not forborne to criticize itself, and perhaps the writer who impressed himself most strongly upon his generation was the one who railed most desperately against the "spirit of the age." Thomas Carlyle (1795–1881) was occupied between 1822 and 1830 chiefly in imparting to the British public a knowledge of German literature. He published, among other things, a *Life of Schiller*, a translation of Goethe's *Wilhelm Meister*, and two volumes of translations from the German romancers—Tieck, Hoffmann, Richter, and Fouqué, and contributed to the *Edinburgh* and *Foreign Review*, articles on Goethe, Werner, Novalis, Richter, German playwrights, the *Nibelungen Lied*, etc. His own diction became more and more tinctured with Germanisms. There was something Gothic in his taste, which was attracted by the lawless, the grotesque, and the whimsical in the writings of Jean Paul Richter. His favorite among English humorists was Sterne, who has a share of these same qualities. He spoke disparagingly of "the sensuous literature of the Greeks," and preferred the Norse to the Hellenic mythology. Even in his admirable critical essays on Burns, on Richter, on Scott, Diderot, and Voltaire, which are free from his later mannerism—written in English, and not in Carlylese—his sense of spirit is always more lively than his sense of form. He finally became so impatient of art as to maintain—half-seriously— the paradox that Shakspere would have done better to write in prose. In three of these early essays—on the *Signs of the Times*, 1829; on *History*, 1830; and on *Characteristics*, 1831—are to be found the germs of all his later writings. The first of these was an arraignment of the mechanical spirit of the age. In every province of thought he discovered too great a reliance upon systems, institutions, machinery, instead of upon men. Thus, in religion, we have Bible Societies, "machines for converting the heathen." "In defect of Raphaels and Angelos and Mozarts, we have royal acade-

mies of painting, sculpture, music." In like manner, he complains, government is a machine. "Its
duties and faults are not those of a father, but of
an active parish-constable." Against the "police
theory," as distinguished from the "paternal" theory of government, Carlyle protested with ever-
shriller iteration. In *Chartism*, 1839; *Past and
Present*, 1843; and *Latter-day Pamphlets*, 1850, he
denounced this *laissez faire* idea. The business
of government, he repeated, is to govern; but this
view makes it its business to refrain from govern-
ing. He fought most fiercely against the conclusions of political economy, "the dismal science,"
which, he said, affirmed that men were guided exclusively by their stomachs. He protested, too,
against the Utilitarians, followers of Bentham and
Mill, with their "greatest happiness principle,"
which reduced virtue to a profit-and-loss account.
Carlyle took issue with modern liberalism; he ridiculed the self-gratulation of the time, all the talk
about progress of the species, unexampled prosperity, etc. But he was reactionary without being
conservative. He had studied the French Revolution, and he saw the fateful, irresistible approach
of democracy. He had no faith in government
"by counting noses," and he hated talking parlia-
ments; but neither did he put trust in an aristoc-
racy that spent its time in "preserving the game."
What he wanted was a great individual ruler, a real
king or hero; and this doctrine he set forth afterward most fully in *Hero Worship*, 1841, and illus-

trated in his lives of representative heroes, such as his *Cromwell's Letters and Speeches*, 1845, and his great *History of Frederick the Great*, 1858–1865. Cromwell and Frederick were well enough ; but as Carlyle grew older, his admiration for mere force grew, and his latest hero was none other than that infamous Dr. Francia, the South American dictator, whose career of bloody and crafty crime horrified the civilized world.

The essay on *History* was a protest against the scientific view of history which attempts to explain away and account for the wonderful. "Wonder," he wrote in *Sartor Resartus*, "is the basis of all worship." He defined history as "the essence of innumerable biographies." "Mr. Carlyle," said the Italian patriot, Mazzini, "comprehends only the individual. The nationality of Italy is, in his eyes, the glory of having produced Dante and Christopher Columbus." This trait comes out in his greatest book, *The French Revolution*, 1837, which is a mighty tragedy, enacted by a few leading characters, Mirabeau, Danton, Napoleon. He loved to emphasize the superiority of history over fiction as dramatic material. The third of the three essays mentioned was a Jeremiad on the morbid self-consciousness of the age, which shows itself in religion and philosophy, as skepticism and introspective metaphysics; and in literature, as sentimentalism, and "view-hunting."

But Carlyle's epoch-making book was *Sartor Resartus* (The Tailor Retailored), published in *Fraser's*

Magazine for 1833-1834, and first reprinted in book form in America. This was a satire upon shams, conventions, the disguises which overlie the most spiritual realities of the soul. It purported to be the life and "clothes-philosophy" of a certain Diogenes Teufelsdröckh, Professor *der Allerlei Wissenschaft*—of things in general—in the University of Weissnichtwo. "Society," said Carlyle, "is founded upon cloth," following the suggestions of Lear's speech to the naked bedlam beggar: "Thou art the thing itself : unaccommodated man is no more but such a poor, bare, forked animal as thou art;" and borrowing also, perhaps, an ironical hint from a paragraph in Swift's *Tale of a Tub :* "A sect was established who held the universe to be a large suit of clothes. . . . If certain ermines or furs be placed in a certain position, we style them a judge ; and so an apt conjunction of lawn and black satin we entitle a bishop." In *Sartor Resartus* Carlyle let himself go. It was willful, uncouth, amorphous, titanic. There was something monstrous in the combination, the hot heart of the Scot married to the transcendental dream of Germany. It was not English, said the reviewers ; it was not sense ; it was disfigured by obscurity and "mysticism." Nevertheless even the thin-witted and the dry-witted had to acknowledge the powerful beauty of many chapters and passages, rich with humor, eloquence, poetry, deep-hearted tenderness, or passionate scorn.

Carlyle was a voracious reader, and the plunder

of whole literatures is strewn over his pages. He flung about the resources of the language with a giant's strength, and made new words at every turn. The concreteness and the swarming fertility of his mind are evidenced by his enormous vocabulary, computed greatly to exceed Shakspere's, or any other single writer's in the English tongue. His style lacks the crowning grace of simplicity and repose. It astonishes, but it also fatigues.

Carlyle's influence has consisted more in his attitude than in any special truth which he has preached. It has been the influence of a moralist, of a practical, rather than a speculative, philosopher. "The end of man," he wrote, "is an action, not a thought." He has not been able to persuade the time that it is going wrong, but his criticisms have been wholesomely corrective of its self-conceit. In a democratic age he has insisted upon the undemocratic virtues of obedience, silence, and reverence. *Ehrfurcht* — reverence — the text of his address to the students of Edinburgh University, in 1866, is the last word of his philosophy.

In 1830 Alfred Tennyson (1809– ——), a young graduate of Cambridge, published a thin duodecimo of 154 pages, entitled *Poems, Chiefly Lyrical.* The pieces in this little volume, like the *Sleeping Beauty*, *Ode to Memory*, and *Recollections of the Arabian Nights*, were full of color, fragrance, melody; but they had a dream-like character, and were without definite theme, resembling an artist's studies, or exercises in music—a few touches of the brush, a few sweet chords, but no *aria.* A number of them —*Claribel, Lilian, Adeline, Isabel, Mariana, Madeline*—were sketches of women; not character portraits, like Browning's *Men and Women,* but impressions of temperament, of delicately differentiated types of feminine beauty. In *Mariana,* expanded from a hint of the forsaken maid, in Shakspere's *Measure for Measure,* "Mariana at the moated grange," the poet showed an art then peculiar, but since grown familiar, of heightening the central feeling by landscape accessories. The level waste, the stagnant sluices, the neglected garden, the wind in the single poplar, re-enforce, by their monotonous sympathy, the loneliness, the hopeless waiting and weariness of life in the one human figure of the poem. In *Mariana,* the *Ode to Memory,* and the *Dying Swan,* it was the fens of Cambridge and of his native Lincolnshire that furnished Tennyson's scenery.

"Stretched wide and wild, the waste enormous marsh,
Where from the frequent bridge,
Like emblems of infinity,
The trenched waters run from sky to sky."

A second collection, published in 1833, exhibited a greater scope and variety, but was still in his earlier manner. The studies of feminine types were continued in *Margaret, Fatima, Eleanore, Mariana in the South,* and *A Dream of Fair Women,* suggested by Chaucer's *Legend of Good*

Women. In the *Lady of Shalott*, the poet first touched the Arthurian legends. The subject is the same as that of *Elaine*, in the *Idylls of the King*, but the treatment is shadowy, and even allegorical. In *Oenone* and the *Lotus Eaters*, he handled Homeric subjects, but in a romantic fashion, which contrasts markedly with the style of his later pieces, *Ulysses* and *Tithonus*. These last have the true classic severity, and are among the noblest specimens of weighty and sonorous blank verse in modern poetry. In general, Tennyson's art is unclassical. It is rich, ornate, composite, not statuesque, so much as picturesque. He is a great painter, and the critics complain that in passages calling for movement and action—a battle, a tournament, or the like—his figures stand still as in a tableau; and they contrast such passages unfavorably with scenes of the same kind in Scott, and with Browning's spirited ballad, *How we brought the Good News from Ghent to Aix*. In the *Palace of Art*, these elaborate pictorial effects were combined with allegory; in the *Lotus Eaters*, with that expressive treatment of landscape, noted in *Mariana ;* the lotus land, "in which it seemed always afternoon," reflecting and promoting the enchanted indolence of the heroes. Two of the pieces in this 1833 volume, the *May Queen* and the *Miller's Daughter*, were Tennyson's first poems of the affections, and as ballads of simple, rustic life, they anticipated his more perfect idyls in blank verse, such as *Dora*, the *Brook*, *Edwin Morris*, and the *Gardener's Daughter*. The songs in the *Miller's Daughter* had a more spontaneous, lyrical movement than any thing that he had yet published, and foretokened the lovely songs which interlude the divisions of the *Princess*, the famous *Bugle Song*, the no-less famous *Cradle Song*, and the rest. In 1833 Tennyson's friend, Arthur Hallam, died, and the effect of this great sorrow upon the poet was to deepen and strengthen the character of his genius. It turned his mind in upon itself, and set it brooding over questions which his poetry had so far left untouched; the meaning of life and death, the uses of adversity, the future of the race, the immortality of the soul, and the dealings of God with mankind.

> " Thou madest man, and, lo, thy foot
> Is on the thing that thou hast made."

His elegy on Hallam, *In Memoriam*, was not published till 1850. He kept it by him all those years, adding section after section, gathering up into it whatever reflections crystallized about its central theme. It is his most intellectual and most individual work, a great song of sorrow and consolation. In 1842 he published a third collection of poems, among which were *Locksley Hall*, displaying a new strength of passion ; *Ulysses*, suggested by a passage in Dante : pieces of a speculative cast, like the *Two Voices* and the *Vision of Sin;* the song *Break, Break, Break,* which preluded *In Memoriam ;* and, lastly, some additional gropings toward the subject of the Arthurian romance, such as *Sir Galahad, Sir Launcelot and Queen Guinevere* and *Morte d'Arthur*. The last was in blank verse, and, as afterward incorporated in the *Passing of Arthur*, forms one of the best passages in the *Idylls of the King*. The *Princess, a Medley*, published in 1849, represents the eclectic character of Tennyson's art; a medieval tale with an admixture of modern sentiment, and with the very modern problem of woman's sphere for its theme. The first four *Idylls of the King*, 1859, with those since added, constitute, when taken together, an epic poem on the old story of King Arthur. Tennyson went to Malory's *Morte d'Arthur* for his material, but the outline of the first idyl, *Enid*, was taken from Lady Charlotte Guest's translation of the Welsh *Mabinogion*. In the idyl of *Guinevere* Tennyson's genius reached its high-water mark. The interview between Arthur and his fallen queen is marked by a moral sublimity and a tragic intensity which move the soul as nobly as any scene in modern literature. Here, at least, the art is pure and not " decorated ; " the effect is produced by the simplest means, and all is just, natural, and grand. *Maud*—a love novel in verse—published in 1855, and considerably enlarged in 1856, had great sweetness and beauty, particularly in its lyrical portions, but it was uneven in execution, imperfect in design, and marred by lapses into mawkishness and excesses in language. Since 1860 Tennyson has added little of permanent

value to his work.   His dramatic experiments, like
Queen Mary, are not, on the whole, successful,
though it would be unjust to deny dramatic power
to the poet who has written, upon one hand, *Guinevere* and the *Passing of Arthur*, and upon the
other the homely, dialectic monologue of the
Northern Farmer.

When we tire of Tennyson's smooth perfection,
of an art that is over exquisite, and a beauty
that is well-nigh too beautiful, and crave a rougher
touch, and a meaning that will not yield itself too
readily, we turn to the thorny pages of his great
contemporary, Robert Browning (1812———). Dr.
Holmes says that Tennyson is white meat and
Browning is dark meat.   A masculine taste, it is
inferred, is shown in a preference for the gamier
flavor.   Browning makes us think; his poems are
puzzles, and furnish business for " Browning Societies."   There are no Tennyson societies, because Tennyson is his own interpreter.   Intellect
in a poet may display itself quite as properly in the
construction of his poem as in its content; we
value a building for its architecture, and not entirely for the amount of timber in it.   Browning's
thought never wears so thin as Tennyson's sometimes does in his latest verse, where the trick of
his style goes on of itself with nothing behind it.
Tennyson, at his worst, is weak.   Browning, when
not at his best, is hoarse.   Hoarseness, in itself,
is no sign of strength.   In Browning, however,
the failure is in art, not in thought.

19

He chooses his subjects from abnormal character types, such as are presented, for example, in
Caliban upon Setebos, the *Grammarian's Funeral*,
My Last Duchess, and *Mr. Sludge, the Medium*.
These are all psychological studies, in which the
poet gets into the inner consciousness of a mon-
ster, a pedant, a criminal, and a quack, and gives
their point of view. They are dramatic soliloquies; but the poet's self-identification with each
of his creations, in turn, remains incomplete. His
curious, analytic observation, his way of looking at
the soul from outside, gives a doubleness to the
monologues in his *Dramatic Lyrics*, 1845, *Men and
Women*, 1855, *Dramatis Personæ*, 1864, and other
collections of the kind. The words are the words
of Caliban or Mr. Sludge ; but the voice is the
voice of Robert Browning. His first complete
poem, *Paracelsus*, 1835, aimed to give the true in-
wardness of the career of the famous 16th century
doctor, whose name became a synonym with char-
latan. His second, *Sordello*, 1840, traced the struggles of an Italian poet who lived before Dante, and
could not reconcile his life with his art. *Paracelsus* was hard, but *Sordello* was incomprehensible.
Mr. Browning has denied that he is ever perverse-
ly crabbed or obscure. Every great artist must be
allowed to say things in his own way, and obscurity has its artistic uses, as the Gothic builders
knew. But there are two kinds of obscurity in
literature. One is inseparable from the subtlety
and difficulty of the thought or the compression

and pregnant indirectness of the phrase.   Instances of this occur in the clear deeps of Dante, Shakspere, and Goethe.   The other comes from a vice of style, a willfully enigmatic and unnatural way of expressing thought.   Both kinds of obscurity exist in Browning.   He is a deep and subtle thinker; but he is also a very eccentric writer, abrupt, harsh, disjointed.   It has been well said that the reader of Browning learns a new dialect.   But one need not grudge the labor that is rewarded with an intellectual pleasure so peculiar and so stimulating. The odd, grotesque impression made by his poetry arises, in part, from his desire to use the artistic values of ugliness, as well as of obscurity; to avoid the shallow prettiness that comes from blinking the disagreeable truth : not to leave the saltness out of the sea.   Whenever he emerges into clearness, as he does in hundreds of places, he is a poet of great qualities.   There are a fire and a swing in his *Cavalier Tunes*, and in pieces like the *Glove* and the *Lost Leader ;* and humor in such ballads as the *Pied Piper of Hamelin* and the *Soliloquy of the Spanish Cloister*, which appeal to the most conservative reader.   He seldom deals directly in the pathetic, but now and then, as in *Evelyn Hope*, the *Last Ride Together*, or the *Incident of the French Camp*, a tenderness comes over the strong verse

> "as sheathes
> A film the mother eagle's eye,
> When her bruised eaglet breathes."

Perhaps the most astonishing example of Browning's mental vigor is the huge composition, entitled *The Ring and the Book*, 1868, a narrative poem in twenty-one thousand lines, in which the same story is repeated eleven times in eleven different ways. It is the story of a criminal trial which occurred at Rome about 1700, the trial of one Count Guido for the murder of his young wife. First the poet tells the tale himself; then he tells what one-half of the world says and what the other; then he gives the deposition of the dying girl, the testimony of witnesses, the speech made by the count in his own defense, the arguments of counsel, etc., and, finally, the judgment of the pope. So wonderful are Browning's resources in casuistry, and so cunningly does he ravel the intricate motives at play in this tragedy and lay bare the secrets of the heart, that the interest increases at each repetition of the tale. He studied the Middle Age carefully, not for its picturesque externals, its feudalisms, chivalries, and the like; but because he found it a rich quarry of spiritual monstrosities, strange outcroppings of fanaticism, superstition, and moral and mental distortion of all shapes. It furnished him especially with a great variety of ecclesiastical types, such as are painted in *Fra Lippo Lippi*, *Bishop Blougram's Apology*, and *The Bishop Orders his Tomb in St. Praxed's Church*.

Browning's dramatic instinct has always attracted him to the stage. His tragedy, *Strafford* (1837),

was written for Macready, and put on at Covent
Garden Theater, but without pronounced success.
He has written many fine dramatic poems, like
Pippa Passes, Colombe's Birthday, and *In a Bal-
cony;* and at least two good acting plays, *Luria*
and *A Blot in the Scutcheon.* The last named has
recently been given to the American public, with
Lawrence Barrett's careful and intelligent presentation of the leading rôle. The motive of the
tragedy is somewhat strained and fantastic, but it
is, notwithstanding, very effective on the stage.
It gives one an unwonted thrill to listen to a
play, by a living English writer, which is really
literature. One gets a faint idea of what it
must have been to assist at the first night of
Hamlet.

1. Dickens. Pickwick Papers, Nicholas Nickleby, David Copperfield, Bleak House, Tale of Two
Cities.

2. Thackeray. Vanity Fair, Pendennis, Henry
Esmond, The Newcomes, The Four Georges.

3. George Eliot. Scenes of Clerical Life, Mill
on the Floss, Silas Marner, Romola, Adam Bede,
Middlemarch.

4. Macaulay. Essays, Lays of Ancient Rome.

5. Carlyle. Sartor Resartus, French Revolution, Essays on History, Signs of the Times, Characteristics, Burns, Scott, Voltaire, and Goethe.

6. The Works of Alfred Tennyson (6 vols.).
London: Strahan & Co., 1872.

7. Selections from the Poetical Works of Robert Browning. (2 vols.) London: Smith, Elder, & Co., 1880.

8. E. C. Stedman's Victorian Poets.

9. Henry Morley's English Literature in the Reign of Victoria. (Tauchnitz Series.)

THE END.

www.ingramcontent.com/pod-product-compliance
Lightning Source LLC
Chambersburg PA
CBHW021038030726
47496CB00006B/1594